iMac® For Dummies, 4th Edition

Cheat Sheet

W9-CIH-057

Finder Shortcut Keys for Mac OS X Tiger

Key Sequence	Action	Key Sequence	Action
⌘+A	Selects all items in the active window	⌘+3	Shows the active window in column mode
⌘+C	Copies selected items	⌘+[	Moves back to the previous Finder location
⌘+D	Duplicates the selected item(s)		
⌘+E	Ejects the selected volume	⌘+]	Moves forward to the next Finder location
⌘+F	Displays the Find Items dialog	⌘+Del	Moves selected items to the Trash
⌘+H	Hides Finder windows	⌘+?	Displays the Mac OS X Help Viewer
⌘+I	Shows info for selected item		
⌘+J	Shows the view options for the active window	⌘+Shift+A	Takes you to your Applications folder
⌘+K	Displays the Connect to Server dialog	⌘+Shift+C	Takes you to the top-level Computer location
⌘+L	Creates an alias for the selected item	⌘+Shift+G	Takes you to a folder that you specify
⌘+M	Minimizes the active window	⌘+Shift+H	Takes you to your Home folder
⌘+N	Opens a new Finder window	⌘+Shift+I	Connects you to your iDisk
⌘+O	Opens (or launches) the selected item	⌘+Shift+Q	Logs you out
⌘+R	Shows the original for selected alias	⌘+Shift+N	Opens a new untitled folder in the active window
⌘+T	Adds the selected item to the Sidebar	⌘+Shift+U	Takes you to your Utilities folder
⌘+V	Pastes items from the Clipboard	⌘+Shift+Del	Deletes the contents of the Trash
⌘+W	Closes the active window	⌘+Option+H	Hides all windows except the Finder window
⌘+X	Cuts the selected items	⌘+Option+T	Hides the Finder window toolbar
⌘+Z	Undoes the last action (if possible)	F9	Shows all open windows using Exposé
⌘+, (comma)	Displays Finder Preferences	F10	Shows all open windows for the current application using Exposé
⌘+1	Shows the active window in icon mode		
⌘+2	Shows the active window in list mode	F11	Hides all windows to display the Desktop using Exposé
		F12	Shows your Dashboard widgets

For Dummies: Bestselling Book Series for Beginners

iMac® For Dummies, 4th Edition

Cheat Sheet

Mark's Recommended iMac Maintenance

Task	Application	How Often?
Check for software updates	Software Update	Daily
Repair disk permissions	Disk Utility	Once a week
Full antivirus scan	Norton Antivirus, Virus Barrier X	Once a week
Back up	Backup, Retrospect	Daily or weekly
Empty Trash	Finder	Daily
Defragment	TechTool Pro, Drive 10	Monthly
Remove inactive user accounts	Accounts pane in System Preferences	Monthly
Check for orphaned files	Spring Cleaning	Monthly
Check hardware status	System Profiler, TechTool Pro	Monthly

Mark's 10-Step iMac Troubleshooting Tree

1. Reboot.

2. Investigate recent changes you've made to your hardware or software.

3. Run Disk Utility and repair your disk permissions.

4. Check all cables.

5. Check the contents of your Trash for files you might have deleted accidentally.

6. Check your Internet, wireless, and network connections to make sure they're still working.

7. Run a virus scan using your antivirus application.

8. Disable your account's login items and reboot.

9. Turn off your screen saver.

10. Run System Profiler and check the status of your hardware. (If you've invested in TechTool Pro, use it to run a full system diagnostic.)

For Dummies: Bestselling Book Series for Beginners

iMac®

FOR

DUMMIES®

4TH EDITION

iMac® FOR DUMMIES®
4TH EDITION

by Mark L. Chambers

WILEY

Wiley Publishing, Inc.

iMac® For Dummies,® 4th Edition

Published by
Wiley Publishing, Inc.
111 River Street
Hoboken, NJ 07030-5774

www.wiley.com

WILEY

About the Author

Mark L. Chambers has been an author, computer consultant, BBS sysop, programmer, and hardware technician for more than 20 years — pushing computers and their uses far beyond "normal" performance limits for decades now. His first love affair with a computer peripheral blossomed in 1984 when he bought his lightning-fast 300 BPS modem for his Atari 400. Now he spends entirely too much time on the Internet and drinks far too much caffeine-laden soda.

With a degree in journalism and creative writing from Louisiana State University, Mark took the logical career choice: programming computers. However, after five years as a COBOL programmer for a hospital system, he decided there must be a better way to earn a living, and he became the Documentation Manager for Datastorm Technologies, a well-known communications software developer. Somewhere in between writing software manuals, Mark began writing computer how-to books. His first book, *Running a Perfect BBS*, was published in 1994 — and after a short decade or so of fun (disguised as hard work), Mark is one of the most productive and best-selling technology authors on the planet.

Along with writing several books a year and editing whatever his publishers throw at him, Mark has also branched out into Web-based education, designing and teaching a number of online classes — called *WebClinics* — for Hewlett-Packard.

His favorite pastimes include collecting gargoyles, watching St. Louis Cardinals baseball, playing his three pinball machines and the latest computer games, supercharging computers, and rendering 3-D flights of fancy with TrueSpace — and during all that, he listens to just about every type of music imaginable. Mark's world-wide Internet radio station, *MLC Radio* (at www.mlcbooks.com), plays only CD-quality classics from 1970 to 1979, including everything from Rush to Billy Joel to the Rocky Horror Picture Show.

Mark's rapidly expanding list of books includes *Mac OS X Tiger All-In-One Desk Reference For Dummies; Building a PC For Dummies,* 5th Edition; *Scanners For Dummies,* 2nd Edition; *CD & DVD Recording For Dummies,* 2nd Edition; *PCs All-In-One Desk Reference For Dummies,* 2nd Edition; *Mac OS X Tiger: Top 100 Simplified Tips & Tricks; Microsoft Office v. X Power User's Guide; BURN IT! Creating Your Own Great DVDs and CDs; The Hewlett-Packard Official Printer Handbook; The Hewlett-Packard Official Recordable CD Handbook; The Hewlett-Packard Official Digital Photography Handbook;*

Computer Gamer's Bible; Recordable CD Bible; Teach Yourself the iMac Visually; Running a Perfect BBS; Official Netscape Guide to Web Animation; and the *Windows 98 Troubleshooting and Optimizing Little Black Book.*

His books have been translated into 14 different languages so far — his favorites are German, Polish, Dutch, and French. Although he can't read them, he enjoys the pictures a great deal.

Mark welcomes all comments and questions about his books. You can reach him at mark@mlcbooks.com, or visit MLC Books Online, his Web site, at www.mlcbooks.com.

Dedication

This book is dedicated to my youngest daughter, Rose Chambers — she of the Green Chair, the Book at Bedtime, and the Barbie blankets — with all the love and happiness I can give her.

Author's Acknowledgments

A guide to Apple's iMac should be as elegantly designed and straightforward as the computer itself . . . and luckily, I had just the right mix of folks to make sure that it turned out that way!

First, my thanks are due to my technical editor, Dennis Cohen, who kept watch on the accuracy of my facts, comments, and step-by-step procedures concerning both the Apple iMac and Mac OS X Tiger. (Nothing quite like tech editing an operating system that's in beta at the time!) And again, copy editor Teresa Artman leant both her superb eye and her humor to another of my books — I can make sense of the most complex actions on Planet Earth if she's there to straighten things up. Thanks, Teresa!

I've often said that Wiley's Production team is the best in the business, and the layout and composition of this book is proof positive — my appreciation to everyone who leant a hand with the graphics, proofing, and cover work for *iMacs For Dummies.*

As with all my books, I'd like to thank my wife, Anne, and my children, Erin, Chelsea, and Rose, for their support and love — and for letting me follow my dream!

Lastly, I'd like to thank the two editorial professionals at Wiley who made this book happen: my good friend Bob Woerner, the acquisitions editor who has guided my way through the jungle of technology yet again; and Pat O'Brien, my project editor, whom I was fortunate to work with for the first time on this great title. Gentlemen, it's folks like you who make this the greatest career on the planet — my heartfelt thanks to you both from a very grateful Mac owner!

Publisher's Acknowledgments

We're proud of this book; please send us your comments through our online registration form located at www.dummies.com/register/.

Some of the people who helped bring this book to market include the following:

Acquisitions, Editorial, and Media Development

Senior Project Editor: Pat O'Brien

Senior Acquisitions Editor: Bob Woerner

Senior Copy Editor: Teresa Artman

Technical Editor: Dennis Cohen

Editorial Manager: Kevin Kirschner

Media Development Supervisor: Richard Graves

Editorial Assistant: Amanda Foxworth

Cartoons: Rich Tennant (www.the5thwave.com)

Composition Services

Project Coordinator: Adrienne Martinez

Layout and Graphics: Carl Byers, Andrea Dahl Kelly Emkow, Stephanie D. Jumper, Barry Offringa, Lynsey Osborn

Proofreaders: TECHBOOKS Production Services, Leeann Harney, Jessica Kramer, Carl William Pierce

Indexer: TECHBOOKS Production Services

Special Help Virginia Sanders

Publishing and Editorial for Technology Dummies

    Richard Swadley, Vice President and Executive Group Publisher

    Andy Cummings, Vice President and Publisher

    Mary Bednarek, Executive Acquisitions Director

    Mary C. Corder, Editorial Director

Publishing for Consumer Dummies

    Diane Graves Steele, Vice President and Publisher

    Joyce Pepple, Acquisitions Director

Composition Services

    Gerry Fahey, Vice President of Production Services

    Debbie Stailey, Director of Composition Services

Contents at a Glance

Table of Contents

Introduction

. . . .

*Q*uerulous about your new iMac? Perhaps you're thinking it's too doggone thin, or you're wondering where all the buttons are. Shouldn't there be places to plug cables? And where the heck is the DVD drive you paid for? (Oh, there it is, on the side, at the top right.)

Ladies and gentlemen, I have great news for you: Not only did you make The Right Decision about which computer to buy, you shot a hole-in-one! The iMac does indeed look much different from the boring beige and black boxes of the Windows bourgeoisie, but it also has everything a computer power user could want: speed, the latest in hardware and standards, a top-of-the-line LCD screen, and all the connectors you need to add just about any device meant for today's computers. And all packaged in a svelte, foxy form that borders on modern art. This is one looker of a computer.

In addition to your iMac having doggone nearly everything you could ever want (okay, I still don't see a frozen yogurt dispenser), here's what it doesn't have: (yawn) bulk. Boasting the smallest *footprint* — the amount of desktop space — of any high-end computer available today, your iMac can practically fit on an end table!

I wrote this book especially for the iMac owner who wants to make the most of this new stunning white computer, so this book is a guide to both the iMac's hardware and *Tiger,* the latest version of Apple's superb Mac OS X operating system. I start by describing the basics that every iMac owner should know and then move on to chapters devoted to the software that comes with your iMac. Along the way are a generous sprinkling of power user tips and tricks that'll save you time, effort, and money.

Like my half-dozen other *For Dummies* titles, I respect and use the same English language you do, avoiding jargon, ridiculous computer acronyms, and confusing techno-babble whenever possible. (Plus, I try to bring out the humor that's hidden inside every computer. Discovering how to use your iMac should be fun and not a chore!)

What's Really (Not) Required

If you're not an engineer with a degree in Advanced Thakamology — imagine that — no need to worry! Here's a reasonably complete list of what's not required to use this book:

✔ I make no assumptions about your previous knowledge of computers and software. I start at the beginning, where every book should start.

✔ Still considering buying an iMac? Heck, you don't even need the computer! If you're evaluating whether the iMac is right for you, this book is a great choice. I introduce you to both the hardware and software you get, so you can easily determine whether the iMac is the machine for you. (It is. Trust me.)

✔ Upgrading from the monster that is Windows XP? I've got tips, tricks, and entire sections devoted to those hardy pioneers called *Switchers!* You can see all about the similarities and differences between the two operating systems — and how you can make the switch as easy and quick as possible.

✔ If your friends and family told you that you're going to spend half your savings on software — or that no "decent" software is available for Mac computers — just smile quietly to yourself! These are two persistent myths about Mac computers, and those same folks are going to be blown away by the images, music, movies, and documents you produce. (Oh, by the way, the iMac comes complete with about a ton more software than any Windows box, and the iLife suite of applications is better than anything available on a PC!) To sum it up: *You can do virtually everything in this book with the software that came with your iMac!*

So what is required? Only your iMac computer and the desire to become a *power user* (someone who produces the best work in the least amount of time, and has the most fun doing it)!

This book was written using the latest iMac computer, so owners of older iMac computers might not be able to follow along with everything I cover. If you upgraded an older iMac G4 with Mac OS X Tiger and the iLife '05 application suite, you should be able to use most of the book with no problem!

About This Book

Each chapter in this book is written as a reference on a specific hardware or software topic. You can begin reading anywhere you like because each chapter is self-contained. However, I recommend that you read the book from front to back because the order of this book makes a great deal of sense.

Conventions Used in This Book

Even with a minimum of techno-speak, this book needs to cover the special keys that you have to press or menu commands that you have to choose in order to make things work — hence this short list of conventions.

Stuff you type

If I ask you to type (or enter) something, like in a text box or field, that text appears in bold, like this:

Type me.

If I ask you to type a command within Mac OS X, that text appears like this:

```
Type me.
```

You usually have to press the Return key before anything happens when entering a manual command.

Menu commands

I list menu paths and commands, using this format:

Edit⇨Copy

This example of shorthand menu instruction indicates that you should click the Edit menu and then choose the Copy menu item.

Web addresses

No up-to-date book on a computer would be complete without a bag full of Web addresses for you to check out. When you see these in the text, they look like this: www.mlcbooks.com.

For the technically curious

Your iMac is an elegant and sophisticated machine — and as easy-to-use as a computer can be — but from time to time, you might be curious about the technical details surrounding your hardware and software. (You probably disassembled alarm clocks as a kid, like I did.) Tangential techy stuff is presented in sidebars, and you don't have to read them unless you want to know what makes things tick. (Pun by accident.)

How This Book Is Organized

After careful thought (read that *flipping a coin*), I divided this book into seven major parts — plus an index, just because you deserve one! For your convenience, cross-references to additional coverage of many topics are also sprinkled liberally throughout the book.

The Seven Parts Shall Be

Part 1: Know Your iMac

This part introduces you to the important features of your iMac — like where all the cables connect (or don't) — and helps you set up your system. I also introduce *Mac OS X Tiger,* Apple's operating system that comes preinstalled on your iMac.

Part 11: Shaking Hands with Mac OS X

Time to familiarize you with Tiger — how to take care of mundane chores (like moving your stuff) as well as how to customize and personalize your system until it fits like the proverbial glove! Switchers from the PC world will be especially interested in mastering the ins and outs of Mac OS X. (Psst. Friends, it ain't hard. The Mac started out easier to use than a Windows PC, and that has not changed.)

Part 111: Connecting and Communicating

Time to jump into the one application you're likely to use every single day: your Safari Web browser! You can also read here about Apple's .Mac Internet subscriber service and how to connect your iMac for printing, scanning, videoconferencing, and faxing. (I told you this thing was powerful, didn't I?)

Part 1V: Living the iLife

Ah, readers, you can begin humming happily to yourself right this second! Yep, this part provides complete coverage of the latest iLife '05 release, with all the names that are the envy of the Windows crowd: iTunes, iPhoto, iMovie

HD, iDVD, and GarageBand. You see how to turn your iMac into the hub for all your digital media. Whether you listen to it, display it, compose it, or direct it, this part of the book explains it!

Part V: Sharing Access and Information

In Part V, I discuss how to share your iMac among a group of people or how to connect your iMac to a network. (Wired or wireless, makes no difference to me!) I also cover how to share data among wireless devices via Bluetooth technology and iSync, and how to broadcast your music around your house like Wolfman Jack.

Part VI: The Necessary Evils: Troubleshooting, Upgrading, Maintaining

This is the stuff my Dad used to call the "*Justin Case* Guide." That is, just in case you want to upgrade your iMac with more memory or new hardware. If you need to troubleshoot a problem with your hardware or software, my should-be-patented troubleshooting guide resides in this part. Finally, I describe what you can do to help keep your iMac running as fast and as trouble-free as the day you took it out of the box!

Part VII: The Part of Tens

The chapters that make up the famous "Part of Tens" section are served in classic Late Night style: Each chapter contains a quick reference of tips and advice on a specific iMac topic. Each list has ten concise tips, and one or two readers have told me that they make excellent tattoos. (Personally, I'm not *that* much of a Mac guru.)

Icons Used in This Book

Like other technology authors, I firmly believe that important nuggets of wisdom should **stand out on the page!** With that in mind, this *For Dummies* book includes a number of margin icons for certain situations:

The most popular icon in the book — you'll find it next to suggestions I make that will save you time and effort. (Once or twice, even cash!)

You don't have to know this stuff, but the technologically curious love high-tech details. (Of course, we're great fun at parties, too.)

Always **read the information for this icon first!** I'm discussing something that could actually harm your hardware or throw a plumber's helper into your software.

The highlighter stuff — not quite as universally accepted (or as important to the author) as a Mark's Maxim but a good reminder! I use these icons to reinforce that which should be remembered.

Speaking of Mark's Maxims. Technically, no, these nuggets aren't decorated with an icon, but you can easily spot them because they appear in bold type and indented on their own, like wee islands of insight. These are My Favorite Recommendations. In fact, I'll bet just about any iMac power user would tell you the same. Follow my Maxims to avoid the quicksand and pitfalls that I've encountered with all sorts of Macs for well over a decade!

Where to Go from Here

My recommendations on how to proceed? You know, I just happen to have three:

- ✔ If you're thinking about buying an iMac, the box is still unopened in your living room, or you'd like help setting things up, I would start with Part I.

- ✔ If your iMac is already running but you'd like guidance with running Mac OS X — Windows Switchers, take note — start with Part II.

- ✔ For all other concerns, use the index or jump straight to the chapter you need. (You can always return later, at your leisure.)

A Final Word

I'd like to thank you for buying this book, and I hope that you find *iMac For Dummies,* 4th Edition valuable! With this book in hand, I believe that you and your iMac will bond together as I have with mine. (That sounds somewhat wrong, but it's really not.) And with that in mind, a concluding Mark's Maxim:

> **Take your time. Learning how to use your computer isn't a race. And don't worry if you're not a graphic artist, a professional photographer, a video editor, a programmer, or a mind reader. With your iMac and its software, you don't *have* to be!™**

Part I
Know Your iMac

The 5th Wave   By Rich Tennant

"Because I can't find my regular cake stand."

In this part . . .

Your iMac odyssey begins with a description of the computer itself, as well as the details you need to know when unpacking and setting up your newest family member. You also find an introduction to Mac OS X Tiger, the latest version of Apple's super-popular operating system.

Chapter 1

Okay, This Machine Looks Really, Really Weird

You bought a brand new iMac, and there it sits, in the box. Waiting. Waiting for you.

If you're a little nervous about unpacking that shiny white rectangle, I completely understand. Face it: The latest iMac follows in the footsteps of many revolutionary iMac designs that have come before it. (In other words, it doesn't *look* like a computer at all, and that can be a bit disconcerting.) And if you're switching from a Windows PC to the Apple universe, you might find yourself floating weightlessly in your office or your living room without a familiar bulky beige box to anchor yourself. Hence the reluctance you might be feeling.

However, dear reader, let me assure you that you've indeed made The Right Choice. I commend you! Your Intel-based iMac is the fastest, leanest, and easiest-to-use self-contained all-in-one computer ever built. Practically everything's in one shining panel (except for your keyboard and mouse). You've got one of the best liquid crystal display (LCD) screens on the planet, a super-fast processor, room for a ton of RAM (memory), and a regular laundry list of the latest technology. Best of all, you don't have to be a techno-nerd to use all that power!

In this chapter, I introduce you to your new dream machine, giving you an overview of the more important locations within iMac City. I show you how to unpack your new computer, what wires go where, and where your iMac should set up housekeeping. I preview the awesome software that's waiting within that powerful panel. Finally, I list the accessories that help keep both you *and* your new iMac computing smoothly.

An Introduction to the Beast

The iMac might look like a sculpture straight out of your local museum of modern art, but it still sports everything that it needs to function as a computer. In this section, I identify the important stuff that you need to live your life — you know, write a term paper in Pages, hear the music you downloaded, or manage the affairs of those lazy Sims.

Major parts of your major appliance

Every computer requires some of the same gizmos. Figure 1-1 helps you track them down. Of course, as you'd expect, a computer has a "body" of sorts in which all the innards and brains are stored (the screen, in this case), a display screen, a keyboard, a mouse/pointing device, and ports for powering and exchanging data with peripherals.

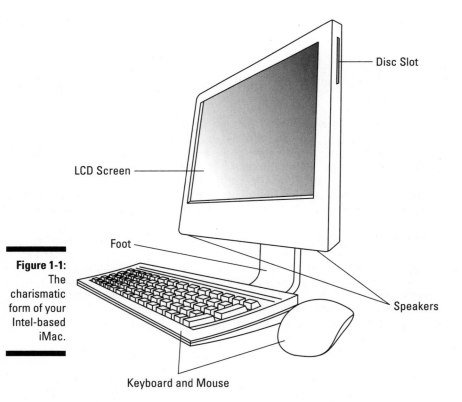

Figure 1-1: The charismatic form of your Intel-based iMac.

Disc Slot

LCD Screen

Foot

Speakers

Keyboard and Mouse

Umm . . . my iMac isn't two inches thick

Believe me, I feel your pain. It seems like only yesterday that Apple introduced its generation of flat-panel iMac G4 models. (You know, the ones that look like a milky-white, half-basketball at the base.) Then came the first generation of "picture frame" iMacs, sporting the G5 processor. The crew at Cupertino tends to update their product line pretty often, so if you have an older flat-panel iMac, you might be feeling like an Edsel owner on his way to catch *Vertigo* at the drive-in.

Ah, but friend, there's good news on your horizon: *Those first-generation flat-panel iMacs and iMac G5 models are still powerful personal platforms for productivity programs and peripherals!* Don't give up on your iMac yet (unless you just plain want to upgrade). You still have a great LCD screen of the same quality, a reasonably fast processor, virtually all the same ports and options, and that spiffy chrome-plated gooseneck to boot.

That magnificent screen

Talk about efficiency: With the iMac, the 2"-thick border surrounding the display is actually your computer's case! And what a view you've got because an Intel iMac is graced with either a 17", 20", or 24" LCD display.

Once upon a time, LCD screens were strictly limited to notebook and laptop computers, whilst desktop computer owners were saddled with huge, heavy cathode ray tube (CRT) monitors. Luckily, the LCD panel has migrated to virtually all the Apple computer product line, so notebook owners can no longer be snobbish (at least about their screens, anyway).

LCD screens use far less electricity than their antique CRT ancestors, and they emit practically no radiation.

All three sizes of iMac screens offer a *widescreen* aspect ratio (the screen is considerably wider than it is tall), which augurs well for those who enjoy watching DVD movies. (A favorite editor of mine loves it when I use the antique word *augur,* meaning *to predict or foretell.*) The larger 24" screen boasts a whopper 1920 x 1200 resolution.

That reminds me: Throw away your printed dictionary! You won't need it because Mac OS X Tiger includes the fantastic Sherlock application that uses the Internet to retrieve definitions from Dictionary.com. More on Sherlock in Chapter 7 . . . and yes, it does contain *augur.*

The keyboard and mouse

Hey, here's something novel for the Intel iMac — something *external* (outside the computer's case). Gotta have a keyboard and mouse, right? And you gotta love the options with iMac: You can fly a little cheaper and remain entangled in a corded world, or you can go nomadic . . . um, that is, wireless and free.

Getting wired

The iMac comes standard with a wired Apple keyboard and multiple-button Mighty Mouse optical mouse. The keyboard is a particular favorite of mine because from here

- ✔ You can either control the sound volume or mute all that noise completely.
- ✔ A handy-dandy Media Eject key lets you eject a CD or DVD.

Read about connecting your keyboard and mouse in the upcoming section, "Absolutely essential connections."

Going wireless

If you're really fancy, you can opt for a truly 21st century computer and order the Apple wireless keyboard and mouse ($60) combo! This dynamic duo lets you sit back and relax with your keyboard in your lap, without being tied down by a cord. (Say it with me: "Death to cords, death to cords.") Just stay within about 30 feet of your iMac screen, and sweet freedom is yours. You can also feel safe using these wireless peripherals because they offer secure 128-bit, over-the-air encryption, which helps keep sensitive information safe while you type and click away.

The wireless mouse needs a flat surface, but that's what TV trays are for, right?

The disc slot

You'll notice a long groove at the right-upper corner of your iMac. No, it's not for your credit card. (If you order online often enough, you'll memorize your card number.) This slot accepts CDs and DVDs into your optical drive. If the drive is empty, loading a disc is as simple as sliding it in an inch or so; the drive sucks in the disc automatically. (And we don't need no stinkin' floppy drive. Macs haven't had floppy drives for years now, and the PC types are just beginning to follow.)

"Luke, the printed label side of the disc should always be *facing you* when you load a disc. Always."

Yes, your computer has a foot . . . just one

You and I — normal human beings — would say that the iMac is supported by a sturdy aluminum stand, but Apple calls it a *foot*. The foot lets you tilt the iMac LCD panel up and down for the best viewing angle. Most important, though, the foot minimizes the computer's desk space requirements (or its *footprint*). (Engineers . . . sheesh.)

If you decide to get really snazzy and mount your iMac to the wall, you can remove the foot and install the VESA mounting adapter (available separately for about $30). You can use any VESA standard mounting bracket on your wall, too.

Hey, Hewlett-Packard or Dell, can you mount one of those monolithic PCs to the wall? *I think not.*

Food for your ears

A machine this nice had better have great sound, and the iMac doesn't disappoint. You have a couple of options for iMac audio:

- ✔ **The iMac sports built-in stereo speakers (and a microphone to boot).**

- ✔ **Use built-in ports to connect your iMac audio to either**

  - • More powerful (and more expensive) external speaker systems

  - • A home stereo system

The power cable

Sorry, can't get a wireless power system . . . yet. (Apple's working hard on that one.) If you opt for the wireless keyboard and mouse setup (see the earlier section, "Going wireless"), the power cable is actually the only required cable that you need to run your computer! Now that's *sassy.*

The power button

Yep, you've got one of these, too. It's on the back of the case.

The iSight Camera

Have you noticed that tiny lens at the top of your computer? Every iMac comes complete with its own iSight digital video camera, ready to add video to your iChat conferences, produce digital snapshots at your whim, or even capture digital video clips for your iMovie HD projects. (Of course, the iSight camera is stationary, so you won't be doing any on-location shooting.

Those holes are called ports

Our next stop on your tour of Planet iMac is Port Central — that row of holes on the back of your computer (see Figure 1-2). Each port connects a different type of cable or device, allowing you to easily add all sorts of extra functionality to your computer.

Each of these stellar holes is identified by an icon to help you identify it. Here's a list of what you'll find as well as a quick rundown on what these ports do.

- ✔ **FireWire:** These ports are the standard in the Apple universe for connecting external hard drives and DVD recorders, but they do double duty as the connector of choice for peripherals like your iPod and your digital video (DV) camcorder. (A *peripheral* is another silly techno-nerd term, meaning a separate device that you connect to your computer.) Note that the iMac offers two FireWire ports — depending on the model you choose, you'll have at least one of the older FireWire 400 specification, and you may have one of the much faster FireWire 800 ports.

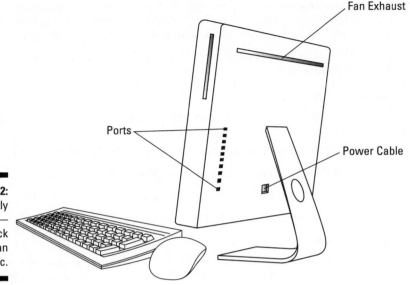

Fan Exhaust

Ports

Power Cable

Figure 1-2:
Only slightly
less sexy —
it's the back
end of an
iMac.

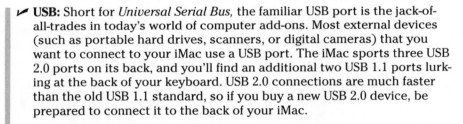

✔ **USB:** Short for *Universal Serial Bus,* the familiar USB port is the jack-of-all-trades in today's world of computer add-ons. Most external devices (such as portable hard drives, scanners, or digital cameras) that you want to connect to your iMac use a USB port. The iMac sports three USB 2.0 ports on its back, and you'll find an additional two USB 1.1 ports lurking at the back of your keyboard. USB 2.0 connections are much faster than the old USB 1.1 standard, so if you buy a new USB 2.0 device, be prepared to connect it to the back of your iMac.

For the specs on connecting your keyboard and mouse, see the upcoming section, "Absolutely essential connections."

For more on FireWire and USB ports, get the lowdown in Chapter 20.

✔ **Ethernet:** The iMac includes a standard 10/100 Ethernet port, so it's ready to join your existing wired Ethernet network. (Alternatively, you can go wireless for your network connection; more on that in the next section and in Chapter 20.)

✔ **VGA/S-Video/Composite Video:** In case that splendid screen isn't quite good enough, you can add an adapter to this port and send the video signal from your iMac to another monitor (VGA) or to an S-Video or composite video device. (Think flatscreen TV or a VCR.)

✔ **Headphone/Optical Output:** You can send the high-quality audio from your rectangular beast to a set of standard headphones or an optical digital audio device like a high-end home theater system.

✔ **Line In:** Last (but certainly not least) is the audio Line In jack, which allows you to pipe the signal from another audio device into your iMac. This one comes in particularly handy when you record MP3 files from your old vinyl albums or when you want to record loops within GarageBand.

Important Hidden Stuff

When you bought your new digital pride and joy, you probably noticed a number of subtle differences between the low-end Intel iMac and the über-expensive top-end model. I call these differences the *Important Hidden Stuff* (or IHS, if you're addicted to acronyms already), and they're just as important as the parts and ports that you can see.

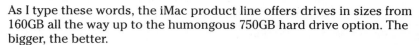

✔ **Hard drive:** The Intel iMac uses the latest in hard drive technology: *serial ATA* hard drives, which are significantly faster than the EIDE hard drives used in previous iMac models. (You don't need to worry about what ATA and EIDE mean here. Really.)

As I type these words, the iMac product line offers drives in sizes from 160GB all the way up to the humongous 750GB hard drive option. The bigger, the better.

✔ **Optical drive:** Okay, I'm cheating a little here. I mention the optical drive in an earlier section, but all you can see is the slot, so it qualifies as an IHS item. Depending on your iMac model, your computer includes either

   • *Best:* A DVD-R SuperDrive (which can play and record both CDs and DVDs)

   • *Not bad:* A DVD/CD-RW combo drive (which can record CDs but only read DVDs)

If your iMac can't burn DVDs with the internal drive, don't give up hope of recording your own DVD movies. Thanks to those handy FireWire ports, it's child's play to add an external DVD recorder.

Time for a plug: If you're interested in recording your own audio and data CDs, or you've got an itch to burn DVD movies, I can highly recommend the bestselling *CD & DVD Recording For Dummies,* 2nd Edition (Wiley). (And written by yours truly; hence the solid recommendation.) Anyway, you'll find everything you need to know to use Roxio's Toast recording software. Within a few minutes, you'll be burning your own shiny digital treasures.

✔ **Wireless Ethernet:** "Look, Ma, no wires!" As I mention earlier, you can connect your iMac to an existing wireless Ethernet network using your Intel iMac's built-in AirPort Extreme card. With wireless connectivity, you can share documents with another computer in another room, share a single high-speed Internet connection betwixt several computers, or enjoy wireless printing. Truly *sassy!*

Although Apple would want you to build your wireless wonderland with an Apple AirPort Extreme Base Station — go figure — you can actually use your iMac with any standard 802.11g wireless network. And yes, PCs and Macs can intermingle on the same wireless network without a hitch. (Scandalous, ain't it?)

✔ **Bluetooth:** Let's get the old "digital pirate" joke out of the way: "Arrgg, matey, I needs me a wireless parrot." (Engineers again . . . sheesh.) Although strangely named, Bluetooth is actually another form of wireless connectivity. This time, however, the standard was designed for accessories like your keyboard and mouse, and devices like your personal digital assistant (PDA) and cellphone. These days, of course, that old pirate Bluetooth is built in to your iMac.

✔ **Apple Remote:** It looks like an old iPod Shuffle, but that's not an MP3 player. Today's Intel iMacs come with a remote control that you can use with Front Row, the multimedia front-end that's built into Mac OS X Tiger. Using your Apple Remote, you can easily listen to your iTunes music collection, watch your iMovie projects and home videos, play a DVD movie, or view your album of digital snapshots in iPhoto. (What? Your old PC didn't have a remote? 'Nuff said.)

✔ **Video card:** If your applications rely heavily on high-speed 3-D graphics, you'll be pleased as punch to find that the iMac can be equipped with an NDIVIA GeForce GT video card. This card is well suited to 3-D modeling, video editing, and well, honestly, blasting the enemy into small smoking pieces with aplomb.

Choosing a Home for Your New Pet

If you pick the wrong spot to park your new iMac, I can guarantee that you'll regret it later. Some domiciles and office cubicles obviously don't offer a choice — you've got one desk at work, for example, and nobody's going to hand over another one — but if you can select a home for your iMac, consider the important placement points in this section.

Picking the right location

You know the mantra: Location, location, location.

✔ **There's always the wall.** Your iMac can disguise itself as a particularly interesting digital picture frame. With the right mounting adapter, you can hang your computer right on the wall and snub your desk altogether.

This wall-mounted solution has two big problems:

- Your VESA mounting plate must be installed safely and correctly (for example, using the studs within your walls).

    The Intel iMac is slim and trim, but it's no lightweight, and it doesn't bounce well. You don't want it to take a high dive!

- External peripherals aren't happy campers — that includes any FireWire and USB cables.

✔ Your iMac must be mounted at the proper height on the wall. It's not good ergonomic practice to sit more than two feet away from your iMac's screen, and the screen should be placed at (or slightly below) eye level.

I see two major requirements for a wall-mounted iMac:

- Don't plan on using any external devices.

- Buy the wireless keyboard and mouse option when you buy your computer!

✔ **Keep things cool.** Your new Intel iMac is nearly silent, but that super-fast G5 processor generates quite a bit of heat. Fans inside the case draw the heat away. (Nothing like an overheated processor to spoil an evening of Doom III.)

Follow these three rules to keep your cool. Make sure that

- The location you choose is far from heating vents.

- The location you choose is shielded from direct sunlight.

- There is plenty of room below the machine (where the air enters the case) and above the machine (where heated air escapes from the slot at the top of the case).

Hot air from a wall-mounted iMac can discolor the wall.

Considering the convenience factor

Technology is nothing if you can't make it convenient:

- ✔ **Outlets, outlets, outlets!** Your computer needs a minimum of at least one nearby outlet, and perhaps as many as three:

    - A standard AC outlet

    - A telephone jack (if you use the iMac's built-in modem for connecting to the Internet or sending and receiving faxes)

    - A nearby Ethernet jack (if you use the iMac's built-in Ethernet port for connecting to a wired Ethernet network)

        If you prefer to send your data over the airwaves, consider wireless networking for your iMac. I discuss everything you need to know in Chapter 17.

- ✔ **Don't forget the lighting.** Let me act as your Mom. (I know that's a stretch, but bear with me.) She'd say, "You can't possibly expect to work without decent lighting! You'll go blind!" She's right, you know. You need a desk or floor lamp at a minimum.

- ✔ **Plan to expand.** If your iMac hangs out on a desk, allow an additional foot of space on each side. That way, you have space for external peripherals, more powerful speakers, and that wired keyboard and mouse.

Unpacking and Connecting

You are going to love this section — it's short and sweet because the installation of an Intel-based iMac on your desktop is a piece of cake. (Sorry about the cliché overload, but this really *is* easy.)

Unpacking your iMac For Dummies

Follow these guidelines when unpacking your system:

- ✔ **Check for damage.** I've never had a box arrive from Apple with shipping damage, but I've heard horror stories from others (who claim that King Kong must have been working for That Shipping Company). Check all sides of your box before you open it.

    Take a photograph of any significant damage (just in case).

- ✔ **Search for all the parts.** When you're removing those chunks o' Styrofoam, make certain that you've checked all sides of each foam block for parts that are snuggled therein or taped for shipment. Make sure you keep track of your diminutive Apple Remote!

✔ **Keep all those packing materials.** Do *not* head for the trash can with that box and those packing materials. Keep your box intact and also keep all packing materials for at least a year until your standard Apple warranty runs out. If you have to ship it to an Apple service center, the box and the original packing is the only way for your iMac to fly.

And now, a dramatic Mark's Maxim about cardboard containers:

Smart computer owners keep their boxes far longer than a year.™

For example, if you sell your iMac or move across the country, you'll want that box. *Trust me on this one.*

✔ **Store the invoice for safekeeping.** Your invoice is a valuable piece of paper, indeed.

Save your original invoice in a plastic bag, along with your computer's manuals and original software, manuals, and other assorted hoo-hah. Keep the bag on your shelf or stored safely in your desk, and enjoy a little peace of mind.

✔ **Read the iMac's manual.** "Hey, wait a minute, Mark — why do I have to read the manual from Apple along with this tome?" Good question, and here's the answer: There might be new and updated instructions in the documentation from Apple that override what I tell you in this book. (For example, *"Never* cut the red wire. Cut the blue wire instead." Or something to that effect.)

Besides, Apple manuals are rarely thicker than a restaurant menu.

Connecting cables like a true nerd

The iMac makes all its connections really simple, but your computer depends on you to get the outside wires and thingamabobs where they go.

Absolutely essential connections

After your new iMac is resting comfortably in its assigned spot (I assume that's a desktop), you need to make a couple of connections:

✔ **The power cable**

Plug the cable into the corresponding socket on the iMac first; then plug 'er in to that handy AC outlet.

✔ **The (wired) keyboard and mouse**

- Plug the USB cable from your keyboard into one of the USB 2.0 ports on the back of the iMac.

- Plug the Mighty Mouse into one of the USB 1.1 ports on the back of the keyboard.

This saves a USB 2.0 port for better uses. (See the earlier section, "Those holes are called ports, " to see what these ports look like.)

If you bought your iMac equipped with the wireless keyboard and mouse options, your batteries might need to be installed. After the batteries are in, you're set to go.

Adding the Internet to the mix

If you have Internet access or a local computer network, you need to make at least one of the following connections.

If you don't already have *any* Internet service, start with local dialup Internet access. You can check high-speed options later — typically, your local cable and telephone companies can provide you with more information on your long-term choice for Internet service.

Dialup Internet access

If you get on the Internet by dialing a standard phone number you'll need an external USB modem, either from Apple or another manufacturer. Once you've installed the modem to a handy USB port, just make two connections.

1. **Plug one of the telephone cable's connectors into your modem port.**

2. **Plug the other telephone cable connector into your telephone line's wall jack.**

After you get your account information from your ISP, Chapters 6 and 17 have the details on configuring your modem and Internet settings for dialup access.

Networks and high-speed Internet access

If you have high-speed Internet service or if you're in an office or school with a local computer network, you can probably connect through the iMac's built-in Ethernet port. You make two connections:

1. **Plug one end of the Ethernet cable into the Ethernet port on the iMac.**

2. **Plug the other end of the Ethernet cable into the Ethernet port from your network. It's probably one of the following:**

    • An Ethernet wall jack

    • An Ethernet hub or switch

    • A cable or DSL Internet router (or sharing device)

Will you be joining a wireless network? If so, you find the information you need on installing an AirPort Extreme wireless card in Chapter 20, and all the details you need to configure Tiger for wireless networking in Chapter 17.

Discovering All the Cool Things You Can Do

This section answers the most common of all novice computer questions: "What the heck will I *do* with this thing?" You find additional details and exciting factoids about the software that you get for free, software you'll want to buy, and stuff you can do on the Internet.

What software do I get?

Currently, all iMac computers ship with these major software applications installed and ready to use:

- ✔ **The iLife suite:** You know you want these applications! They turn your iMac into a digital hub for practically every kind of high-tech device on the planet, including DV camcorders, digital cameras, portable music players, PDAs, and even cellphones.

 Chapters 11–15 of this book focus on the five applications that make up iLife: iMovie HD, iDVD, iTunes, iPhoto, and GarageBand.

- ✔ **A trial version of iWork:** A try-before-you-buy version of Apple's powerful office productivity suite is included with your iMac. You can create documents, spreadsheets, databases, and presentations within Pages and Keynote. It's much like that other Office Suite (the one that costs a bundle) from those guys in Redmond.

 Figure 1-3 illustrates an AppleWorks drawing document.

  AppleWorks is such a humongous application that it takes an entire Dummies book to cover it all. To wit, you'll find *AppleWorks 6 For Dummies* (written by Bob LeVitus and Dennis Cohen, and published by Wiley) nestled on the shelves of your local bookstore.

- ✔ **Quicken:** Track your expenses, build a budget (and watch it evaporate), and plan for your financial future. Your checkbook suddenly becomes manageable and tax time becomes easier when you organize your financial world with Quicken.

The installed software on your iMac might change as new programs become available.

Looking forward to fun on the Internet

What is a modern computer without the Internet? Apple gives you great tools to take full advantage of every road sign and off-ramp on the Information Superhighway right out of the box:

- ✔ **Web surfing:** I use Tiger's Apple Safari Web browser every single day. It's faster and better designed than Internet Explorer, with unique features like tabbed browsing and built-in RSS feeds.

  If *tabbed browsing* and *RSS feeds* sound like ancient Aztec to you, don't worry. Chapter 8 is devoted entirely to Safari.

- ✔ **Web searches:** Sherlock can search the entire Internet for stocks, movie listings, airline schedules, dictionaries, and foreign language translations. I explain this Internet sleuth in Chapter 7.

✔ **Chat:** *iChat* lets you use your iMac to chat with others around the world for free via the Internet — by keyboard, voice, or (using your built-in iSight Web camera) full-color video. This is awesome stuff straight out of Dick Tracy and Buck Rogers. If you've never seen a video chat, you'll be surprised by just how good your friends and family look!

Always wear a shirt when videoconferencing.

✔ **E-mail:** Soldier, Apple's got you covered. The Mail application is a full-featured e-mail system, complete with defenses against the torrent of junk mail awaiting you. (Imagine a hungry digital saber-tooth tiger with an appetite for spam.) Send pictures and attached files to everyone else on the planet, and look doggone good doing it.

Applications that rock

Dozens of small applications are built into Mac OS X. I mention them in later chapters, but here are three good examples to whet your appetite:

✔ **iCal:** Keep track of your schedule and upcoming events, and even share your calendar online with others in your company or your circle of friends. See how to keep your life in order in Figure 1-3.

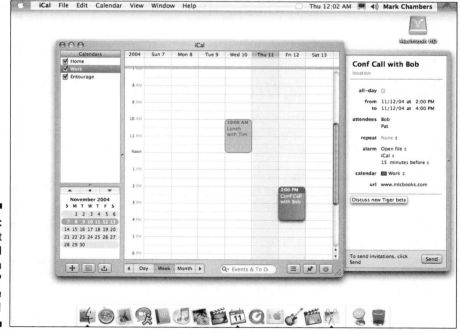

Figure 1-3: Hey, isn't that iCal running on your iMac? You are iTogether!

- **DVD Player:** Put all that widescreen beauty to work and watch your favorite DVD movies with DVD Player! You have all the features of today's most expensive standalone DVD players, too, including a spiffy onscreen control that looks like a remote.

- **Photo Booth:** You can use your iMac's built-in iSight camera to take digital snapshots right from your computer, just like the carnival photo booths of old!

- **Address Book:** Throw away that well-thumbed collection of fading addresses. Tiger's Address Book can store, search, and recall just about any piece of information on your friends, family, and acquaintances.

You can use the data you store in your Address Book in other Apple applications that are included with Tiger, like Apple Mail and iChat.

Would you like to play a game?

"All productivity and no play. . . ." Hey, Steve Jobs likes a good video game as much as the next guy, so you can look forward to playing games on your iMac right out of the box:

- **Board Games:** A selection of the favorite Mac board games — no cleanup afterwords, either.

- **Chess:** Ah, but this isn't the chessboard your Dad used! Play the game of kings against a tough (and configurable) opponent — your iMac — on a beautiful 3-D board. Heck, your Mac even narrates the game by speaking the moves!

Stuff You Oughta Buy Right Now

No man is an island, and no computer is either. I always recommend the same set of stuff for new PC and Mac owners. These extras help keep your new computer clean and healthy (and some make sure you're happy as well):

- **Surge suppressor or UPS (uninterruptible power supply):** Even an all-in-one computer like your iMac can fall prey to a power surge. I recommend one of these:

  - A *basic surge suppressor* with a fuse can help protect your iMac from an overload.

  - A *UPS* costs a little more, but it does a better job of filtering your AC line voltage to prevent brownouts or line interference from reaching your computer.

  A UPS provides a few minutes of battery power during a blackout so you can save your documents and safely shut down your iMac.

✔ **Screen wipes:** Invest in a box of premoistened screen wipes. Your iMac's screen can pick up dirt, fingerprints, and other unmentionables faster than you think.

Make sure your wipes are especially meant for LCD or laptop computer screens.

✔ **Blank CDs and DVDs:** Depending on the type of optical drive that's installed in your computer — and the type of media you're recording, like computer data CDs, DVD movies, or audio CDs — you'll want blank discs for

- CD-R (record once)

- CD-RW (record multiple times)

- DVD-R (record once)

✔ **Cables:** Depending on the external devices and wired network connectivity you'll be using, these are

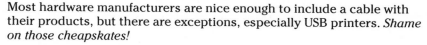

- A standard Ethernet cable (for wired networks or high-speed Internet)

- FireWire or USB cables for devices you already have

Most hardware manufacturers are nice enough to include a cable with their products, but there are exceptions, especially USB printers. _Shame on those cheapskates!_

✔ **A wrist rest for both your keyboard and mouse:** You might have many reasons to buy a new iMac, but I know that a bad case of carpal tunnel syndrome is not one of them. Take care of your wrists by adding a keyboard and mouse rest (even for a wireless keyboard/mouse combo, even on a TV tray).

Chapter 2

Life! Give My iMac Life!

In This Chapter

▶ Turning on your iMac

▶ Checking your iMac for proper operation

▶ Setting up Mac OS X Tiger

▶ Registering your iMac

▶ Using Migration Assistant

▶ Copying information from a Windows PC

---

*I*n Chapter 1, you got as far as unpacking your iMac and connecting a number of cables to it, but unless you solely bought this computer as a work of modern art, it's time to actually turn on your iMac and begin living The Good Life. (Plus, you still get to admire that Apple design whilst using iTunes.) After you get your new beauty powered on, I help you with an initial checkup on your iMac's health.

I also familiarize you with the initial chores that you need to complete — such as using the Mac OS X Setup and moving the data and settings from your existing computer to your iMac — before you settle in with your favorite applications.

In this chapter, I assume that Mac OS X Tiger was preinstalled on your iMac or that you just completed an upgrade to Tiger from an earlier version of Mac OS X. (If you're upgrading, your iMac is already turned on, and you can skip the next section!)

Throwing the Big Leaf Switch

Your iMac's power switch is located on the back of the computer, at the bottom of the line of ports. Press it now to turn on your iMac, and you hear the pleasant start-up tone that's been a hallmark of Apple computers for many years now. The power status light on the front of your iMac's case will also light up. Don't be alarmed if you don't immediately see anything onscreen because it takes a few seconds for the initial Apple logo to appear.

In my personal experience, a simple quick press of the power button on some iMacs sometimes just doesn't do it. Rather, you actually have to hold the button down for a count of two or so before the computer turns on. However, if your iMac ever locks up tight (and you can't quit an application, as I demonstrate in Chapter 4), the power button gives you another option — hold it down for a count of five, and your iMac shuts off.

As the Apple logo appears, you see a twirling, circular high-tech progress indicator appear that looks like something from a *Star Wars* movie. That's the sign that your iMac is loading Tiger and checking your internal drive for problems. Sometimes the twirling circle can take a bit longer to disappear. As long as it's twirling, though, something good is happening. *Note:* There is no On switch for the display on the iMac.

Next, Tiger displays the soon-to-be-quite-familiar Aqua Blue (yup, that's its name) background while it loads certain file sharing, networking, and printing components (and such). This time, you get a more conservative progress bar, but the end result is the same. Just wait patiently a bit longer.

At last, your patience of a whole 10–15 seconds is rewarded, and you see the Tiger Setup Assistant appear.

Mark's Favorite Signs of a Healthy iMac

Before you jump into the fun stuff, don't forget an important step — a quick prelim check of the signs that your iMac survived shipment intact and happy. (Although the shipping box that Apple uses for the iMac is one of the best I've ever encountered in 20+ years of shipping computer hardware, your computer could still have met with foul play.)

If you can answer Yes to each of these questions, your iMac likely made the trip without serious damage:

1. **Is there any obvious damage?**

   It's pretty easy to spot damage to your iMac's svelte white design. Look for scratches, puncture damage, and misalignment of the screen.

2. **Does the LCD screen work, and is it undamaged?**

I'm talking about obvious scratches or puncture damage to your screen. Additionally, you should also check whether any individual dots (or *pixels*) on your LCD monitor are obviously malfunctioning. Bad pixels either appear black or in a different color than everything surrounding them.

Techs call these irritating anarchists *dead pixels*. Unfortunately, many new LCD screens include one or two. After all, there are literally over a million of pixels on a 20" iMac screen.

3. **Can you feel a flow of air from the vent on top?**

   Your iMac's processor generates quite a bit of heat, so the fan system never turns off completely. If you don't feel warm air from the fan system after your iMac has been on for a minute or two, you might have a problem.

4. **Do the keyboard and mouse work?**

   Check your iMac's USB (Universal Serial Bus) ports by moving the mouse; the cursor should move on your screen. To check the keyboard, press the Caps Lock key on the left and observe whether the green Caps Lock light turns on and off.

If you do notice a problem with your iMac (and you can still use your Safari browser and reach the Web), you can make the connection to an Apple support technician on at www.apple.com. If your iMac is lying on its back with its foot in the air and you can't get to the Internet, you can check your phone book for a local Apple service center. Chapter 19 also offers troubleshooting information.

Harriet, It's Already Asking Me Questions!

After your iMac is running and you've given it the once-over for obvious shipping damage, your next chore is to set up your iMac. Unlike other tasks in this book, I won't cover the setup process step by step. Apple contextually tweaks the questions that you see during setup on a regular basis, and the questions are really very easy to answer. Everything is explained onscreen, complete with onscreen Help if you need it.

However, I do want you to know what to expect as well as what information you need to have at hand. I also want you to know about support opportunities like the AppleCare Protection Plan and the Apple .Mac Internet services. Hence this section: Consider it a study guide for whatever your iMac's setup procedure has to throw at you.

Setting up Mac OS X Tiger

After you start your iMac for the first time — or if you just upgraded from Mac OS 9 or an earlier version of Mac OS X — your iMac will likely automatically launches the Tiger setup procedure. (Note that some custom install options, like the *Archive and Install* option, might not launch the Setup procedure.) The set-up process takes care of a number of different tasks:

✔ **Setup provides Tiger with your personal information.**

As I mention in Chapter 1, your iMac ships with a bathtub full of different applications, and many of those use your personal data (like your address and telephone number) to automatically fill out your documents.

If that personal stored information starts you worrying about identity theft, I congratulate you. If you're using your common sense, it should. However, in this case, Apple doesn't disseminate this information anywhere else, and the applications that use your personal data won't send it anywhere, either. And *Safari,* the Apple Web browser, fills out forms on a Web page automatically only if you give your permission.

✔ **Setup configures your language and keyboard choices.**

Mac OS X is a truly international operating system, so Setup offers you a chance to configure your iMac to use a specific language and keyboard layout.

✔ **Setup configures your e-mail accounts within Apple Mail.**

If you already have an e-mail account set up with your ISP, keep that e-mail account information that the ISP provided handy to answer these questions. (The list should include the incoming POP3 and outgoing SMTP mail servers you'll be using, your e-mail address, and your login name and password. Don't worry about those crazy acronyms — your ISP will know exactly what you mean when you ask for this information.)

✔ **Setup allows you to open a trial subscription with Apple's .Mac service.**

Apple's *.Mac* subscription service provides you with online file storage, iSync capability across multiple computers, backups to your online storage, Apple e-mail accounts (through both Web mail and the Apple Mail application), and your own acre of Web site on the Internet. I go into all these in detail in Chapter 9. For now, just sign up and take the opportunity to feel smug about owning an Apple computer.

✔ **Setup sends your registration information to Apple.**

As a proud owner of an iMac, take advantage of the year of hardware warranty support and the free 90 days of telephone support. You have to register to use 'em, but rest assured that all this info is confidential.

✔ **Setup launches Migration Assistant.**

This assistant guides you through the process of *migrating* (an engineer's term for *moving*) your existing user data from your old Mac or PC to your new iMac. Naturally, if your iMac is your first computer, you can skip this step with a song in your heart! (Read more on Migration Assistant in the section, "Importing Documents and Data from Your Old Mac.")

Registering your Mac

I'll be honest here: I know that many of us, myself included, don't register every piece of computer hardware we buy. For example, I didn't register my wireless Bluetooth adapter that I bought for my older iBook because the total expenditure was only around $40, the gizmo has no moving parts, and I'm never likely to need technical support to use it or get it fixed.

However, your iMac is a different kettle of fish altogether, and I *strongly* recommend that you register your purchase with Apple during the setup process. You spent a fair amount on your computer, and it's an investment with a significant number of moving parts.

Even the hardiest of techno-wizards would agree with this important Mark's Maxim:

If you don't register your iMac, you can't receive support.™

And rest assured that Apple is not one of those companies that constantly pesters you with e-mail advertisements and near-spam. I've registered every Apple computer I've owned, and I've never felt pestered. (And I have an extremely low tolerance for spam.)

Importing Documents and Data from Your Old Mac

If you're upgrading from an older Mac running Mac OS X to your new iMac, I have great news for you: Apple includes the *Migration Assistant* utility application that can help you copy (whoops, I mean, *migrate*) all sorts of data from your old Mac to your new machine. The list of stuff that gets copied over includes

✔ **User accounts:** If you set up multiple user accounts (so that more than one person can share the computer), the utility ports them all to your new iMac.

✔ **Network settings:** Boy, howdy, this is a real treat for those with manual network settings provided by an ISP or network administrator! Migration Assistant can re-create the entire network environment of your old Mac on your new iMac.

✔ **System Preference settings:** If you're a fan of tweaking and customizing Mac OS X to fit you like a glove, then rejoice. The Assistant actually copies over all the changes that you've made within System Preferences on your old Mac! (Insert sound of angelic chorus of cherubim and seraphim: *Hallelujah!*)

✔ **Documents:** The files in your Documents folder(s) are copied to your new iMac.

✔ **Applications:** Migration Assistant tries its best to copy over the third-party applications that you've installed in your Applications folder on the older Mac. I say *tries its best* because you might have to reinstall some applications, anyway. Some developers create applications that spread out all sorts of files across your hard drive, and the Assistant just can't keep track of those nomadic files. Too, some other applications make the trek just fine, but you might have to reenter their serial numbers.

Setup launches its Migration Assistant automatically if you indicate that you need to transfer stuff during the Setup process, but you can always launch the Assistant manually at any time. You'll find it in the Utilities folder inside your Applications folder; just double-click the Migration Assistant icon.

To use Migration Assistant to copy your system from your older Mac, you need a FireWire cable to connect the computers. If you don't already have one, you can pick up a standard FireWire cable at your local Maze o' Wires electronics store or at your computer store. (This cable will probably come in handy in the future as well, so it's not a one-use wonder.)

Follow these steps to use Migration Assistant:

1. **Click Continue on the opening screen.**

   The Assistant prompts you for your account name and password that you created during the Setup procedure, as shown in Figure 2-1. Your account is an *admin account,* meaning that you have a higher security level that allows you to change things within Tiger. (Much more detail on user accounts is covered in Chapter 16.)

2. **Type your password and click OK.**

   Characters in your password are displayed as bullet characters for security.

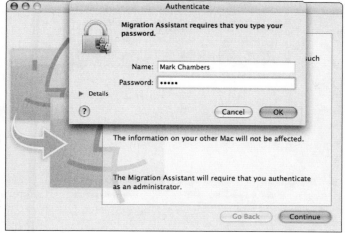

3. **Select the From Another Mac radio button and then click Continue.**

4. **Connect a FireWire cable between the two computers and click Continue.**

5. **Restart your older Mac while holding down the T key.**

   This restarts your older computer in *FireWire Target Disk mode,* in which your older Mac essentially becomes a huge external FireWire hard drive. (Neat trick.)

   You must hold down the T key until you see the FireWire symbol appear on your older machine.

6. **Click Continue.**

7. **Select the check boxes next to the user accounts that you want to transfer from your older machine (as shown in Figure 2-2) and then click Continue.**

   The assistant displays how much space is required to hold the selected accounts on your iMac's hard drive.

8. **Select the check boxes next to the applications and files that you want to copy (see how in Figure 2-3) and then click Continue.**

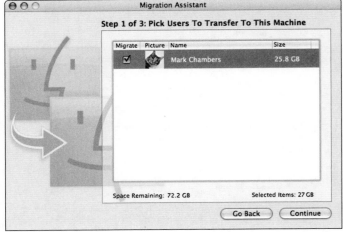

Figure 2-2:
Select
the user
accounts
you want to
migrate.

9. **Select the check boxes next to the settings that you want to transfer (as shown in Figure 2-4).**

   Normally, you want to migrate all three of these settings groups.

10. **Click the Migrate button.**

11. **After everything is copied, you can press and hold the power button on your older Mac to shut it off. Then disconnect the FireWire cable.**

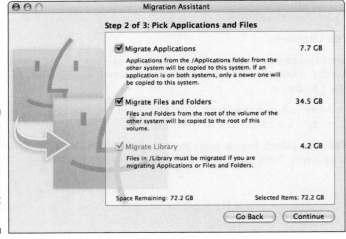

Figure 2-3:
Would
you like
applications
and files
with that
migration?

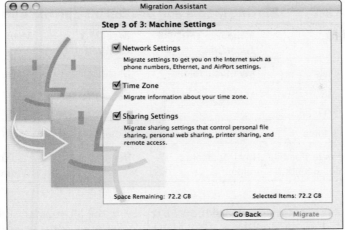

Figure 2-4:
Copy
Mac OS X
settings
with
Migration
Assistant.

Importing Documents and Data from Windows

If you're a classic Windows-to-Mac *Switcher,* you made a wise choice, especially if you're interested in the creative applications within the iLife suite! Although you can choose to start your Apple computing life anew, you probably want to migrate some of your existing documents and files from that tired PC to your bright, shiny, new iMac.

Unfortunately, no Windows Migration Assistant exists within Mac OS X. However, if you're moving from a Windows PC to an iMac, you can copy your files manually from a CD or DVD, a USB Flash drive, or over a network. (Note, however, that the iMac doesn't come with a floppy drive. And trust me, you wouldn't want to use one to move anything that matters, anyway.)

The Mac OS X Help system contains an entire subsection on specific tricks that you can use when switching from Windows to Mac, including how to connect to a Windows network and how to connect the two computers together directly.

Because Tiger can't run Windows programs (at least, not without extra software), moving applications (think Paint Shop Pro) won't do you any good. In general, however, you can move documents, movies, photos, and music without a problem. Table 2-1 illustrates what can be moved between Windows XP and Mac OS X as well as the application that you use in Tiger to open those files and documents.

Table 2-1	Moving Media and Documents betwixt Computers		
File Type	*Windows XP Location*	*Mac OS X Location*	*Mac Application*
Music files	My Music folder	Music folder	iTunes
Video and movie files	My Videos folder	Movies folder	QuickTime/DVD Player
Digital photos	My Pictures folder	Pictures folder	iPhoto
Excel/PowerPoint/ Word documents	My Documents folder	Documents folder	Mac Office/ iWorks

If you don't mind investing around $50, try using the Move2Mac software utility, which does most of the work of Migration Assistant for those switching from a Windows PC. From Detto Technologies (www.detto.com/move2mac), Move2Mac comes complete with a special USB-to-USB cable that connects your two computers for high-speed copying. With Move2Mac, you can choose what you want to transfer to your new iMac (use Table 2-1 as a guide), and the copying is done automatically for you. Plus, Move2Mac also transfers goodies like your home page and bookmarks from Internet Explorer, desktop backgrounds, and even your Address Book contacts and account settings from Outlook Express. Move2Mac makes switching much easier, and I can highly recommend it.

Chapter 3

Introducing the Apple of Your iMac

*I*n the other books that I've written about Mac OS X Tiger, I use all sorts of somewhat understated phrases to describe my operating system of choice, like *elegantly reliable, purely powerful,* and *supremely user-friendly.*

But *why* is Tiger such a standout? To be specific, why do creative professionals and computer techno-wizards across the globe hunger for the very same Mac OS X that runs your iMac? Why is Tiger so far ahead of Windows XP in features and performance? Good questions, all!

In this chapter, I answer those queries and satisfy your curiosity about your new big cat. I introduce the main elements of the Tiger Desktop, and I show you the fearless UNIX heart that beats underneath Tiger's sleek exterior. I also point out the most important similarities between Tiger and Windows XP, and I outline the resources available if you need help with Mac OS X.

Oh, and I promise to use honest-to-goodness English in my explanations, with a minimum of engineer-speak and indecipherable acronyms. (Hey, you've got to boast about Tiger in turn to your family and friends. Aunt Harriet might not be as technologically savvy as we are.)

A Quick Tour About the Premises

Tiger is a special type of software called an *operating system.* You know, OS, as in *Mac OS X?* That means that Tiger essentially runs your iMac and also allows you to run all your other applications, like AppleWorks or Photoshop. It's the most important computer application — or *software* — that you run.

Think of a pyramid, with Tiger as the foundation and other applications running on top.

You're using the operating system when you aren't running a specific application, such as these actions:

- ✔ Copying files from a CD to your hard drive
- ✔ Choosing a different screensaver

Sometimes, Tiger even peeks through an application while it's running. For example, actions like these are also controlled by Tiger:

- ✔ The Open, Save, and Save As dialogs that you see when working with files in Photoshop CS
- ✔ The Print dialog that appears when you print a document in Microsoft Word 2004

In this section, I escort you personally around the most important hotspots in Tiger, and you meet the most interesting onscreen thingamabobs that you use to control your iMac. (I told you I wasn't going to talk like an engineer!)

The Tiger Desktop

This particular Desktop isn't made of wood, and you can't stick your gum underneath. However, your Tiger Desktop does indeed work much like the surface of a traditional desk. You can store things there, organize things into folders, and take care of important tasks like running other applications. Heck, you've even got a clock and a trash can.

Gaze upon Figure 3-1 and follow along as you venture to your Desktop and beyond.

Meet me at the Dock

The Dock is the closest thing to the dashboard of a car that you're likely to find on a Macintosh. It's a pretty versatile combination — it's one part organizer, one part application launcher, and one part system monitor. From here, you can launch applications, see what's currently running, and display or hide the windows shown by your applications.

Finder menu   Finder window

Figure 3-1:
Everything
Tiger starts
here — the
Mac OS X
Desktop.

Dock   Icons

Each icon in the Dock represents one of the following:

- ✔ An application that you can run (or is currently running)
- ✔ An application window that's minimized (shrunk)
- ✔ A Web page
- ✔ A document or folder on your system
- ✔ A network server or shared folder
- ✔ Your Trash

I cover the Dock in more detail in Chapter 5.

The Dock is highly configurable:

- ✔ It can appear at different sides of the screen.
- ✔ It can disappear until you move your mouse pointer to the edge to call it forth.
- ✔ You can resize it larger or smaller.

Dig those crazy icons

By default, Tiger always displays at least one icon on your Desktop: your Mac's internal hard drive. To open a hard drive and view or use the contents, you double-click the icon. Other icons that might appear on your Desktop can include

- CDs and DVDs
- An iPod
- External hard drives or USB Flash drives
- Applications, folders, and documents
- Files you've downloaded from the Internet
- Network servers you've accessed

Chapter 4 provides the good stuff on icons and their uses within Tiger.

There's no food on this menu

The Finder menu isn't found in a restaurant. You find it at the top of the Desktop, where you can use it to control your applications. Virtually every application that you run on your iMac has a menu.

To use a menu command, follow these steps:

1. **Click the menu group (like File or Edit).**

2. **Choose the desired command from the list that appears.**

Virtually every Macintosh application has some menu groups, like File, Edit and Window. You're likely to find similar commands within these groups. However, only two menu groups are in *every* Mac OS X application:

- The *Apple menu* (which is identified with that jaunty Apple Corporation icon,).
- The *application menu* (which always bears the name of the active application). For instance, the DVD Player menu group appears when you run Tiger's DVD Player, and the Word menu group appears when you launch Microsoft Word 2004.

I cover these two common groups in more detail in Chapters 4 and 5.

There's always room for one more window

You're probably already familiar with the ubiquitous window itself. Both Tiger and the applications that you run use windows to display things like

- The documents that you create
- The contents of your hard drive

Isn't Windows XP the latest thing?

You've seen highly customized "pocket rocket" compact cars with the flashy paint jobs, huge noisy mufflers, and aerodynamic fiberglass stuff. You might think that these cars are real road racers, but what's underneath is different. The 4-cylinder engine that you *don't* see is completely stock. These cars don't perform any better than a mundane model straight from the factory.

The same holds true for Microsoft Windows XP, which was another attempt by the folks at Redmond to put a modern face on an antique operating system. Forget the flashy colors and the visual effects: Windows XP is simply more of the same (and it's now several years old to boot). Sure, it's more reliable and faster than Windows 98 and Windows Me, but forget real performance or innovation. (Unfortunately, if you're running PC hardware, the only other practical choice for a computing novice is Linux, which is still regarded as too complex by major manufacturers like Dell and Hewlett-Packard. Therefore, with a PC, you're usually stuck with Windows XP, or you've picked up a very expensive paperweight.)

The window in Figure 3-1 is a Finder window, where Tiger gives you access to the applications, documents, and folders on your system.

Windows are surprisingly configurable. I cover them at length in Chapter 4.

What's going on underneath?

How the core is designed makes more of a difference than all the visual bells and whistles, which tend to be similar between Windows XP and Mac OS X Tiger (and Linux as well, for that matter). Time for a Mark's Maxim:

> **Sure, Tiger's elegant exterior is a joy to use, but Mac OS X is a better operating system than Windows because of the unique UNIX muscle that lies underneath!**™

So what should you and I look for in an operating system? Keep in mind that today's computer techno-wizard demands three requirements for a truly high-powered software wonderland — and Mac OS X Tiger easily meets all three:

✔ **Reliability:** Your operating system has to stay up and running reliably for as long as necessary — I'm talking *months* here — without lockups or error messages. If an application crashes, the rest of your work should remain safe, and you should be able to shut down the offending software.

It's Apple to the rescue!

UNIX is the super-reliable operating system that powers most of the high-performance servers that make up the Internet. UNIX has built-in support for virtually every hardware device ever wrought by the hand of Man (including all the cool stuff that came with your iMac), and UNIX is well designed and highly efficient.

Unfortunately, standard UNIX looks as hideous as DOS, complete with a confusing command line, so ease-of-use for normal human beings like you and me goes out the door. Enter the genius types at Apple, who figured several years ago that all UNIX needed was a state-of-the-art, novice-friendly interface! To wit: Mac OS X was developed with a UNIX foundation (or *core*), so it shares the same reliability and performance as UNIX. However, the software engineers at Apple (who know a thing or two about ease-of-use) made it good-looking and easy to use.

This is the secret to the worldwide fever over Mac OS X: It blends the best of UNIX (an established, super-powered operating system) with the

best of earlier Macintosh operating systems like Mac OS 9. Mac OS X is not only easy to use, but it runs tight, concentric *sassy* rings around anything that Microsoft is likely to offer before 2006.

That's as far as I delve into the foundation of Tiger in this volume — understandable, because there's lots more iMac to cover! It's my job to help you use the features and controls within Tiger, not turn you into a bearded UNIX nerd with a pocket protector and suspenders. In fact, you never see the UNIX running underneath Tiger (unless you want to, by running the Terminal application). Instead, iMac owners can stay safely in the elegant world of drag-and-drop and point-and-click.

If you are interested in all the details about what makes Mac OS X tick, as well as its settings and features, I can heartily recommend another of my books, the bestselling (and extremely heavy) *Mac OS X Tiger All-in-One Desk Reference For Dummies* (Wiley). It comprehensively covers everything Tiger — over 700 pages devoted entirely to Mac OS X and its companion applications!

✔ **Performance:** If your computer has advanced hardware, your operating system must be able to use those resources to speed things up big-time. The operating system has to be highly configurable, and it has to be updated often to keep up with the latest in computer hardware.

"Mark, what do you mean by advanced hardware?" Well, if you're already knowledgeable about state-of-the-art hardware, examples include

- True 64-bit computing

- Multiple processors (like more than one chip in your computer)

- A huge amount of RAM (4GB or more)

- Enough hard drive space to make use of a RAID array

If all that sounds like ancient Sumerian, gleefully ignore this technical drabble and keep reading.

✔ **Ease of use:** All the speed and reliability in the world won't help an operating system if it's difficult to use.

DOS was the PC operating system of choice before the arrival of Windows. It was doomed because it wasn't intuitive or easy to master, requiring a PC owner to remember all sorts of commands that looked like hieroglyphics. (This is one of the reasons why the Macintosh was so incredibly popular in the days of DOS-based PCs — Macs had a mouse, and they were a snap to master and use.)

Similarities with That Windows Behemoth

You might have heard of the *Windows Switcher:* a uniquely intelligent species that's becoming more and more common these days. Switchers are former PC owners who have abandoned Windows and bought a Macintosh, thereby joining the Apple faithful running Mac OS X. (Apple loves to document this migration on its Web site.) Because today's Macintosh computers are significantly faster than their PC counterparts — and you get neat software like Tiger and the iLife suite when you buy a new Mac — switching makes perfect sense.

Like Windows, but better

Switchers aren't moving to totally unfamiliar waters. Windows XP and Tiger share a number of important concepts. Familiarizing yourself with Tiger takes far less time than you might think.

Here's an overview of the basic similarities between the two operating systems:

✔ **The Desktop:** The Tiger Desktop is a neat representation of a real physical desktop, and Windows XP uses the same idea:

- You can arrange files, folders, and applications on your Desktop to help keep things handy.

- Application windows appear on the Desktop.

✔ **Drives, files, and folders:** Data is stored in files on your hard drive(s), and those files can be organized in folders. Both Tiger and Windows XP use the same file/folder concept.

✔ **Specific locations:** Both Windows XP and Tiger provide every user with a set of folders to help keep various types of files organized. For example, the My Videos folder that you can use in Windows XP corresponds to the Movies folder that you find in your Home folder within Tiger.

✔ **Running programs:** Both Tiger and Windows XP run programs (or applications) in the same manner:

   • Double-clicking an application icon launches that application.

   • Double-clicking a document runs the corresponding application and then automatically loads the document.

✔ **Window control:** Yep, both operating systems use windows, and those windows can be resized, hidden (or minimized), and closed in similar fashions. (Are you starting to see the connections here?)

✔ **Drag-and-drop:** One of the basics behind a GUI (a ridiculous acronym that stands for *graphical user interface*) like Windows XP and Tiger is the ability to drag documents and folders around to move, delete, copy, and load them. Drag-and-drop is one of the primary advantages of both of these operating systems — copying a file by dragging it from one window to another is intuitive and easy enough for a kid to accomplish.

✔ **Editing:** Along the same lines as drag-and-drop, both Tiger and Windows XP offer similar cut-and-paste editing features. You've likely used Cut, Copy, and Paste for years, so this is familiar stuff.

Loading the truck

Most folks use a high-capacity external hard drive when moving their documents from a PC to an iMac. Remember, you won't have to copy any applications or support files, so all that you'll be transferring are the files that you created yourself. For example, a Switcher is likely to copy media files (like music tracks and video clips), word processing and spreadsheet documents, and the like.

Keep in mind that a folder you create on your PC's hard drive will copy just fine under Tiger, so you can leave your files arranged in their current folders to help keep them organized. For example, if you store all your Quicken data files for the last few years in a folder named Financial Archives, go ahead and copy that entire folder to the external drive.

If you're undertaking a switch from Windows XP to Tiger, I highly recommend using Move2Mac ($50) from Detto Technologies (www.detto.com). This application takes care of most migration chores automatically, like moving the files that you select from XP to their corresponding locations in Tiger. Move2Mac also transfers your contacts, e-mail settings, and Internet configuration to your new Mac. The package comes complete with a specially designed USB cable for connecting the two computers, so you don't even need an external hard drive to make the switch.

Wondering what you can do about Windows-only applications that you leave behind if you switch? Are you a Mac owner who must run a program that's available only for Windows? Believe it or not, Microsoft comes to the rescue with Virtual PC 7 (as shown in Figure 3-2). Virtual PC allows your iMac to run multiple "virtual copies" of Windows 98, Me, 2000, or XP . . . you can even run Linux! (The operating system and software that you install and run within your virtual PC hardware environment can't tell the difference.) I discuss Virtual PC 7 again in a little more detail in Chapter 23.

Figure 3-2:
Hey, isn't that Windows running on my Tiger Desktop?

Calling for Help

You can call on these resources if you need additional help while you're discovering how to tame the Tiger.

Some of the help resources are located on the Internet, so your Web browser will come in handy.

Tiger's built-in Help system

Sometimes the help you need is as close as the Help group on the menu. You can get help for either

- **A specific application:** Just click Help.
- **Actions and functions (topics):** Click a Finder window and then press ⌘+? to summon the top-level Mac OS Help menu.

After the Help viewer appears, click in the Ask a Question box and type a short phrase that sums up your query (such as *startup keys*). Press Return to list the topics that most closely match your search phrase. To display the Help text for an entry in the topic list, just double-click it.

Apple's Web-based support center

Apple has online product support areas for every hardware and software product that it manufactures. Visit www.apple.com and click the Support tab at the top of the Web page.

The Search box works just like the Mac OS Help system, but the Knowledge Base that Apple provides online has a *lot* more answers.

Magazines

Many magazines (both in print and online) offer tips and tricks on using and maintaining Mac OS X Tiger.

My personal online favorites are Macworld (www.macworld.com) and MacAddict (www.macaddict.com).

Mac support Web sites

A number of private individuals and groups offer support forums on the Web, and you can often find help from other Mac owners on these sites within a few hours of posting a question.

I'm very fond of MacFixIt (www.macfixit.com) and MacMinute (www.mac minute.com).

Mac newsgroups on Usenet

If you're familiar with Usenet newsgroups, you can find lots of help (typically dispensed with a healthy dose of opinion) in newsgroups like comp.sys.mac. system and comp.sys.mac.applications. Simply post a message and then check back within a few hours to read the replies.

Local Mac user groups

I'm remiss if I don't mention your local Mac user group. Often a user group maintains its own Web site and discussion forum. If you can wait until the next meeting, you can even ask your question and receive a reply from a real-live human being . . . quite a thrill in today's Web-riffic world!

Part II
Shaking Hands with Mac OS X

The 5th Wave   By Rich Tennant

DARRYL PREPARES TO ENGAGE WITH THE AQUA INTERFACE

In this part . . .

In this part, you delve deeper into the works of Mac OS X Tiger. I show you how to perform all sorts of common tasks, as well as how to customize your system, how to change settings in System Preferences, where your personal files are stored, and how to use the latest Spotlight search technology to find *anything* you've stored on your iMac!

Chapter 4

Opening and Closing and Clicking and Such

A h, the Finder — many admire its scenic beauty, but don't ignore its unsurpassed power nor its many moods. And send a postcard while you're there.

Okay, so Tiger's Finder might not be *quite* as majestic as the mighty Mississippi River, but it's the basic toolbox that you use every single day while piloting your iMac. The Finder includes the most common elements of Mac OS X: window controls, common menu commands, icon fun (everything from launching applications to copying files), network connections, keyboard shortcuts, and even emptying the Trash. In fact, one could say that if you master the Finder and find how to use it efficiently, you're on your way to becoming a power user! (My editor calls this the Finder "window of opportunity." She's a hoot.)

That's what this chapter is designed to do: This is your Finder tour guide, and we're ready to roll.

Working within the Finder

This is a hands-on tour, with none of that "On your right, you'll see the historic Go menu" for you! Time to get off the bus and start the tour with Figure 4-1, in which I show you around the most important elements of the Finder.

(In the upcoming section, "Performing Tricks with Finder Windows," I give you a close-up view of window controls.)

The popular attractions include

- **The Apple menu ():** This is a special menu because it appears both in the Finder and within every application menu that you run: It doesn't matter whether you're in iTunes or Photoshop or Word — if you can see a menu bar, the Apple menu is there. The Apple menu contains common commands to use no matter where you are in Tiger, such as Restart, Shut Down, and System Preferences.

- **The Finder menu bar:** Whenever the Finder itself is ready to use (or, in Mac-speak, whenever the Finder is the *active* application rather than another application), the Finder menu bar appears at the top of your screen. You know the Finder is active and ready when the word *Finder* appears at the left of the menu bar.

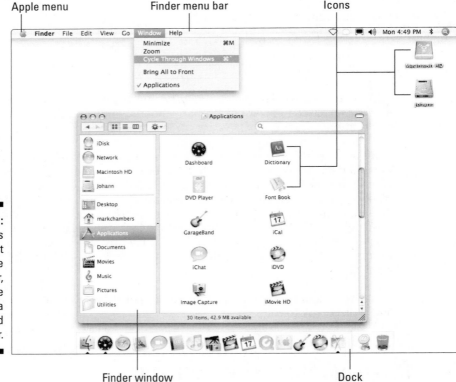

Figure 4-1: Tiger's friendliest face — the Finder, complete with a window and menu bar.

If you're brand new to computers, a *menu* is simply a list of commands. For example, you click the File menu and then choose to save a document. When you click a menu, it extends down so that you can see the commands it includes. While the menu is extended, you can choose any enabled menu item (just click it) to perform that action. You can tell that an item is enabled if its name appears in black; conversely, a menu command is disabled if it is grayed-out — clicking it does nothing.

When you see a menu path like this — File⇨Save — it's just a visual shortcut that tells you to click the File menu and then choose Save from the drop-down menu that appears.

✔ **The Desktop:** Your Finder Desktop serves the same purpose as your physical desktop: You can store stuff here (files, alias icons, and so on), and it's a solid, stable surface where you can work comfortably. Application windows appear on the Desktop, for example, as do other applications such as your Stickies notes and your DVD player. Just click an application there to launch it.

Your Desktop is easily customized in many ways. For example, you can use your own images to decorate the Desktop, organize it to store new folders and documents, arrange icons how you like, or put the Dock in another location. Don't worry — I cover all this in other areas of the book — I just want you to know that you don't have to settle for what Apple gives you as a default Desktop.

✔ **All sorts of icons:** This is a Macintosh computer, after all, replete with tons of make-your-life-easier tools. Check out the plethora of icons on your Desktop as well as icons within the Finder window itself. Each icon is a shortcut of sorts to a file, folder, network connection, or device in your system, including applications that you run and documents that you create. Refer to Figure 4-1 to see the icon for my iMac's hard drive icon, labeled Macintosh HD. Sometimes you click an icon to watch it do its thing (like icons in the Dock, which I cover next), but usually you double-click an icon to make something happen.

✔ **The Dock:** The Dock is a launching pad for your favorite applications, network connections, and Web sites. You can also refer to it to see what applications are running. Click an icon there to open the item (for example, the postage stamp icon represents Apple's Mail application, while the spiffy compass will launch your Safari Web browser).

✔ **The Finder window:** Finally! The simple Finder window in Figure 4-1 displays the contents of my Home folder. You'll use Finder windows to launch applications, perform disk chores like copying and moving files, and navigate your hard drive.

Mousing in a Mac World

Tiger takes a visual approach to everything, and what you see in Figure 4-1 is designed for point-and-click convenience because the mouse is your primary navigational tool while you're using your iMac. You click an item, it opens, you do your thing, and life is good. If you've grazed on the other side of the fence — one of Those Who Were Once Windows Users — you are probably accustomed to using a mouse with at least two buttons. This brings up the nagging question: "Hey, Mark! Where the heck is the right mouse button?"

In a nutshell, the right mouse button simply ain't there. At least, if you're using your iMac original equipment mouse, it simply ain't there. The entire top of an original-equipment iMac (or any Mac) mouse is one huge button, and you click something by pressing down anywhere on the top surface of the aforementioned rodent.

Lean in closer, and I'll tell you a secret. (Dramatic pause.) This is one of the few disagreements that I have with my friends at Apple Computer, Inc. Apple feels that a mouse needs but one button. And before the arrival of Mac OS X, I used to agree that the world needed only one mouse button, but now I feel that a right mouse button is pretty doggone essential. In fact, my iMac's Logitech optical trackball (a really fancy mouse, in effect) has both a right mouse button and a scroll wheel. (You use the scroll wheel to move up and down through the pages of a document or to move up and down through a long Web page.) So here's a Mark's Maxim that I think you'll appreciate more and more as you use your iMac:

> **If you can afford a new mouse or trackball with more than one button,** *buy it.* **You can thank me later with an e-mail message, which you can send to** mark@mlcbooks.com.™

Clicking the right mouse button performs the same default function in Tiger that it does in Windows. Namely, when you click the right mouse button on most items — icons, documents, even your Desktop — you get a *contextual menu* of things. That is, you get more commands specific to that item. (Boy howdy, I hate that word *contextual*, but that's what engineers call it. I call it the right-click menu, and I promise to refer to it as such for the rest of the book.)

Figure 4-2 illustrates a typical convenient right-click menu within a Finder window. I have all sorts of cool items at my disposal on this menu because it's on an application that makes use of a right-click menu.

Don't despair, though, if you're the owner of the Apple One-Button Wonder-Mouse. You can still display a right-click menu: You just have to hold down either Control key while you click. (The mouse cursor gains a tiny funky-looking menu sidecar when you hold down Control to indicate that you're going to right-click something.)

Figure 4-2:
Well-
adjusted
folks call
this a right-
click menu.

Pressing an extra key, as you might imagine, can be a real downer, especially if your non-mouse-holding hand is busy doing something else. Hence my preceding Mark's Maxim. Someday, Apple will finally throw in the towel and add a second mouse button. I'm hoping it's before the arrival of our next President.

Launching and Quitting for the Lazy iMac Owner

Now it's time for you to pair your newly found mouse acumen with Tiger's Finder window. Follow along this simple exercise. Move your mouse cursor over the iTunes icon in the Dock (this icon looks like an audio CD with a green musical note on it) and click once. Whoosh! Tiger *launches* (or starts) the iTunes application, and you see a window much like the one in Figure 4-3.

If an application icon is already selected (which I discuss in the next section), you can simply press ⌘+O to launch it. The same key shortcut works with documents, too.

Close window button

Named menu

Figure 4-3:
Clicking a
Dock icon to
launch that
application.

Besides the Dock, you have several other ways to launch an application or open a document in Tiger:

✔ **From the Apple menu (🍎):** A number of different applications can always be launched anywhere within Tiger from the Apple menu:

   • *System Preferences:* This is where you change all sorts of settings, such as your display background and how icons appear.

   • *Software Update:* This uses the Internet to see whether update patches are available for your Apple software.

   • *Mac OS X Software:* This launches the Safari browser and displays software you can download for your iMac.

✔ **From the Desktop:** If you have a document that you've created or an application icon on your Desktop, you can launch or open it here by *double-clicking* that icon (clicking the mouse twice in rapid succession when the mouse cursor is on top of the icon).

Double-clicking a device or network connection on your Desktop opens the contents in a Finder window. This works for CDs and DVDs that you've loaded as well as external hard drives and USB Flash drives. Just double-click 'em to open them and display their contents in a Finder window. Applications and documents launch from a CD, a DVD, or an external drive just like they launch from your internal drive (the one that's named Macintosh HD), so you don't have to copy stuff from the external drive just to use it. (You can't change the contents of most CDs and DVDs; they're read-only, so you can't write to them.)

✔ **From the Recent Items selection:** When you click the Apple menu and hover your mouse over the Recent Items menu item, the Finder displays all the applications and documents you've used over the last few computing sessions. Click an item in this list to launch or open it.

✔ **From the Login Items list:** Login Items are applications that Tiger launches automatically each time you log in to your user account.

I cover Login Items in detail in Chapter 16.

✔ **From the Finder window:** You can also double-click an icon within the confines of a Finder window to open it (for documents), launch it (for applications), or display the contents (for a folder).

After you finish using an application, you can quit that application to close its window and return to the Desktop. Here are a number of different ways to quit an application:

✔ **Press ⌘+Q.** This keyboard shortcut quits virtually every Macintosh application on the planet.

✔ **Choose the Quit command in the menu.** To display the Quit command, click the application's name — its menu — from the menu bar. This menu is always to the immediate right of the Apple menu. (For example, Safari displays a Safari menu, and that same spot in the menu is taken up by iCal when iCal is the active application. In Figure 4-3, look for the iTunes menu, right next to .)

✔ **Choose Quit from the Dock.** You can Control-click (or right-click) an application's icon on the Dock and choose Quit from the right-click menu that appears.

A running application displays a small black triangle under its icons on the Dock.

✔ **Click the Close button on the application window (refer to Figure 4-3).** Some applications quit entirely when you close their window, like the System Preferences window or Apple's DVD Player. Other applications might continue running without any window, like Safari or iTunes; to close these applications, you have to use another method in this list.

> ✔ **Choose Force Quit from the Apple menu.** *This is a last-resort measure!* Use this only if an application has frozen and you can't use another method in this list to quit. Force-quitting an application doesn't save any changes to any open documents within that application!

Juggling Folders and Icons

Finder windows aren't just for launching applications and opening the files and documents you've created. You can also use the icons within a Finder window to select one or more specific items or to copy and move items from place to place within your system.

A field observer's guide to icons

Not all icons are created equal. Earlier in this chapter, I introduce you to your iMac's hard drive icon on the Desktop, but here is a little background on the other types of icons that you might encounter during your iMac travels:

- ✔ **Hardware:** These are your storage devices, like your hard drive and DVD drive, as well as external peripherals like your iPod and printer.

- ✔ **Applications:** These icons represent the applications (or programs) that you can launch. Most applications have a custom icon that incorporates the company's logo or the specific application logo, so they're very easy to recognize, as you can see in Figure 4-4. Double-clicking an application usually doesn't load a document automatically; you typically get a new blank document, or an Open dialog box from which you can choose the existing file you want to open.

- ✔ **Documents:** Many of the files on your hard drive are documents that can be opened within the corresponding application, and the icon usually looks similar to the application's icon. Double-clicking a document automatically launches the required application (as long as Mac OS X recognizes the file type).

- ✔ **Files:** Most of the file icons on your system are mundane things (like preference and settings files, text files, log files, and miscellaneous data files), yet most are identified with at least some type of recognizable icon that lets you guess what purpose the file serves. You also come across generic file icons that look like a blank sheet of paper (used when Tiger has no earthly idea what the file type is).

- ✔ **Aliases:** An *alias* acts as a link to another item elsewhere on your system. For example, to launch Adobe Acrobat, you can click an Adobe

Acrobat alias icon that you created on your Desktop rather than the actual Acrobat application icon. The alias essentially acts the same way as the original icon, but it doesn't take up the same space — only a few bytes for the icon itself, compared with the size of the actual application. Plus, you don't have to go digging through folders galore to find the original application icon. (Windows Switchers know an alias as a *shortcut*, and the idea is the same although Macs had it *first*. Harrumph.) You can always identify an alias by the small curved arrow at the base of the icon — and the icon might also sport the tag alias at the end of its name.

Figure 4-4: A collection of some of my favorite application icons.

You have two ways to create an alias. Here's one:

   a. Select the item.

   The following section has details about selecting icons.

   b. Choose File⇨Make Alias, or press ⌘+L.

   Figure 4-5 illustrates a number of aliases, arranged beneath their linked files.

Here's another way to create an alias:

   a. Hold down ⌘+Option.

   b. Drag the original icon to the location where you want the alias.

   Note that this funky method doesn't add the alias tag to the end of the alias icon name!

Figure 4-5:
No, not the famous girl-spy TV show. These are alias icons in Tiger.

So why bother to use an alias? Two good reasons:

Launch an application or open a document from anywhere on your drive. For example, you can start Pages directly from the folder where you store the documents for your current Pages project. Speed, organization, and convenience . . . life is good.

Send an alias to the Trash without affecting on the original item. When that AppleWorks project is finished, you can safely delete the entire folder without worrying about whether AppleWorks will run the next time you double-click the application icon!

If you move or rename the original file, Tiger is actually smart enough to update the alias, too! However, if the original file is deleted (or if the original is moved to a different volume, like an external hard drive), the alias no longer works. (Go figure.)

Selecting items

Often, the menu commands or keyboard commands that you perform in the Finder need to be performed on something: Perhaps you're moving an item to the Trash, or getting more information on the item, or creating an alias for that item. In order to identify the target of your action to the Finder, you need to select one or more items on your Desktop or in a Finder window. In this section, I show you just how to do that.

Selecting one thing

Tiger gives you a number of options when selecting just one item for an upcoming action:

✔ **Move your mouse pointer over the item and click.** A dark border (or *highlight*) appears around the icon, indicating that it's selected.

✔ **Type the first few letters of the icon's name.** As soon as you type enough letters to match an item name uniquely, Tiger highlights (and selects) that item.

✔ **If an icon is already highlighted on your Desktop or within a window, move the selection highlight to another icon in the same location by using the arrow keys.** To move through the icons alphabetically, press Tab to go forward or press Shift+Tab to go backward. To shift the selection highlight alphabetically, press Tab (to move in order) or Shift+Tab (to move in reverse order).

Selecting items in the Finder doesn't actually *do* anything to them by itself. You have to perform an action on the selected items to make something happen.

Selecting a whole bunch of things

You can also select multiple items with aplomb by using one of these methods:

✔ **Adjacent items**

• *Drag a box around them.* If that sounds like ancient Sumerian, here's the explanation: Click a spot above and to the left of the first item; then hold down the mouse button and drag down and to the right. (This is *dragging* in Mac-speak.) A box outline like the one in Figure 4-6 appears, indicating what you're selecting. Any icons that appear within the box outline are selected when you release the mouse button.

Figure 4-6:
Drag a box
around
icons to
select them.

> • *Click the first item to select it and then hold down the Shift key while you click the last item.* Tiger selects both items and everything between them.

✔ **Nonadjacent items:** Select these by holding down the ⌘ key while you click each item.

Check out the status line at the bottom of a Finder window. It tells you how much space is available on the drive you're working in as well as how many items are displayed in the current Finder window. When you select items, it shows you how many you highlighted.

Copying items

Want to copy items from one Finder window to another, or from one location (like a CD-ROM) to another (like your Desktop). Très easy. Just use one of these methods:

✔ **On the same drive**

> • *To copy one item to another location:* Hold down the Option key (you don't have to select the icon first) and then click and drag the item from its current home to the new location.
>
> To put a copy of an item within a folder, just drop the item on top of the receiving folder. If you hold the item that you're dragging over the destination folder for a second or two, Tiger opens up a new window so you can see the contents of the target.
>
> • *To copy multiple items to another location:* Select them all first (see the earlier section, "Selecting a whole bunch of things") and then drag and drop one of the selected items where you want it. All the items that you selected follow the item you drag. (Rather like lemmings. Nice touch, don't you think?)

To help indicate your target when you're copying or moving files, Tiger highlights the location to show you where the items will end up. (This works whether the target location is a folder or a drive icon.) If the target location is a window, Tiger adds a highlight to the window border.

✔ **On a different drive**

> • *To copy one or multiple items:* Click and drag the icon (or the selected items if you have more than one) from the original window to a window you've opened on the target drive. You can also drag one item (or a selected group of items) and simply drop the items on top of the drive icon on your Desktop.
>
> The items are copied to the top level, or *root,* of the target drive.

My, what an attractive sidebar . . . and so useful!

I like as few icons on my Desktop as possible. I created a separate folder, named Incoming, and put all the items that might otherwise end up on my Desktop into that folder. In fact, I recently added my Incoming folder to my Finder window

Sidebar so that it's available immediately from any Finder window. To do this, just drag the folder into the column at the left side of the Finder window and drop it in the Sidebar's list of folder icons.

If you try to move or copy something to a location that already has an item with the same name, Figure 4-7 illustrates the answer: You get a dialog that prompts you to decide whether to replace the file or to stop the copy/move procedure and leave the existing file alone. Good insurance, indeed.

Figure 4-7:
It's your choice, but replace the existing file only if you're sure of what you're doing.

Moving things from place to place

Moving things from one location to another location on the same drive is the easiest action you can take. Just drag the item (or selected items) to the new location. The item disappears from the original spot and reappears in the new spot.

Duplicating in a jiffy

If you need more than one copy of the same item within a folder, use Tiger's Duplicate command. I use Duplicate often when I want to edit a document but ensure that the original document stays pristine, no matter what. I just create a duplicate and edit that file instead.

To use Duplicate, you can

- ✔ Click an item to select it and then choose File➪Duplicate.
- ✔ Control-click the item and choose Duplicate from the right-click menu.
- ✔ Hold down the Option key and drag the original item to another spot in the same window; when you release the mouse button, the duplicate file appears like magic!

The duplicate item has the word `copy` appended to its name. A second copy is named `copy2`, a third is `copy3`, and so on.

Duplicating a folder also duplicates all the contents of that folder, so creating a duplicate folder can take some time to create if the original folder was stuffed full. The duplicate folder has `copy` appended to its name, as well.

Keys and Keyboard Shortcuts to Fame and Fortune

Your iMac's keyboard might not be as glamorous as your mouse, but any Macintosh power user will tell you that using keyboard shortcuts is usually the fastest method of performing certain tasks in the Finder, like saving or closing a file. I recommend committing these shortcuts to memory and putting them to work as soon as you begin using your iMac so that they become second nature to you as quickly as possible.

Special keys on the keyboard

Apple's standard keyboard has a number of special keys that you might not recognize — especially if you've made the smart move and decided to migrate from the chaos that is Windows to Mac OS X! Table 4-1 lists the keys that bear strange hieroglyphics on the Apple keyboard as well as what they do.

Table 4-1	Too-Cool Key Symbols	
Action	*Symbol*	*Purpose*
Media Eject	⏏	Ejects a CD or DVD from your optical drive
Audio Mute	◀	Mutes (and restores) all sound produced by your iMac
Volume Up	◀))	Increases the sound volume
Volume Down	◀)	Decreases the sound volume
Control	⌃	Displays right-click/Control-click menu
Command	⌘	Primary modifier for menus and keyboard shortcuts
Del	⌦	Deletes selected text
Option	⌥	Modifier for shortcuts

Using Finder and application keyboard shortcuts

The Finder is chock full of keyboard shortcuts that you can use to take care of common tasks. Some of the handiest shortcuts are in Table 4-2.

But wait, there's more! Most of your applications also provide their own set of keyboard shortcuts. While you're working with a new application, display the application's Help file and print out a copy of the keyboard shortcuts as a handy cheat sheet.

Table 4-2	Tiger Keyboard Shortcuts of Distinction	
Key Combination	**Location**	**Action**
⌘+A	Edit menu	Selects all (works in the Finder too)
⌘+C	Edit menu	Copies the highlighted item to the Clipboard
⌘+H	Application menu	Hides the application
⌘+M	Window menu	Minimizes the active window to the Dock (also works in the Finder)
⌘+O	File menu	Opens an existing document, file, or folder (also works in the Finder)
⌘+P	File menu	Prints the current document
⌘+Q	Application menu	Exits the application
⌘+V	Edit menu	Pastes the contents of the Clipboard at the current cursor position
⌘+X	Edit menu	Cuts the highlighted item to the Clipboard
⌘+Z	Edit menu	Reverses the effect of the last action you took
⌘+?	Help menu	Displays the Help system (works in the Finder, too)
⌘+Tab	Finder	Switches between open applications
⌘+Option+M	Finder	Minimizes all Finder windows to the Dock
⌘+Option+W	Finder	Closes all Finder windows

If you've used a PC before, you're certainly familiar with three-key shortcuts — the most infamous being Ctrl+Alt+Delete, the beloved shut down shortcut nicknamed the Windows Three-Finger Salute. Three-key shortcuts work the same way in Tiger (but you'll be thrilled to know you won't need to reboot using that notorious Windows shortcut)! If you're new to computing, just hold down the first two keys simultaneously and press the third key.

Performing Tricks with Finder Windows

In this section of your introduction to Mac OS X, I describe basic windows management within Tiger: how to move things around, how to close windows, and how to make 'em disappear and reappear like magic.

Scrolling and resizing windows

Can you imagine what life would be like if you couldn't see more than a single window's worth of stuff? Shopping would be curtailed quite a bit — and so would the contents of the folders on your hard drives!

That's why Tiger adds *scroll bars* that you can click and drag to move through the contents of the window. You can either

- Click the scroll bar and drag it.
- Click anywhere in the empty area above or below the bar to scroll pages one at a time.

Figure 4-8 illustrates both vertical and horizontal scroll bars in a typical Finder window.

Often, pressing your Page Up and Page Down keys moves you through a document one page at a time. Also, pressing your arrow keys moves your insertion cursor one line or one character in the four compass directions.

You can also resize most Finder and application windows by enlarging or reducing the window frame itself. Move your mouse pointer over the resize handle in the lower-right corner of the window (which smartly bears a number of slashed lines to help it stand out) and then drag the handle in any direction until the window is the precise size you need.

Minimizing and restoring windows

Resizing a window is indeed helpful, but maybe you simply want to banish the doggone thing until you need it again. That's a situation for the Minimize button, which also appears in Figure 4-8. A *minimized* window disappears from the Desktop but isn't closed: It simply reappears in the Dock as a miniature icon. Minimizing a window is easy: Move your mouse pointer over the yellow Minimize button at the top-left corner of the window — a minus sign appears in the button to tell you that you're on target — and then click.

Figure 4-8:
A plethora
of helpful
window
controls.

Hold down the Shift key whilst you minimize, and prepare to be amazed when the window shrinks in slow motion like Alice in Wonderland!

To restore the window to its full size again (and its original position on the Desktop), just click its window icon on the Dock.

Only one can be active at once™

Yes, here's a very special Mark's Maxim in the Mac OS X universe.

Only one application window can be active in Tiger at any time.™

You can always tell which window is active:

✔ **The active window is on top of other windows.**

✔ **The Close, Minimize, and Zoom buttons of the active window are in color.**

Tip: You can still use a window's Close, Minimize, and Zoom buttons when it's inactive.

✔ **Any input you make by typing or by moving your mouse appears in the active window.**

✔ **Mac OS X *dims* inactive windows that you haven't minimized.**

Toggling toolbars the Tiger way

Time to define a window control that's actually *inside* the window for a change. A *toolbar* is a strip of icons that appears under the window's title bar. These icons typically perform the most common actions within an application; the effect is the same as if you use a menu or press a keyboard shortcut. Toolbars are very popular these days. You see 'em within everything from the Finder window to most application windows.

You can banish a window's toolbar to make extra room for icons, documents, or whatever it happens to be holding. Just click the little lozenge-shaped button at the right corner of the window. (You guessed it — the Toolbar button is also shown in Figure 4-8.) *Note:* By toggling the Finder toolbar to off, you also lose the Finder window Sidebar.

Moving and zooming windows

Perhaps you want to move a window to another location on the Desktop so you can see the contents of multiple windows at the same time. Click the window's *title bar* (that's the top frame of the window, which usually includes a document or application name) and drag the window anywhere you like. Then release the mouse button.

Many applications can automatically arrange multiple windows for you. Choose Window⇨Arrange All menu item (if it appears).

To see all that a window can show you, use the Zoom feature to expand any Finder or application window to its maximum practical size. Note that a zoomed window can fill the entire screen, or (if that extra space isn't applicable for the application) the window might expand only to a larger part of the Desktop. To zoom a window, move your mouse pointer over the green Zoom button (refer to Figure 4-8 yet again) at the top-left corner of the window. When the plus sign appears in the Zoom button, click to claim the additional territory on your Desktop. (You can click the Zoom button again to automatically return the same window to its original dimensions.)

Closing windows

When you're finished with an application or no longer need a window open, move your mouse pointer over the red Close button at the top-left corner of the window. When the X appears in the button, click it. (And yes, I can get one more reference out of Figure 4-8, which I'm thinking of nominating as Figure of the Year.)

If you have more than one window open in the same application and you want to close 'em all in one swoop, hold down the Option key whilst you click the Close button on any of the windows.

If you haven't saved a document and you try to close that application's window, Tiger gets downright surly and prompts you for confirmation. "Hey, human, you don't really want to do this, do you?" If you answer in the affirmative — "Why, yes, machine. Yes, indeed, I do want to throw this away and not save it." — the application discards the document that you were working on. If you decide to keep your document (thereby saving your posterior from harm), you can either save the document under the same filename or under a new name.

Chapter 5

A Plethora of Powerful Fun

*W*hen you're no longer a novice to Tiger and the basics of the Finder, turn your attention to a number of more advanced topics 'n' tricks to turn you into an iMac power user — which, after all, is the goal of every civilized consciousness on Planet Earth.

Consider this chapter a grab bag of Tiger knowledge. Sure, I jump around a little, but these topics are indeed connected by a common thread: They're all surefire problem-solvers and speeder-uppers. (I can't believe the latter is really a word, but evidently it is. My editors told me so.)

Home, Sweet Home Folder

Each user account that you create within Tiger is actually a self-contained universe. For example, each user has a number of unique characteristics and folders devoted just to that person, and Tiger keeps track of everything that user changes or creates. (In Chapter 16, I describe the innate loveliness of multiple users living in peace and harmony on your iMac.)

This unique universe includes a different system of folders for each user account on your system. The top-level folder uses the short name that Tiger assigns when that user account is created. Naturally, the actual folder name is different for each person, so Mac techno-types typically refer to this folder as your *Home folder.*

Each account's Home folder contains a set of subfolders, including

- ✔ Movies
- ✔ Music
- ✔ Pictures
- ✔ Sites (for Web pages created by the user)
- ✔ Documents (created by the user)

Although you can store your stuff at the *root* (top level) of your hard drive, that crowd of files, folders, and aliases can get very crowded and confusing very quickly. Here's a Mark's Maxim to live by:

> **Your Home folder is where you hang out and where you store your stuff. Use it to make your computing life *much* easier!™**

Create subfolders within your Documents folder to organize your files and folders even further. For example, I always create a subfolder in my Documents folder for every book that I write so that I can quickly and easily locate all the documents and files associated with that book project.

I discuss security within your Home folder and what gets stored where in Chapter 16. For now, Figure 5-1 shows how convenient your Home folder is to reach because it appears in the Finder window Sidebar. One click of your Home folder, and all your stuff is in easy reach.

In addition to the Finder window Sidebar, you can also reach your Home folder in other convenient ways:

- ✔ **From the Go menu:** Choose Go➪Home to display your Home folder immediately from the Finder window. Alternatively, you can press ⌘+Shift+H to accomplish the same thing.

- ✔ **From within Open and Save dialogs:** Tiger's standard File Open and File Save dialogs also include the same Home folder (and subfolder) icons as the Finder window Sidebar.

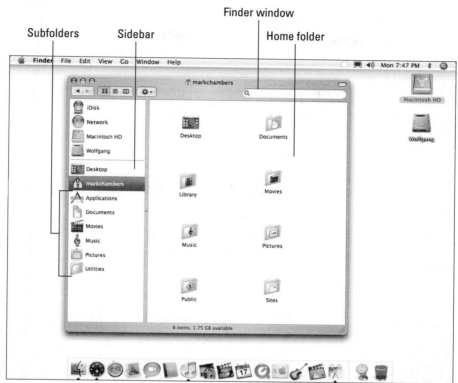

Subfolders   Sidebar   Finder window   Home folder

Figure 5-1:
Your Home
folder is the
central
location for
all your stuff
on your
iMac.

✔ **Within any new Finder window you open:** If you like, you can set every Finder window that you open to open automatically within your Home folder.

   a. *Choose Finder⇨Preferences to display the dialog that you see in Figure 5-2.*

   b. *Click the arrow button at the right side of the New Finder Windows Open pop-up menu.*

   A menu pops up (hence the name).

   c. *Click the Home entry in the menu.*

   d. *Click the red Close button at the top-left corner of the dialog.*

   You're set to go. From now on, every Finder window you open displays your Home folder as the starting location!

Figure 5-2:
Set Tiger to
open your
Home folder
within new
Finder
windows.

Here's another reason to use your Home folder to store your stuff: Tiger
expects your stuff to be there when you use Apple's Backup application or
when you migrate your files from an older Mac to a new Mac.

Arranging Your Desktop

Most folks put all their documents, pictures, and videos on their Tiger
Desktop because the file icons are easy to locate! Your computing stuff is
right in front of you . . . or *is* it?

Call me a finicky, stubborn fussbudget — go ahead, I don't mind — but I
prefer a clean Tiger Desktop without all the iconic clutter. In fact, my Desktop
usually has just three or four icons even though I use my iMac several hours
every day. It's an organizational thing; I work with literally hundreds of applications, documents, and assorted knickknacks daily. Sooner or later, you'll
find that you're using that many, too. When you keep your stuff crammed on
your Desktop, you end up having to scan your screen for one particular file,

an alias, or a particular type of icon, which ends up taking you more time to locate it on your Desktop than in your Documents folder!

Plus, you'll likely find yourself looking at old icons that no longer mean anything to you or stuff that's covered in cobwebs that you haven't used in years. Stale icons . . . *yuck.*

I recommend that you arrange your Desktop so you see only a couple of icons for the files or documents that you use the most. Leave the rest of the Desktop for that cool image of your favorite actor or actress.

Besides keeping things clean, I can recommend a number of other favorite tweaks that you can make to your Desktop:

✔ **Keep Desktop icons arranged as you like.**

   a. *From the Finder menu, choose View⇨Show View Options.*

   b. *Select the Keep Arranged By check box.*

   c. *From the pop-up menu, choose the criteria that Tiger uses to automatically arrange your Desktop icons, including the item name, the last modification date, or the size of the items.*

   I personally like things organized by name.

✔ **Choose a favorite background.**

   a. *Hold down the Control key while you click any open spot on your Desktop. (Or, if you use a pointing thing with a right mouse button, click that instead.)*

   b. *From the contextual menu that appears, choose Change Desktop Background.*

   You see the Desktop & Screen Saver pane appear, as shown in Figure 5-3. Browse through the various folders of background images that Apple provides or use an image from your iPhoto library.

✔ **Display everything that's connected.**

   a. *Choose Finder⇨Preferences.*

   b. *Make sure that all three of the top checkboxes (Hard Disks; CDs, DVDs, and iPods; and Connected Servers) are enabled.*

   If you're connected to an external network or you've loaded an external hard drive or device, that shows up on your Desktop. You can double-click that Desktop icon to view your external stuff.

Figure 5-3:
Choose a
Desktop
background
of more
interest.

Putting the Dock to the Test

If the Dock seems like a nifty contraption to you, you're right again — it's like one of those big control rooms that NASA uses. From the *Dock* — that icon toolbar at the bottom of Tiger's Desktop — you can launch an application, monitor what's running, and even use the pop-up menu commands to control the applications that you launch. (Hey, that NASA analogy is even better than I thought!)

When you launch an application — either by clicking an icon on the Dock or by double-clicking an icon in a Finder window or the Desktop — the icon begins to bounce hilariously on the Dock to indicate that the application is loading. (So much for my Mission Control analogy.) After an application is running, the application icon appears on the Dock with a tiny triangle underneath. Thusly, you can easily see what's running at any time just by glancing at the Dock.

You can hide most applications by pressing ⌘+H. Although the application itself is still running, it might not appear on the Dock.

Some applications run in the *background* — that is, they don't show up on the Dock. You generally don't even know that these applications are working for you. However, if you need to see in detail what's going on, you can always use the Activity Monitor utility to view everything that's happening on your iMac. (For example, an Apple support technician might ask you to run Activity Monitor to help troubleshoot a problem.) To run the Activity Monitor

1. **Open a Finder window.**

2. **Click the Utilities folder in the Sidebar.**

3. **Double-click the Activity Monitor icon.**

Adding Dock icons

Ah, but there's more: The Dock can offer more than just a set of default icons! You can add your own MIS (or *Most Important Stuff*) to the Dock, making it the most convenient method of taking care of business without cluttering up your Desktop. You can add

- ✔ **Applications:** Add any application to your Dock by dragging the application icon into the area to the left of the *separator line* (which appears between applications and folders or documents). The existing Dock icons move aside so that you can place the new neighbor in a choice location.

  Do not try to add an application anywhere to the right of the separator line. You can't put applications there — and Tiger might even think that you want the application dumped in the Trash!

- ✔ **Files and folders:** Here's where you want to add things to the area to the right of the separator line. Again, drag the desired folders and volume icons to the Dock and deposit them in the desired spot.

- ✔ **Web URLs:** Sure, you can add your favorite Web site from Safari! Drag it right from the Safari Address bar into the area to the right of the separator line. When you click the URL icon, Safari opens the page automatically.

Removing Dock icons

You can remove an icon from the Dock at any time (as long as the application isn't running). In fact, I always recommend that every Tiger user remove the default icons that never get used to make more room available for your favorite icons. The only two icons you can't remove are the Finder and Trash icons. To remove an icon from the Dock, just click and drag it off the Dock. You're rewarded with a ridiculous puff of smoke straight out of a Daffy Duck cartoon! (One of the Mac OS X developers was in a fun mood, I guess.)

When you delete an icon from the Dock, all you delete is the Dock icon: The original application, folder, or volume is not deleted.

Using Dock icon menus

From the Dock menu, you can open documents, open the location in a Finder window, set an application as a Login Item, control the features in some applications, and other assorted fun, depending on the item.

To display the contextual Dock menu for an icon

1. **Move your mouse over the icon.**
2. **Click and hold the mouse button for a second or two.**

   Note that you can also press the Control key and click the icon. Or you can even click the right mouse button (if you have one) to display the menu.

I cover the Dock settings that you can change within System Preferences in Chapter 6. You can also change the same settings from the Apple menu if you hover your mouse over the Dock item, which displays a submenu with the settings.

What's with the Trash?

Another sign of an iMac power user is a well-maintained Trash bin. It's a breeze to empty the discarded items you no longer need, and you can even rescue something that you suddenly discover you still need!

The Tiger Trash bin resides on the Dock, and it works just like the Trash has always worked in Mac OS X: Simply drag selected items to the Trash to delete them.

Note one very important exception: If you drag an external device or removable media drive icon on your Desktop to the Trash (like an iPod, DVD, or an external hard drive), the Trash bin icon automagically turns into a giant Eject icon, and the removable device or media is ejected or shut down — not erased. Repeat, *not erased*. (That's why the Trash icon changes to the Eject icon — to remind you that you're not doing anything destructive.)

Here are other methods of chunking items you select to go to the wastebasket:

- Choose File➪Move to Trash.
- Click the Action button on the Finder toolbar and choose Move to Trash from the list that appears.

Previewing images and documents the Tiger way

Tiger offers a Swiss Army knife application for viewing image files and documents in Adobe's PDF format Preview. You can use Preview to display digital photos in several popular image formats, including TIFF, GIF, PICT, PNG, JPEG, and Windows Bitmap.

I know, if that were the sum total of Preview's features, it wouldn't deserve coverage here. So, what else can it do? Here's a partial list (just my favorites, mind you):

✔ **Use Preview to add a bookmark at the current page within a PDF document by choosing Bookmarks⇨Add Bookmark.**

✔ **Fill out a form in a PDF document by choosing Tools⇨Text Tool.**

Click a field; if a blue highlight appears, you can type text into that field. After you complete the form, you can fax or print it.

✔ **Take a screen snapshot (saving the contents of your screen as a digital photo) by choosing File⇨Grab⇨Timed Screen.**

✔ **Convert an image into another format or into a PDF file by choosing File⇨Save As.**

✔ **Resize or rotate an image by using the commands on the Tools menu.**

Tiger automatically loads Preview when you double-click an image in a format that it recognizes or when you double-click a PDF file. It also acts as the Print Preview window, as you can read elsewhere in this chapter. However, if you want to launch Preview manually, open a Finder window, click the Applications folder in the Sidebar, and then double-click the Preview icon.

✔ Press ⌘+Delete.

✔ Hold down Control (or press the right mouse button) while clicking the item; then choose Move to Trash from the contextual menu.

You can always tell when the Trash contains at least one item because the basket icon is full of crumpled paper! However, you don't have to unfold a wad of paper to see what the Trash holds: Just click the Trash icon on the Dock to display the contents of the Trash. To rescue something from the Trash, drag the item(s) from the Trash folder to the Desktop or any other folder in a Finder window. (If you're doing this for someone else who's not familiar with Tiger, remember to act like it was a lot of work, and you'll earn big-time DRP, or *Data Rescue Points.*)

When you're sure that you want to permanently delete the contents of the Trash, use one of these methods to empty the Trash:

✔ **Choose Finder⇨Empty Trash.**

✔ **Choose Finder⇨Secure Empty Trash.**

If security is an issue around your iMac and you want to make sure that no one can recover the files you've sent to the Trash, using the Secure

Empty Trash command takes a little time but helps to ensure that no third-party hard drive repair or recovery program could resuscitate the items you discard.

- **Press ⌘+Shift+Delete.**

- **Hold down Control while clicking the Trash icon on the Dock and then choose Empty Trash from the contextual menu.**

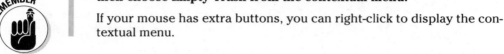

If your mouse has extra buttons, you can right-click to display the contextual menu.

Working Magic with Dashboard and Exposé

iMac power users tend to wax enthusiastic over the convenience features built into Tiger. In fact, we show 'em off to our PC-saddled friends and family. Two of the features that I've demonstrated the most to others are Tiger's brand-new Dashboard display and the amazing convenience of Exposé. In this section, I show 'em off to you as well. (Then you can become the Tiger evangelist on *your* block.)

Using Dashboard

The idea behind Dashboard is deceptively simple yet about as revolutionary as it gets for a mainstream personal computer operating system. *Dashboard* is an alternate Desktop that you can display at any time by using the keyboard or your mouse; the Dashboard desktop holds *widgets* (small applications that each provide a single function). Examples of default widgets that come with Tiger include a calculator, world clock, weather display, and dictionary/thesaurus.

Oh, did I mention that you're not limited to the widgets that come with Tiger? Simply click the plus button at the bottom of the Dashboard display and drag new widgets to your Dashboard from the menu at the bottom of the screen. To remove a widget while you're in this mode, click the X icon that appears next to each widget. When you're done with your widgets — that sounds a bit strange, but I mean no offense — press the Dashboard key again to return to your Desktop.

Widgets can also be rearranged any way you like by dragging them to a new location.

Simple applications like these are no big whoop — after all, Tiger has always had a calculator and a clock. What's revolutionary is how you access your widgets. You can display and use them anywhere in Tiger, at any time, by simply pressing the Dashboard key. The default key is F12 although you can change the Dashboard key via the Dashboard & Exposé pane within System Preferences (or even turn it into a key sequence, like Option+F12). You can also click the Dashboard icon on the Dock to summon your Dashboard widgets and then banish the Dashboard when you're done.

Switching between apps with Exposé

Exposé is a rather racy-sounding feature, but (like Dashboard) it's really all about convenience. If you typically run a large number of applications at the same time, Exposé can be a real timesaver, allowing you to quickly switch between a forest of different application windows (or display your Desktop instantly without those very same windows in the way). The feature works in three ways:

✔ **Press the All Windows key (or key sequence) to display all your application windows on a single screen, as shown in the truly cool Figure 5-4.**

Click the window that you want to make active. By default, F9 is the All Windows key.

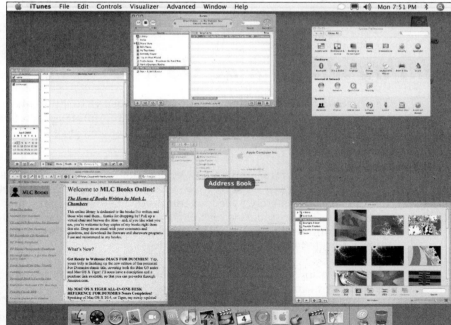

Figure 5-4: With Exposé, you can instantly see every open application's window(s).

✔ **Press the Application Windows key (or key sequence) to display all the windows that have been opened by the active application.**

This comes in handy with those mega-applications like Photoshop Elements or FileMaker Pro, in which you often have three or four windows open at one time. Again, you can click the window that you want to make it active. By default, F10 is the Application Windows key.

✔ **Press the Desktop key (or key sequence) to move all your application and Finder windows to the sides of your Desktop so you can access your Desktop icons.**

After you're done with your Desktop and you want to restore your windows to their original locations, press the Desktop key again to put things right again. The default Desktop key is F11.

You can activate both Exposé and Dashboard by using your mouse rather than the keyboard:

1. **Click the System Preferences icon on the Dock.**

2. **Click the Dashboard & Exposé icon to display the settings.**

3. **Click the desired screen corner pop-up menu to choose what function that screen corner will trigger.**

4. **Press ⌘+Q to save your changes and exit System Preferences.**

When you move your mouse pointer to that corner, Dashboard or Exposé automatically kicks in!

Printing within Mac OS X

Tiger makes document printing a breeze. Because virtually all Mac printers use a Universal Serial Bus (USB) port, setting up printing couldn't be easier. Just turn on your printer and connect the USB cable between the printer and your iMac; Tiger does the rest.

Printer manufacturers supply you with installation software that might add cool extra software or fonts to your system. Even if Tiger recognizes your USB printer immediately, I recommend that you still launch the manufacturer's Mac OS X installation disc. For example, my new Epson printer came with new fonts and a CD/DVD label application, but I wouldn't have 'em if I hadn't installed the Epson software package.

After your printer is connected and installed, you can use the same procedure to print from within just about every Mac OS X application on the

planet! To print with the default page layout settings — standard 8½-x-11"
paper, portrait mode, no scaling — follow these steps:

1. **Within the active application, choose File⇨Print or press the ⌘+P
   shortcut.**

Mac OS X displays the Print dialog, as shown in Figure 5-5.

From this dialog, you can

- *Print from a different printer connected to your iMac or print over a
  network connection to a shared printer on another computer.*

  Click the Printer pop-up menu. In this pop-up menu, Tiger displays
  all the printers that you can access.

- *Check what the printed document will look like.*

  Click Preview to open it within the very same Preview application I
  discuss earlier in this chapter.

If you have to make changes to the document or you need to change the
default print settings, click Cancel to return to your document. (You
have to repeat Step 1 again to display the Print dialog again.)

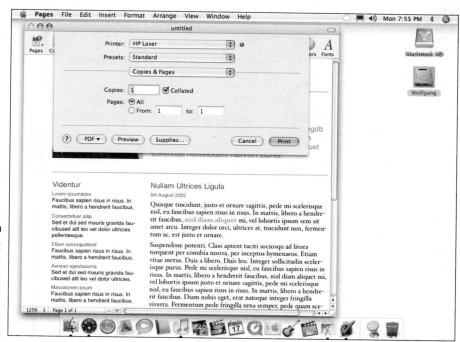

Figure 5-5:
Preparing to
print the
Great
American
Novel.

If everything looks good at this point and you don't need to change any settings (like multiple copies or to print only a portion of the document), click Print — you're done! If not, proceed with these steps:

1. **(Optional) For more than one copy, click in the Copies field and type the number of copies that you need.**

   Collation (separating copies) is also available, and it doesn't cost a thing!

2. **(Optional) To print a range of selected pages, select the From radio button and then enter the starting and ending pages.**

   To print the entire document, leave the default Pages option set to All.

3. **(Optional) If the application offers its own print settings, such as collating and grayscale printing, make any necessary changes to those settings.**

   To display these application-specific settings, click the pop-up menu in the Print dialog and choose the desired settings pane that you need to adjust. (You can blissfully ignore these settings and skip this step entirely if the defaults are fine.)

4. **When you're set to go, click Print.**

You can also save an electronic version of a document in the popular Adobe Acrobat PDF format from the Print dialog — without spending money on Adobe Acrobat. *(Slick.)*

1. **Click the PDF button to display the destination list.**

2. **Click Save as PDF.**

   Tiger prompts you with a Save As dialog, where you can type a name for the PDF document and specify a location on your hard drive where the file should be saved.

Heck, if you like, you can even fax a PDF or send it as an e-mail attachment! Just choose these options from the destination list rather than Save as PDF.

Chapter 6

A Nerd's Guide to System Preferences

Remember the old TV series *Voyage to the Bottom of the Sea?* You always knew you were on the bridge of the submarine Seaview because it had an entire wall made up of randomly blinking lights, crewmen darting about with clipboards, and all sorts of strange and exotic-looking controls on every available surface. You could fix just about anything by looking into the camera with grim determination and barking out an order. After all, you were On The Bridge. That's why virtually all the dialog and action inside the sub took place on that one (expensive) set: It was the nerve center of the ship, and a truly happenin' place to be.

In the same vein, I devote this entire chapter to the System Preferences window and all the settings within it. After all, if you want to change how Tiger works or customize the features within our favorite operating system, this one window is the nerve center of Mac OS X, and a truly happenin' place to be. (Sorry, no built-in wall of randomly blinking lights — but there are exotic controls just about everywhere.)

A Not-So-Confusing Introduction

The System Preferences window (as shown in Figure 6-1) is a self-contained beast, and you can reach it in a number of ways:

- Clicking the System Preferences icon on the Dock, which resembles a light switch next to the Apple logo. (Don't ask me, I just work here.)

- Clicking the Apple menu (🍎) and choosing the System Preferences menu item.

✔ Clicking the Apple menu, choosing Dock, and choosing the Dock Preferences menu item.

✔ Clicking the Time and Date display in the Finder menu and choosing the Open Date and Time menu item.

✔ Control-clicking (or right-clicking) any uninhabited area of your Desktop and choosing Change Desktop Background.

✔ Clicking most of the Finder menu status icons and choosing the Open Preferences menu item. (This includes the Bluetooth, AirPort, Display, Modem, and Clock.)

When the System Preferences window is open, you can click any of the group icons to switch to that group's *pane;* the entire window morphs to display the settings for the selected pane. For example, Figure 6-2 illustrates the Sound pane, which allows you to set a system alert sound, configure your iMac's built-in microphone, and choose from several different output options.

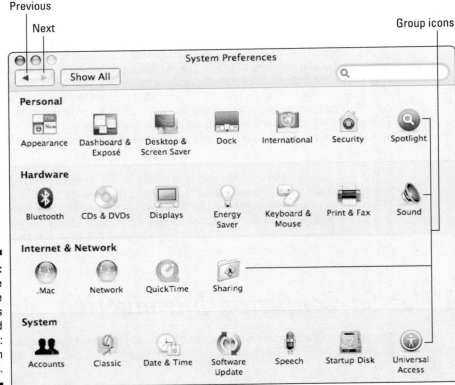

Figure 6-1:
The powerhouse of settings and switches: System Preferences.

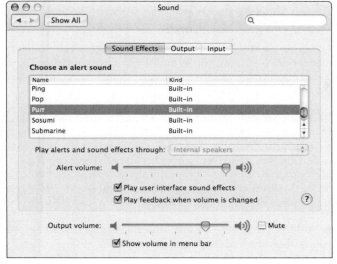

Figure 6-2:
The Sound
pane,
proudly
showing off
the Sound
Effects
panel.

Many panes also include a number of tabbed buttons at the top — in this case, Sound Effects, Output, and Input. You can click these tabs to switch to another *panel* within the same pane. Many panes within System Preferences have multiple panels. This design allows our friends at Apple to group a large number of similar settings together in the same pane (without things getting too confusing).

To return to the top-level System Preferences panel from any pane, just click the Show All button (top left) or press ⌘+L. You can also click the familiar Previous and Next buttons to move backward through the panes you've already visited and then move forward again, in sequence. (Yep, these buttons work just like the browser controls in Safari. Sometimes life is funny that way.)

You won't find an Okay button that you have to click to apply any System Preference changes — Apple's developers do things the right way. Your changes to the settings in a pane are automatically saved when you click Show All or when you click the Close button on the System Preferences window. You can also press ⌘+Q to exit the window and save all your changes automatically . . . a favorite shortcut of mine.

If you see an Apply Now button in a pane, you can click it to immediately apply any changes you made, without exiting the pane. This is perfect for some settings that you might want to try first before you accept them, like many of the controls on the Network pane. However, if you're sure about what you changed and how those changes will affect your system, you don't have to click Apply Now. Just exit the System Preferences window or click Show All as you normally would.

Searching for Settings

Hey, wouldn't it be great if you could search through all the different panes in System Preferences — with all those countless radio buttons, check boxes, and slider controls — from one place? Even when you're not quite sure exactly what it is you're looking for?

Figure 6-3 illustrates exactly that kind of activity taking place. Just click in the System Preferences Search box (upper right, with the magnifying glass icon) and type in just about anything. For example, if you know part of the name of a particular setting you need to change, type that. Tiger highlights the System Preferences panes that might contain matching settings. And if you're a *Switcher* from the Windows world, you can even type in what you might have called the same setting in Windows XP!

The System Preferences window dims, and the group icons that might contain what you're looking for stay highlighted. *Slick.*

You can also search for System Preferences controls by using the Spotlight menu and Spotlight window. Find more on this cool feature in Chapter 7.

If you need to reset the Search box to try again, click the X icon that appears at the right side of the box to clear it.

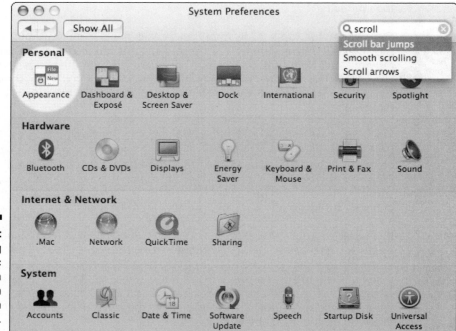

Figure 6-3: Searching for specific settings is a breeze with the Search box.

Popular Preference Panes Explained

Time to get down to brass tacks. Open up the most often-used panes in System Preferences to see what magic you can perform! I won't discuss every pane because I cover many of them in other chapters. (In fact, you might never need to open some System Preferences panes at all, like the Universal Access or Classic panes.) However, this chapter covers just about all the settings that you're likely to use on a regular basis.

The Displays pane

If you're a heavy-duty game player or you work with applications like video editing and 3-D modeling, you probably find yourself switching the characteristics of your monitor on a regular basis. To easily accomplish switching, visit the Displays panel (see Figure 6-4), which includes two panels:

✔ **Display:** Click a screen resolution to choose it from the Resolutions list on the left. Tiger displays the number of colors (or *color depth*) allowed at that resolution, and you can pick a color depth from the Colors pop-up menu. (Typically, it's a good idea to use the highest resolution and the highest number of colors.) Because most iMacs running Tiger have a flat-panel LCD, the refresh rate is disabled. However, if you're using a CRT display, I recommend choosing the highest refresh rate allowed. Drag the Brightness slider to change the brightness level of your display.

When you enable (mark) the Show Displays in Menu Bar check box, you can switch resolutions and color levels right from the Finder menu!

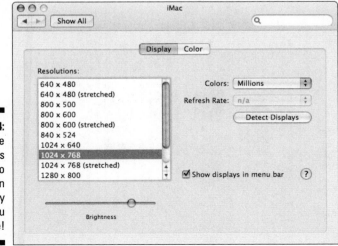

Figure 6-4: The Displays panel also comes in a handy Finder menu bar size!

✔ **Color:** Your iMac can use a *color profile* file that controls the colors on your display. This setting comes in handy for graphic artists and illustrators who need color output from their printers that closely matches the colors displayed by the iMac. Click the Calibrate button to launch the Display Calibrator, which can create a custom ColorSync profile and calibrate the colors that you see on your monitor.

The Desktop & Screen Saver pane

Hey, no offense to the Aqua Blue Desktop background, but who doesn't want to choose their own background? And what about that nifty screensaver you just downloaded from the Apple Web site? You can change both your background and your screen saver by using these options on the Desktop & Screen Saver pane.

The settings on the Desktop panel (as shown in Figure 6-5) include

✔ **Current Desktop picture:** To change your Desktop background, click a thumbnail. You can also drag a picture from a Finder window or the desktop and drop it into the *well* (the fancy Apple word for the square box with the sunken look). Tiger automatically updates your Desktop so you can see the results. To open another collection of images from Apple, click the collection folder in the list on the left of the panel. (I recommend the stunning images in the Nature folder.) If you want to open a different folder with your own images, click the Choose Folder entry in the left column and navigate to that folder.

Figure 6-5:
Show
The Man
who's boss
and pick
your own
Desktop
background.

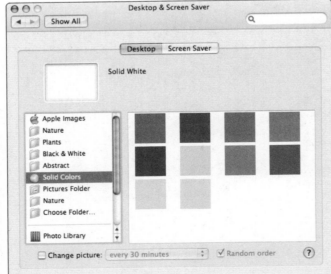

To add your own folder as a collection in the list, drag the folder to the well from a Finder window.

✓ **Arrangement:** You can *tile* your background image (repeat it across the Desktop), center it, and stretch it to fill the screen. Because the images from Apple are all sized correctly already, the Arrangement control appears only when you're using your own pictures.

✓ **Change picture:** If you like a bit of automatic variety on your desktop, select the Change Picture check box. You can click the drop-down list box to set the delay period. The images in the current collection or folder are then displayed in the sequence in which they appear in the thumbnail list.

✓ **Random Order:** Select this check box to throw caution utterly to the wind and display random screens from the current collection or folder!

The settings on the Screen Saver tab include

✓ **Screen Savers:** Click the screen saver that you want to display from the Screen Savers list. Tiger displays an animated preview of the selected saver on the right. You can also click the Test button to try out the screen saver in full-screen mode. (Move your mouse a bit to end the test.)

If the selected screen saver has any settings you can change, the Options button displays them.

✓ **Start Screen Saver:** Drag this slider to choose the period of inactivity that triggers the screen saver. Choose Never to disable the screen saver entirely.

✓ **Use Random Screen Saver:** Another chance to rebel against conformity! Enable this check box, and Tiger picks a different screen saver each time.

✓ **Hot Corners:** Click any of the four pop-up menus at the four corners of the screen to select that corner as an *activating hot corner.* (Moving your mouse pointer there immediately activates the screen saver.) You can also specify a corner as a *disabling hot corner* — as long as the mouse pointer stays in that corner, the screen saver is disabled. Note that you can also set the Dashboard and Exposé activation corners from here. (Read on for the entire lowdown.)

The Dashboard & Exposé pane

The pane you see in Figure 6-6 illustrates the settings that control Tiger's Dashboard and Exposé features. The settings include

✔ **Active Screen Corners:** The screen corners pop-up menus that I describe in the preceding section operate just like those in the Screen Savers panel. Click a corner's list box to set it as

- An Exposé *All Windows* corner (displays all windows on your Desktop).

- An Exposé *Application Windows* corner (displays only the windows from the active application).

- An Exposé *Desktop* corner (moves all windows to the outside of the screen to uncover your Desktop).

- A *Dashboard* corner (displays your Dashboard widgets). *Widgets* are small applications that each perform a single task; they appear when you invoke the awesome power of Dashboard.

These pop-up menus can also set the Screen Saver activate and disable hot corners.

✔ **Keyboard and Mouse Shortcuts:** Pretty straightforward stuff here. Click each pop-up menu to set the key sequences (and mouse button settings) for all three Exposé functions as well as Dashboard.

If you hold down a modifier key (Shift, Control, Option, or ⌘) while a shortcut pop-up menu is open, Tiger adds that modifier key to the selections you can choose! (Perfect for those folks who already have the F11 key in use by another application. Make your Desktop shortcut key the Shift+F11 key sequence instead.)

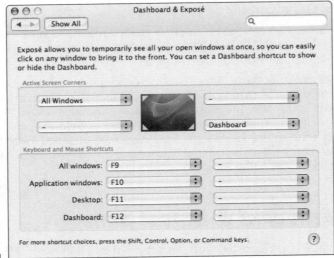

Figure 6-6:
The
Dashboard
and Exposé
pane in
System
Preferences.

The Appearance pane

This talented pane (as shown in Figure 6-7) determines the look and operation of the controls that appear in application windows and Finder windows.
It looks complex, but I cover each option here.

The settings include

- ✔ **Appearance:** Click this pop-up menu to specify the color Tiger uses for
  buttons, menus, and windows.

- ✔ **Highlight Color:** Click this pop-up menu to choose the color that highlights selected text in fields, pop-up menus, and drop-down list boxes.

- ✔ **Place Scroll Arrows:** Select a radio button here to determine whether
  the arrows that control the scroll bar in a window appear together at the
  bottom of the scroll bar, or separately at the top and bottom of the
  scroll bar.

- ✔ **Click in the Scroll Bar To:** By default, Tiger scrolls to the next or previous page when you click in an empty portion of the scroll bar. Select the
  Jump to Here radio button to scroll the document to the approximate
  position in relation to where you clicked. (Smooth scrolling slows down
  scrolling, which some people prefer.)

Figure 6-7:
Appear-
ances might
not be
everything,
but they're
easy to find
here.

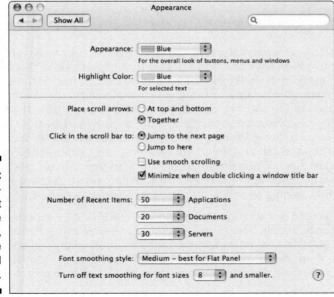

You can minimize a Finder or application window by simply double-clicking the window's title bar. To enable this feature, mark the Minimize When Double Clicking a Window Title Bar check box.

✔ **Number of Recent Items:** By default, Tiger displays ten recent applications, documents, and servers within Recent Items in the Apple menu. Need more? Just click the corresponding pop-up menu and specify up to 50 items.

✔ **Font Smoothing Style:** This feature performs a little visual magic that makes the text on your monitor or flat-panel look more like the text on a printed page. Most iMac owners should choose Standard (for a typical CRT monitor) or Medium (for a typical flat-panel LCD display).

✔ **Turn Off Text Smoothing for Font Sizes:** Below a certain point size, text smoothing doesn't help fonts look any smoother onscreen. By default, any font displayed at 8 point or smaller isn't smoothed, which is a good choice for an iMac with a flat-panel LCD screen.

The Energy Saver pane

I'm an environmentalist — it's surprising how many techno-types are colored green — so these two panels are pretty doggone important. When you use them correctly, you not only save electricity but also even invoke the Power of Tiger to automatically start and shut down your iMac whenever you like!

The panels (as shown in Figure 6-8) include

✔ **Sleep:** To save electricity, drag the Put the Computer to Sleep When It Is Inactive For slider to a delay period that triggers sleep mode when you're away from the keyboard for a significant period of time. (I prefer 30 minutes.) If your iMac must always remain alert and you want to disable sleep mode entirely, choose Never. You can set the delay period for blanking your monitor separately from the sleep setting with the Put the Display to Sleep When the Computer Is Inactive For slider. To conserve the maximum juice and cut down on wear, enable the Put the Hard Disk(s) to Sleep When Possible check box to power-down your hard drives when they're not needed. (This might cause a delay of a second or two while loading or saving files because the drives must spin back up.)

You can set Tiger to start or shut down your iMac at a scheduled time. Click the Schedule button and then select the desired schedule (the Start Up/Wake check box and the Shut Down/Sleep pop-up menu) to enable them. Set the trigger time by clicking the up and down arrows next to the time display for each schedule. Click OK to return to the Energy Saver pane.

✔ **Options:** From this panel, you can specify events that can awake your iMac from sleep mode, like a ring signal from your modem. If you prefer to send your iMac to sleep by pressing the Power button, enable the Allow Power Button to Sleep the Computer check box. Tiger can also restart your iMac automatically after a power failure — a good feature for those running Apache Web server.

If you're running an iMac, the Processor Performance pop-up menu appears in the Options panel. You can use this control to fine-tune the performance of your Mac's processor to reduce its power consumption and heat buildup. Choose Automatic to allow Tiger to monitor and tweak your processor's performance whenever possible. Choose Highest if you want the best possible performance at all times — my favorite setting for use with my iMac because (unlike a laptop) you don't have to worry about heat buildup. Don't pick the Reduced option, however, which is meant for laptop owners who need to conserve battery power.

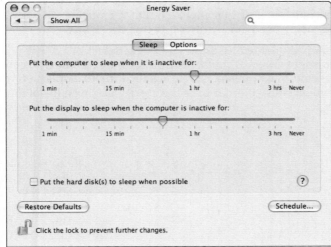

Figure 6-8: Reduce your iMac's power consumption from the Energy Saver pane.

The Dock pane

I'll come clean: I think the Dock is the best thing since sliced bread! (I wonder what people referred to before sliced bread was invented?) You can use the settings, shown in Figure 6-9, to configure the Dock's behavior until it fits your personality like a glove:

✔ **Dock Size:** Pretty self-explanatory. Just drag the slider to change the scale of the Dock.

✔ **Magnification:** When you select this check box, each icon in your Dock swells like a puffer fish when you move your mouse cursor over it. (Just how much it magnifies is determined by the Magnification slider.) I really like this feature because I resize my Dock smaller, and I have a large number of Dock icons.

✔ **Position on Screen:** Select a radio button here to position the Dock on the left, bottom, or right edge of your iMac's Desktop.

✔ **Minimize Using:** Tiger includes two cool animations that you can choose from when shrinking a window to the Dock (and expanding it back to the Desktop). Click the Minimize Using pop-up menu to specify the genie-in-a-bottle effect or a scale-up-or-down-incrementally effect.

If animation isn't your bag or you want to speed up the graphics performance of an older G3 iMac, you can turn off these minimizing effects.

✔ **Animate Opening Applications:** Are you into aerobics? How about punk rock and slam dancing? Active souls who like animation likely get a kick out of the bouncing application icons in the Dock. They indicate that you've launched an application and that it's loading. You can turn off this bouncing behavior by disabling this check box.

✔ **Automatically Hide and Show the Dock:** Select this check box, and the Dock disappears until you need it. (Depending on the size of your Dock, the Desktop that you gain can be significant.) To display a hidden Dock, move your mouse pointer over the corresponding edge of the Desktop.

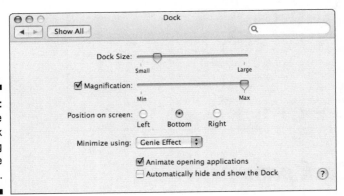

Figure 6-9:
Customize
your Dock
by using
these
controls.

The Sharing pane

So you're in a neighborly mood, and you want to share your toys with others on your local wired or wireless network. Perhaps you'd like to start your own

Web site, or protect yourself against the Bad Guys on the Internet. All these fun diversions are available from the Sharing pane in System Preferences, as shown in Figure 6-10. Here's the lowdown on the three panels it offers:

The three tabs here are

✔ **Services:** Each entry in the services list controls a specific type of sharing, including Personal File Sharing (with other Macs), Windows Sharing (with PCs running Windows), Personal Web Sharing, Remote Login, FTP Access, Apple Remote Desktop, Remote Apple Events, Printer Sharing, and Xgrid. To turn on any of these services, select the On check box for that service. To turn off a service, choose it from the list and click the Stop button that appears or just disable the On check box for that service.

To change the default network name assigned to your iMac during Tiger's set up process, click in the Computer Name text box and type the new name.

✔ **Firewall:** You can enable Tiger's powerful built-in Internet firewall from this panel — and I strongly urge you to do so! A *firewall* blocks communication to any sharing service not allowed in the list. To enable communications with a service, select the entry in the list and select the On check box to enable it. (Note that Tiger takes care of this automatically when you start a service on the Services panel.)

Need to create an opening (or *port*) in your firewall for an application? Click the New button to specify a new port by entering a port number and assigning it a name. The new port appears in the list, and you can turn it on and off like any other port. You can also edit or delete the selected port.

If you find that your iMac suddenly can't connect to other computers (or share services that you were able to share) after you turn on your firewall, one (or more) of your ports is incorrectly set. (This often happens if you turn off a port manually.) Review each service that you've turned on, and then make sure the corresponding ports are opened on the Firewall panel.

✔ **Internet:** To share an Internet connection from your iMac to the rest of the computers on your network, click the Share Your Connection From pop-up menu and choose the proper port. For just about every network, you should pick the Built-in Ethernet port. (Naturally, wireless folks can choose AirPort.). Then click Start.

Figure 6-10:
Share your
toys with
others by
using the
controls on
the Sharing
pane.

Chapter 7

Searching amidst iMac Chaos

. . . .

. . . .

*W*hat would you say if I told you that you could search your entire system for every single piece of data connected with a person — and in only the time it takes to type that person's name? And I'm not just talking about files and folders that might include that person's name. I mean *every* e-mail message and *every* iCal calendar or event that references that person and even that person's Address Book card to boot? Heck, how about if that search could dig up every occurrence of the person's name inside your electronic PDF documents?

You'd probably say, "That makes for good future tech — I'll bet I can do that in five or ten years. It'll take Apple at least that long to do it . . . and just in time for me to buy a new iMac! (Harrumph.)"

Don't be so hasty: You can do all this, right now. The technology is a new Mac OS X feature named *Spotlight,* built right into Tiger. In this chapter, I show you how to use it like an iMac power guru. I also show you how to take advantage of Sherlock, the best Internet search tool ever. (From what I hear, there's good stuff on the Internet, too.)

Spotlight Explained

Invoking the magic of Spotlight is a snap. As you can see in Figure 7-1, the Spotlight search field always hangs out on the right side of the Finder menu bar. You can either click once on the magnifying glass icon or just press F5. Either way, Tiger displays the Spotlight search box.

Figure 7-1:
Soon to be a
very good
friend of
yours — the
Spotlight
search box.

Spotlight works by *indexing* — in other words, searching for and keeping track of keywords within your files. In fact, Tiger indexes the contents of your iMac's hard drives into a huge file, which it constantly maintains while you create new files and modify existing files. Tiger can search this index file in a fraction of a second after you enter your search criteria. The index file contains all sorts of data, including quite a bit of information from inside various documents — hence Spotlight's ability to present matching data inside your files and application records.

When you first boot Tiger, it spends anywhere from a few minutes to an hour or two creating the Spotlight index file. If you click the Spotlight icon whilst indexing is taking place, you see a progress bar indicating how much longer you have to wait before you can use Spotlight. Creating this full index happens only once, so it's no great burden to bear.

You can search for any string of text characters in Spotlight, and you'll be surprised at everything this plucky feature will search. For example, Spotlight searches through your Address Book contacts, Mail messages, iCal calendars, iChat transcripts, and even System Preferences! Yep, you can even use it to find specific settings in all those System Preferences panes, like *printer sharing* or *Dashboard*. Of course, Spotlight includes matching files and folders — like that other operating system — but it does it in the blink of an eye.

Spotlight matches only those items that include all your search text: Therefore, if you enter just the word *horse,* you're likely to get far more matches than if you enter a word string, like *horse show ticket.*

If you add *metadata* to your documents (like the Comments field in a Word document or the keywords embedded in a Photoshop image), Spotlight can match that information as well. Other recognized file formats include AppleWorks documents, Excel spreadsheets, Keynote presentations, Pages documents, and third-party applications that offer a Spotlight plug-in.

Spotlight works so seamlessly — and so doggone fast — because it's literally built into the core of Tiger (unlike that other operating system that begins with a W, which uses a separate program to search and can take a couple of minutes to return just matching filenames). Spotlight's integration into the heart of Tiger allows those high-IQ Apple developers (and even smart folks outside the company) to easily use it elsewhere within Tiger — more on this later in the chapter.

Searching with Spotlight

To begin a Spotlight search, display the Spotlight box, click in it, and start typing. As soon as your finger presses the first key, you'll see matching items start to appear. Check out Figure 7-2, in which I only typed a single character. (No need to press Return, by the way. This is all automatic from here on.) As you continue to type, Spotlight's results are updated in real time to reflect the new characters.

Spotlight displays what it considers the top 20 matching items within the Spotlight menu itself. These most relevant hits are arranged into categories like Documents, Images, and Folders. You can change the order in which categories appear (via the Spotlight pane within System Preferences, which I cover a bit later in this chapter).

Using internal magic, Spotlight presents the category Top Hit (with what it considers the single most relevant match) at the top of the search results, as also shown in Figure 7-2. You'll find that the Top Hit is often just what you're looking for. To open or launch the Top Hit item from the keyboard, press ⌘+Return.

Didn't find what you were after? Click the X icon that appears at the right side of the Spotlight box to reset the box and start over.

If all you know about the item you're searching for is what type of file it is — for example, you know it's a QuickTime movie, but you know nothing about the title — just use the file type, like *movies,* all by itself as the keyword in the Searchlight field. This trick also works with *image* files and *audio* files, too.

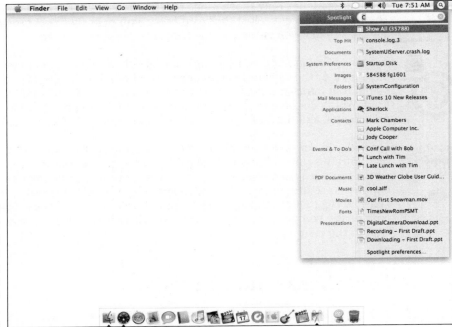

Here's another trick that's built into Spotlight: You can type in a relative time period — like *yesterday, last week,* or *last month* — and Spotlight matches every item that was created or received within that period. One hundred percent *sassy!*

Working with Spotlight matches

After you run a fruitful search, and Spotlight finds the proverbial needle in your system's haystack, what's next?

Just click the item — that's all it takes. Depending on the type of item, Tiger does one of four things:

- ✔ Launches an application
- ✔ Opens a specific pane in System Preferences (if the match is the name of a setting or contained in the text on a Preferences pane)
- ✔ Opens a document or data item, like an Address Book card
- ✔ Displays a folder within a Finder window

To see all sorts of useful info about each Spotlight menu item, click the Show All item (above the Top Hit listing) to expand your Spotlight menu into the

Spotlight Results window, as shown in Figure 7-3. From the keyboard, you can press the Results window shortcut key, which you can set from System Preferences (more on this in a page or two).

Figure 7-3:
The Spotlight Results window offers more ways to group and sort your matches.

The category groups at the upper-right side of the Results window allow you to group your results by different categories. You can also specify how items are sorted within each group by clicking the option you want under the Sort Within Group By heading. Spotlight displays images as thumbnails to make them easier to differentiate. To display the details about any item in the list (without selecting it, which closes the Results window), click the Info icon (lowercase italic *i* in a circle) at the right side of the item entry. After you locate the item you want, click it to open, launch, or display it, just like you would in the Spotlight menu.

TIP

Use the filter settings at the bottom of the column to display or hide items by the date they were created or last saved, or by their source (such as your hard drive or Home folder).

Fine-tuning Spotlight in System Preferences

The System Preferences window boasts a new Spotlight icon, which you can use to customize what search matches you see and how they are presented. To adjust these settings, click the System Preferences icon on the Dock (look for the light switch) and then click the Spotlight icon (under Personal).

Configuring the Search Results settings

Figure 7-4 illustrates the Search Results tab of the Spotlight Preferences pane. From here, you can

- ✔ **Pick your categories.** To disable a category (typically because you don't use those types of files), select the check box next to the unnecessary category to clear it.

- ✔ **Specify the order that categories appear within Spotlight.** Drag the categories into the order that you want them to appear in the Spotlight menu and Results window.

- ✔ **Select new Spotlight menu and Spotlight Results window keyboard shortcuts.** In fact, you can enable or disable either keyboard shortcut, as you like. Click the pop-up menu to choose a key combination.

Marking stuff off-limits

Click the Privacy tab (as shown in Figure 7-5) to add disks and folders that should never be listed as results in a Spotlight search. The disks and folders that you add to this list won't appear even if they actually match your search string. This safeguard can come in handy for organizations (such as hospitals) that are required by law to protect their patient or client data. However, you can select a removable hard drive here, which is often stored in a safe after business hours.

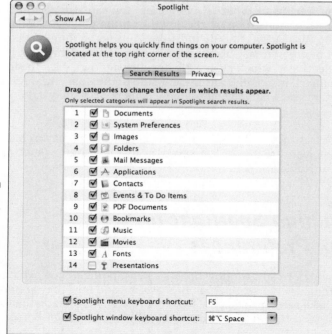

Figure 7-4:
These settings control how your matches are presented within Spotlight.

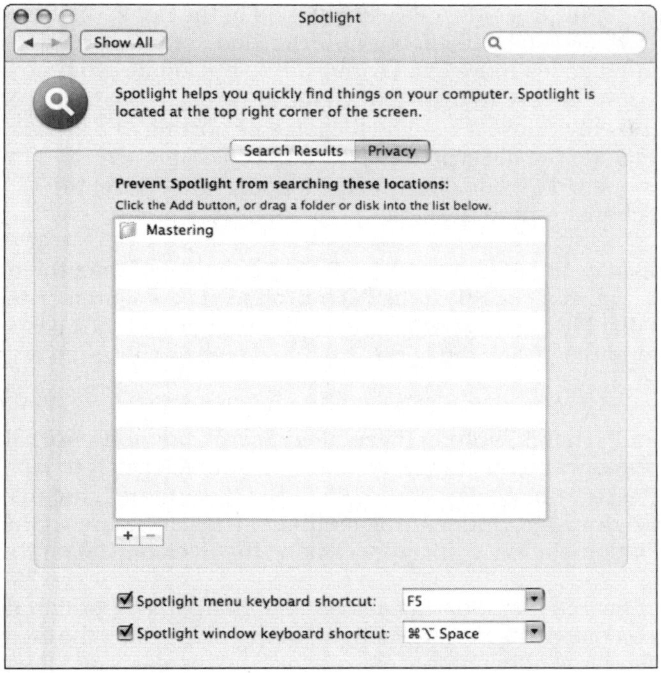

Figure 7-5:
Some things
should
never been
seen;
specify
them within
Spotlight.

To add a private location, click the Add button (which bears a plus sign) and navigate to the desired location. Then click the location to select it and click Choose. (If you already have the location open in a Finder window, you also can drag folders or disks directly from the window and drop them into the list.)

Searching the Old-Fashioned Way

The Finder window toolbar has featured a Search box for a few years now (and Tiger includes a Find dialog), but even the older Search features within Tiger have been updated to take advantage of Spotlight technology. Now you can even use file types (like *image* or *movie*) and relative time periods (like *yesterday* and *last week*) in the Finder window Search box and Find displays!

Typically, I use the Finder window Search box if I need to do a simple file or folder name search: It works the same as using the Spotlight search field. Just begin typing, and use the X button in the Search box to reset the field. To choose a specific location for your search — like your Home folder or a hard drive volume — click the desired button along the top of the Search results display. The Finder window automatically turns into a Results display.

Tiger also includes the oldest Search method in the book: the Find display. (It used to be a dialog all by itself, but now the Find controls are displayed in the Finder window, so it's more of an extension to the Finder window.) Choose File⇨Find or press ⌘+F to display the Find controls. From here, you can click pop-up menus to choose a specific filename or portion of a filename. Other modifiers include the file type, content, label color, file size, and the last date the file was opened. Again, click the location buttons at the top of the window to choose where to search.

The Find display, however, is a little more sophisticated than the toolbar Search box. You can click the plus (+) button next to a search criterion field in the Find display to add another field, allowing for matches based on more than one condition. Click the minus (–) button next to a search criterion field to remove it.

After you find a match, both of these older Search methods work the same: Click the item once to display its location, or double-click it to launch or open it. Files can also be moved or copied from the Results and Find displays with the standard drag and Option+drag methods. You can return to the more mundane Finder window display by clicking the Back button on the toolbar.

These older Search methods can also do one thing that Spotlight doesn't offer: You can use them to create a new *Smart Folder*. Click the Save button in either the Finder window Search Results or Find display. You'll be prompted to specify the name and location for the new Smart Folder and whether it should appear in the Finder window Sidebar. After you create the folder, Tiger automatically updates the contents of the Smart Folder with whatever items match the criterion(a) you saved. You never have to search using the same text or criterion(a) again! (Each icon in a Smart Folder is a link to the actual file or folder, so nothing gets moved, and no extra space is wasted with multiple copies of the same items.) You can work with the files and folders inside a Smart Folder as if they were the actual items themselves.

With Sherlock, the Search Is Afoot

No chapter on searching within Mac OS X would be complete without that famous Internet sleuth, *Sherlock* (as shown in Figure 7-6). Conan Doyle himself would be proud indeed if he could see just how much information Tiger's Sherlock application can pluck from Web pages, Internet search engines, and all sorts of content providers.

Each channel in Sherlock has a different function. To see a short description of what each can do, just click the Channels button. In this section, I demonstrate how to use three of the most useful channels to track down the information you need.

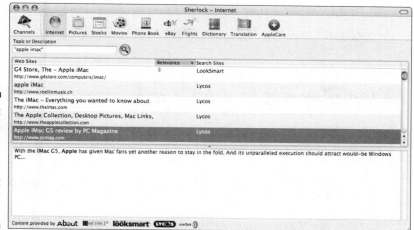

Figure 7-6:
Elementary, dear reader. If it's on the Internet, I wager that Sherlock can find it!

Okay, I know you're going to roll your eyes, but I have to remind you that you need an Internet connection to use Sherlock. Otherwise, Sherlock is about as useful as a pair of swim fins in the Sahara Desert.

Searching the Internet for data and pictures

If you're using Safari, check out the Google search box conveniently located on the Safari toolbar. (Still, Sherlock can perform the same duties if you choose the Internet channel.) Find Sherlock within your Applications folder on your iMac's boot drive. (Click the Applications icon in the Sidebar that appears in any Finder window to get there.) After you double-click the Sherlock icon to launch the application, follow these steps to track down specific information from Web sites around the world, using a number of Internet search engines:

1. **Click the Internet channel button.**

2. **Type the phrase** Elvis Parade **into the Topic or Description box and then click the Search button (the button with the magnifying glass).**

   To force a search for an exact phrase, surround it with quotes.

3. **When you find the perfect match for your search, click that entry to display the summary text.**

   I bet you didn't know that there were so many parades featuring Elvis impersonators, did you?

4. **To display the entire Web page in all its glory, double-click the entry.**

   Sherlock launches Safari (or whatever you installed as a default browser).

Tracking down movie information

Ready to take in a good movie? Yep, you guessed it, Sherlock can help! Follow these steps to scope out the best in cinematic entertainment in your neighborhood:

To search local theaters for information on a movie — and watch the trailer to boot — follow these steps:

1. **Click the Movies channel button.**

2. **Click the Movies button to search by movie name.**

   (Optional) You can also search by theater name by clicking the Theaters button.

   (Optional) You can filter the results you get by entering a different city/state combination or Zip code in the Find Near box.

3. **Click the Showtime pop-up menu and then select today's date.**

4. **When you find a listing that looks good, click that entry to display the summary text.**

   See the results for *Sideways* in Figure 7-7.

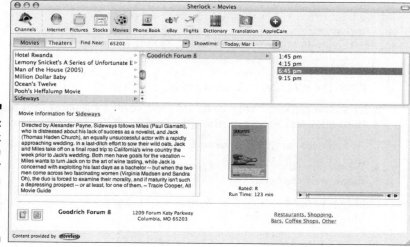

Figure 7-7:
Sherlock displays the movies near you with movie posters and trailers.

Sherlock automatically downloads a thumbnail of the movie poster (and, if available, the QuickTime movie trailer). If you have a broadband or network Internet connection, click the Play button in the QuickTime viewer window to watch the trailer.

5. **Click the theater you want in the center column to display a list of the show times for the selected film.**

Get those stock tickers here

What better stock to monitor than Apple? I use the Stocks channel (as shown in Figure 7-8) all the time to keep up on the latest news and information on a number of stocks. Follow these steps to monitor a stock:

1. **Click the Stocks channel button.**

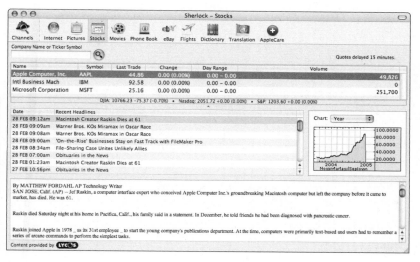

Figure 7-8: I would check Microsoft stock, but it hasn't been doing so well recently.

2. **Type** Apple **(or its ticker symbol** AAPL**) into the Company Name or Ticker Symbol box; then press Return or click the Search button.**

3. **To display the text of a news item (or a link to the story on the Web), click the desired headline.**

Sherlock displays the text of the news item in the summary section, and Safari launches automatically to display Web pages.

4. **To switch to another stock you've recently been watching, click the stock entry in the list at the top of the window.**

Like any other public-access stock ticker, the quotes you see on the Stocks channel are delayed 15 minutes. (Go figure.)

Part III
Connecting and Communicating

The 5th Wave   By Rich Tennant

JERRY AND LYLE ATTEMPT TO LOAD THE NEWEST VERSION OF "TOAST," CD-BURNING SOFTWARE

OK, I got the Sunbeam firewired to the iMac. Try putting the CD in the slot again.

In this part . . .

You want to do the Internet thing, don't you? Sure you do — and in this part, I describe and demonstrate your Safari Web browser. You also get to know all about Apple's .Mac Internet subscription service, and how you can store, back up, and synchronize your data online. Finally, this part fills you in on connecting important stuff like printers, scanners, and that cool-looking iSight Webcam.

Chapter 8

Let's Go on Safari!

Looking for that massive Microsoft monster of a Web browser on your iMac? You know, the one that practically everyone uses in the Windows world. What's it called? I forget the name.

You see, I use an iMac, and I proudly surf the Web via a lean, mean — and *very* fast — browser application. That's Safari, of course, and it just keeps getting better with each new version of Mac OS X. Safari delivers the Web the right way, without the wait.

If you need a guide to Safari, this is your chapter. Sure, you can start using it immediately, but wouldn't you rather read a few pages in order to surf like a power user?

It Doesn't Even Look Like That Other Web Browser

Safari could almost be mistaken for a Finder window! Figure 8-1 illustrates the Safari window, with the most important controls and whatnot marked. To launch Safari, click the spiffy-looking compass icon on the Dock.

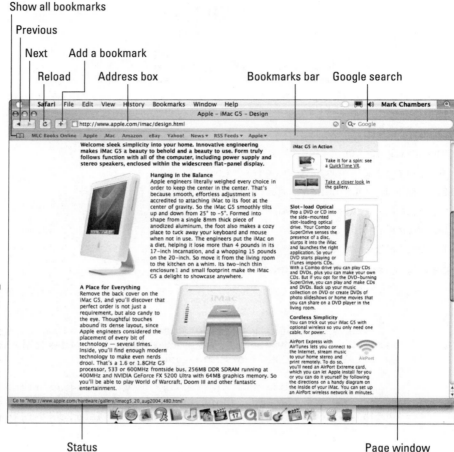

Show all bookmarks

Previous

Next   Add a bookmark

Reload   Address box   Bookmarks bar   Google search

Figure 8-1:
The Web
doesn't get
any better
than this —
the default
Safari
window.

Status   Page window

Let's begin with introductions all around to the stuff in Figure 8-1:

- **Previous/Next buttons:** Click the Previous button (left-facing triangle) to surf backwards — no small feat on water, but no big deal here. Safari simply returns you to the last page that you visited, and each additional click takes you back one page farther. If you've moved one or more pages backward, you can click the Next button (right-facing triangle) to move forward through those same pages again.

- **Reload button:** Clicking this button (circular arrow) reloads *(refreshes)* the current page, updating the page with the latest information from the Web server. This feature is useful for Web sites that change periodically, like www.cnn.com or your stockbroker's Web site.

✔ **Add a Bookmark:** Click this button (a plus sign) to add the current page to your collection of *bookmarks,* which are favorite sites that you return to regularly. (More about bookmarks later in the section, "Collecting and using bookmarks.")

✔ **Address box:** You can enter a Web site's address (URL) manually in this box (the big one in the middle of the toolbar), or you can drag a Web address from another application here to jump directly to that page.

✔ **Google search box:** One of the slicker features of Safari, this box (look for the magnifying glass) allows you to search Google for keywords that you type without having to visit www.google.com first.

✔ **Show All Bookmarks button:** Clicking this button (looks like an open book) displays (or hides) a special screen from which you can organize your bookmark collections and select a specific bookmark. You can also add or remove bookmarks from the Bookmarks bar and Bookmarks menu from this screen.

✔ **Bookmarks bar:** This button strip (which appears underneath the Safari toolbar) allows you to jump directly to your most important bookmarks.

✔ **Page window:** No surprises here! This window displays the contents of the current Web page, including all sorts of stuff such as links to other pages, images, animated graphics, pop-up windows (if you want them), and anything else that appears on a Web page.

✔ **Status bar:** Not particularly flashy, but I like the status bar nevertheless because it updates you with information on what you're doing, what's currently loading, or what will load if you click a link.

Basic Navigation While on Safari

Sure, you're likely saying, "Mark, I already know this stuff. I can operate a Web browser blindfolded — while listening to *The Best of Air Supply,* even." I know that most browsers work in the same way, and Safari shares most of those mechanics. However, I'm a thorough guy (just ask my editors). Therefore, just in case you've never used a browser before, let me show you how to surf.

And no giggling from the Peanut Gallery.

Entering Web addresses

The most mundane method of crossing the Web and visiting a specific site is manually typing the Web page address — more technically called a URL, short for *Uniform Resource Locator* — directly into the Address box. Click the tiny image icon that appears at the beginning of the Address box, start typing, and then press Return after you enter the entire address. Boom, you're there.

However, other methods of entering addresses are a bit easier than all that hunt-and-peck action:

- ✔ **Click a link.** If the page that's currently displayed includes an underlined link to another page, you can click the colored link text to jump to that page.

  Links can also be attached to images. And you know when you're over a link because the mouse cursor changes to a pointing hand.

- ✔ **Use the Google search box.** A Google results page contains links to Web pages that match your search criteria. (More on Google later in the upcoming section, "It's a snap to search with Google.")

- ✔ **Double-click an HTML file.** If an application saves an HTML file on your drive, you can display that page by double-clicking the file icon to make Safari launch and load the page automatically. (HyperText Markup Language [HTML] is the computer "language" of Web pages. When you visit a Web site on the Internet, you're actually receiving a series of commands that tell Safari what text to display and how to display it. These commands can also be saved as a file to your hard drive.)

- ✔ **Click a bookmark.** Bookmarks can appear on the Bookmarks menu or the Bookmarks bar, and a single click automatically sends you to that site.

- ✔ **Click a Web address icon.** A Web address icon looks like a spring-loaded @ symbol. By default, the Tiger Dock contains the perfect example. On the right side of the Dock, you see a Web address icon. Clicking that icon takes you to the Mac OS X home page on the Apple Web site, as shown in Figure 8-2. You can drag any Web address to the right side of the Dock (on the right of that funny vertical line) to create your own Dock Web address icon.

- ✔ **Drag and drop; cut/copy and paste.** You can cut or copy a Web address from a document and paste it into the Safari Address box; often you can drag and drop the address into the Address box as well.

Putting the toolbar to work

You can specify which controls — buttons — should appear on the Safari toolbar from the View menu. For example, if you don't use the Add a Bookmark button very often, you can hide it to make room for another control that sees more action:

✔ **To add a toolbar control:** Choose View➪Customize Address Bar.

A sheet appears in which you can drag controls to and from the toolbar.

✔ **To return to the default set of Safari toolbar controls:** Drag the preset default group back to the toolbar.

Although I discuss most of the Safari toolbar buttons earlier in this chapter, two or three don't appear on the default toolbar configuration, but you can see them in Figure 8-3. Here's a rundown on the controls that you can add to the toolbar:

✔ **Home:** Click this button (a house) to return immediately to your home page. Find more on selecting a home page later in the section, "Selecting a new home page."

✔ **AutoFill:** This button (look for the pencil) is great if you do a lot of online shopping or have to regularly fill out forms online. Click Auto-Fill, and Safari does its best to automatically complete online forms with the information that you provide in the AutoFill section of the Safari Preferences dialog. (Choose Safari➪Preferences to display this dialog.) You can choose to AutoFill with data from your personal Address Book card, and you can also specify whether AutoFill should take care of names and passwords.

Figure 8-2:
The Safari
window.

AutoFill works its magic for *anyone* who's sitting at the keyboard. If your iMac is in a public location and you can't guarantee that you'll be the one using it (or you're worried about security in general), *fill out forms manually.* We're talking about *your* personal information here — even your login names and passwords, if you choose!

Don't provide any personal information to any Web site unless the connection is secure. Skip to the upcoming section, "Using secure connections."

✔ **Text size:** These two buttons (small and large capital As) allow you to increase or decrease the point size of the text on your Web pages. This feature is great for those who prefer larger text for better readability.

✔ **Bug:** Strange name, but a click of the Bug button (um, look for the spider-ant critter) helps Apple improve Safari! If you visit a Web page that doesn't display properly in Safari (hence the name *Bug,* which is developer-speak for an error in an application), click this button to display a sheet in which you can describe the problem. When you then click Submit, your Bug report is automatically sent to the hardworking Apple developers responsible for Safari, who check out the page themselves to see whether they can fix what's wrong for a future version of Safari. In fact, the Bug feature is one of the reasons why Apple was able to fine-tune Safari's compatibility so quickly after the browser was introduced.

✔ **Print Page:** Click this icon (a printer, natch) to print the current page displayed in Safari.

Tabs: Love 'em or leave 'em

Safari offers an alternate method of displaying multiple Web pages — Tabbed browsing mode. With Safari open, just choose Safari⇨ Preferences to display the Preferences dialog and then click the Tabs button on the Preferences dialog toolbar. From here, you can mark the Enable Tabbed Browsing check box to turn on tabs.

In *Tabbed browsing mode,* Safari doesn't open a new window or replace the current Web page when you click a link. Instead, a tab representing the new page appears under the Bookmarks bar, and you can click it to switch pages. The trick is, however, that you have to open a link or a bookmark as a tab by holding down the ⌘ key while you click. Otherwise, Safari acts as it usually does and replaces the contents of the window with the new page.

In fact, this area below the Bookmarks bar becomes a separate strip called the *Tab bar.* To remove a tabbed page from the Tab bar, click the X button next to the tab's title. (If less than two tabs are active, the Tab bar automatically disappears altogether unless you've enabled the Always Show Tab Bar check box on the Tabs pane of the Preferences dialog.)

To be honest, I'm not a huge fan of tabs because I tend to surf the Web in a linear fashion and don't often keep multiple windows open. (Evidently, Apple thinks that most people fall in the same category because Tabbed browsing is disabled by default.) However, if you do a lot of comparison shopping (or research), or you find yourself with a dozen Safari windows open at once), tabs might be just the ticket for you.

Home

Autofill   Text size

Bugs

Figure 8-3:
The lesser-known buttons on the Safari toolbar.

What about downloading?

The default Safari configuration can handle just about any type of download file you throw at it, including movies, MP3 audio, disk images, and executable applications. Just click the download link, and the Downloads window pops up to keep you informed on the status of the transfer. Things work the way they're supposed to, even the first time you run Safari after you unpack your iMac.

However, I am going to persist in reminding you about the possibility of malicious files and the damage they can do to your system. This includes viruses, *Trojan horses* (applications that appear to be harmless that are actually designed to do Very Bad Things), and Java applets. Here's the rule: *Never download or run any application from a Web site that you don't trust, and always run an antivirus application to scan anything you download.* 'Nuff said.

Searching for That Special Something

I honestly can't imagine how anyone could find anything on the Web without today's modern Web search engines. In my opinion, the best online Web search on the Internet can be found at the familiar Google.com home page. I've been using Google now for the last several years (long before it became oh-so-very trendy and fashionable). There's no better way to find the proverbial needle in the Internet haystack.

However, searching isn't always about where you're going — sometimes, it's more important to look where you've *been*. If you need to search through the Web sites that you visited in the recent past and return to a specific page, you need to comb Safari's History list.

Finally, Safari allows you to find specific text within the current page. And believe me, with some of the humongous, 23-screen behemoth pages that I've recently visited, you really appreciate the ability to zero in on the phrase *ripe avocado* in two or three seconds! (It gives me a headache just to imagine manually scanning all 23 screens for a single occurrence of a phrase!)

In this section, I jaw about all three of these search resources. Read along, and you'll be well prepared to search the Web sites behind you, under you, and in front of you.

It's a snap to search with Google

Before Safari arrived on the scene, Mac owners had to bookmark Google.com, or make Google their home page — or, in the worst case, actually type the address manually. (Oh, the horror!) The designers and bigwigs at Apple knew that they wanted to beat Microsoft at the browser game, so they added the Google search box to the Safari toolbar . . . and knocked the pitch right out of the ballpark.

To search for something, simply click your mouse cursor within the Google search box on the Safari toolbar, type a word or short phrase, and press Return. Figure 8-4 illustrates the result of a search that I did using the phrase *Stradivarius violins*. (If you need to narrow a search to the most relevant pages, you can enclose the search text in quotes — like "Stradivarius violins" — to search for precisely that text.)

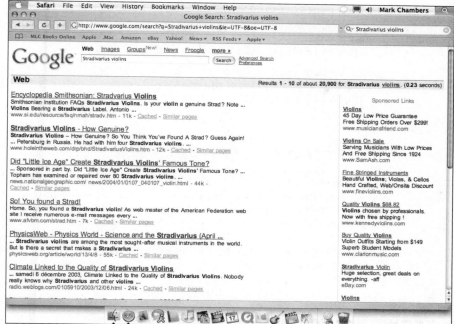

Figure 8-4:
The results
of a Google
search for
the finest
violins.

Looking back with the History list

Safari's History list records any page visit. Click the History menu at any
time to

- **Return to your home page.** You can also press ⌘+Shift+H at any time.

- **Mark a page for SnapBack.** The first page that you open in a window (or
  the page that appears when you click a bookmark) is automatically set
  as the *SnapBack* page.

    - To return immediately to the SnapBack page, just click the orange
      SnapBack button that appears at the right end of the Address box.

    - To mark the active page as the SnapBack page, you can choose this
      command from the History menu. (For example, if you were visit-
      ing the Apple site and you decide that you prefer to SnapBack to
      the Support page rather than the Apple welcome page, you would
      display the Support page and choose Mark Page for SnapBack.)

> ✔ **Visit pages ordered by date.** You see a number of submenus, including Earlier Today, and then previous days. To view the History list for an earlier date, move your mouse pointer over the desired date and then click the desired page.
>
> ✔ **Clear History.** If you want to clear the History list — for security reasons, or if you just want to remove old entries — you can do so from the History menu.

Searching the current page

You can always press ⌘+F (or choose Edit⇨Find⇨Find) to display the Find dialog. Type the word or phrase that you're looking for in the Find box and then click Next to display each occurrence in order, all the way to the bottom of the page. To search upward to the top of the page, click Previous.

Safari highlights any match that it finds and jumps to that spot within the page. Convenient indeed.

Safari Power User Features

Safari is easy to use and handles simple Web surfing as well as any other browser — click here, click there, and you're navigating the Web. But what about the features that a power user needs? They're here as well!

In this section, I mention the most popular features among the experienced Mac surfing set.

Selecting a new home page

You have a number of different ways to jump to your home page but how do you *set* your home page in the first place? Follow these steps to move in to your new home page:

1. **Visit the page that you want to use as your home page.**

2. **Choose Safari⇨Preferences, which displays the Safari Preferences dialog.**

3. **Click the Set to Current Page button.**

4. **Click the Close button on the Preferences dialog to return to your (new) home page.**

Collecting and using bookmarks

Bookmarks make it easy to return to your favorite hangouts in cyberspace.

Sometimes a technology author has to use the same word over and over and yet even over again. In this section, I claim the world record for using the term *bookmark* — it's a small triumph, but I take whatever comes my way.

To set a bookmark for the current page, just click the Add a Bookmark button on the Safari toolbar, which looks like a big plus sign. (There's high intelligence at work here, I'm telling you.)

Figure 8-5 illustrates the sheet that appears, in which you can

- ✔ Enter a new name for the bookmark.
- ✔ Specify whether you want the bookmark to appear in the Bookmarks bar, the Bookmarks menu, or an existing Bookmarks folder.

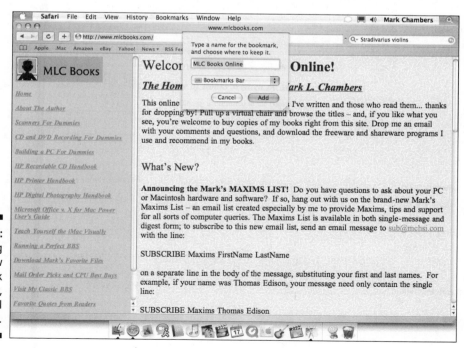

Figure 8-5: Creating a new bookmark — heady, powerful stuff.

To return to a bookmark, use one of these methods:

- ✓ **Click a bookmark button on the Bookmarks bar.**

- ✓ **Click the Bookmarks menu and select a bookmark.**

- ✓ **Press a Bookmark keyboard shortcut.** Safari assigns a keyboard shortcut to the keys that appear on the Bookmarks bar. For example, pressing ⌘+1 is the same as clicking the first Bookmark button on the Bookmarks bar.

- ✓ **Click the All Bookmarks button at the left side of the Bookmarks bar.** A full-screen Bookmarks Library appears (see Figure 8-6), in which you can drag and drop all your bookmarks to the Bookmarks bar, the Bookmarks menu, or to collection folders that you can create.

  Collection folders are great for organizing; I have over 200 bookmarks, and I'd need a separate computer to keep track of 'em if I didn't use collections. Anyway, you can Control-click (or right-click) any bookmark on the All Bookmarks screen to display the pop-up menu, and then click Open to display the page. To close the Bookmarks Library screen, just click the All Bookmarks button in the Safari toolbar a second time.

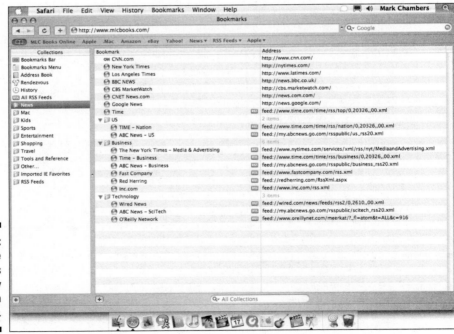

Figure 8-6:
The
Bookmarks
Library
screen in
action.

Your Address Book appears in the Bookmarks Library screen. You can click this collection to immediately access all Web sites stored as contact information in your Address Book; then you can create bookmarks directly from those sites.

I now hereby close my record-setting *bookmark* section. Thank you.

Using secure connections

I love shopping on the Web, but I'm always cautious — and you should be, too. Safari indicates that your connection to the current Web page is secure (or encrypted) by displaying a padlock icon in the upper-right corner of the Safari window, as shown in Figure 8-7. Here comes the only rule that you have to remember about secure connections in Safari. (In fact, it's a Mark's Maxim.)

> *Never* — I mean *never* — **enter any valuable personal or financial information on a Web page unless you see the secure connection padlock symbol.**™

This includes

- ✔ Obvious things such as your credit card number, address, or telephone number
- ✔ Not-so-obvious things such as your Social Security number or a login/password combination

If a site doesn't provide a secure connection and asks you for personal information, *find another spot in cyberspace to do your business.* Your identity should remain *yours.*

Working with RSS feeds

Almost time to exit stage right, but before leaving this discussion of Safari, I want to cover a feature that's new with Tiger: Safari now has the ability to receive *RSS* (short for RDF Site Summary) newsfeeds. A Web site that provides RSS content sends updated news or information in a short headline format — almost like the old AP and UPI teletype machines that newspapers once used. RSS Web addresses can be recognized by their feed:// prefixes.

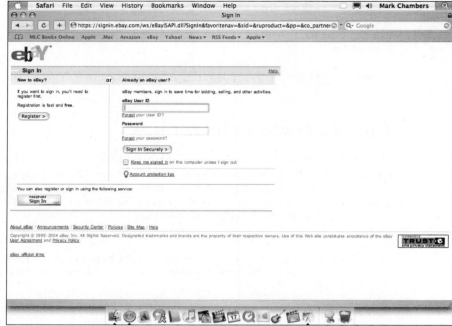

Figure 8-7:
eBay
provides a
secure
connection
when you're
entering
your ID and
password.

Safari displays RSS headlines in a list format. They're easy to scan with a glance, with no pop-up advertisements or unnecessary graphics, either.

A square blue RSS icon appears at the right side of the Address box to let you know that the Web server you're visiting has RSS feeds available. Click this RSS icon to display the newsfeed provided by that Web server.

The RSS feature has its own pane in the Safari Preferences dialog, in which you can specify the time delay before Safari checks for updated articles. You can also assign a color to new articles, which is a great help for those who like to ride the latest tech wave (like I do). RSS feeds can be bookmarked just like a typical Web page, too, and Apple provides a number of RSS sites as a default drop-down list on the Bookmarks bar.

Chapter 9

Moving to .Mac

Readers often ask me to name my favorite reasons why they should switch — that is, why should a Windows user who *thinks* all is well move to the Apple universe? Of course, I always mention the superior hardware and how much better of a job Tiger does as an operating system. Here's my favorite selling point: "Apple simply does things right the first time, and everyone else plays catch-up."

And then I pose this question: "What if you could reach a hard drive with 125MB of your files over any Internet connection — anywhere in the world — and it just *showed up* on your Desktop automatically?" Usually, I get a thoughtful silence after that one, and another person decides to find out more — about Apple's .Mac online hosting service, that is.

In this chapter, I save you the trouble of researching all the benefits of .Mac. Heck, that's one of the reasons why you bought this book, right?

Wait a Minute: Where Exactly IS My .Mac Storage?

Yep, that's what everyone asks. Best that I answer this one first.

I'll begin with a definition. The online hard drive offered to .Mac subscribers (read about subscribing in the following section) is an *iDisk,* and it's well integrated into Mac OS X. In fact, if you didn't know the background, you might think that iDisk were simply another internal hard drive. Figure 9-1 illustrates my iDisk icon on my Desktop. The Finder window displays the contents; notice the folders visible there. (More on these folders later in the chapter.)

Figure 9-1: My iDisk at work. Looks like a normal hard drive, doesn't it?

The files that I add to my iDisk are stored on an Apple server, location unknown. Literally. The physical storage (a massive file server that holds uncounted gigabytes of data) could be in Cupertino, or it might be in Timbuktu. There's a whole bunch of 'em, too. You and I don't need to care about the where part because

- ✔ **Your iDisk is always available.** Oh, yes. 24/7, your files are waiting for you.

- ✔ **Your iDisk is secure.** Apple goes to great lengths to guarantee the security of your data, encrypting the transfer of files and folders whenever you use your iDisk. You can also password-protect any data that you want to offer to others, just in case.

- ✔ **Your iDisk works even when you aren't on the Internet.** Yep, you read that right: You can create new documents and modify files to your heart's content while you're on a flight or relaxing on the beach. iDisk automatically updates whatever's changed the next time you connect to the Internet.

Now that I've piqued your interest (and answered the most common question about iDisk), return to the .Mac service for a moment so I can show you how to set up your account.

Opening a .Mac Account

If you haven't already opened your .Mac account, you get a chance to sign up when you turn on your iMac for the first time and also when you install (or upgrade) Mac OS X. However, if you decided to pass on .Mac at that time, you can always join in the fun by following these steps:

1. **Click the System Preferences icon on the Dock.**

2. **Click the .Mac icon.**

3. **Click the Sign Up button.**

   This launches Safari and displays Apple's .Mac Welcome page (www. mac.com, .Mac tab). Follow the onscreen instructions to choose a member name and password.

   When you're done with the clicking and you're rewarded with your login information, close Safari and then enter your name and password into the text boxes in the .Mac System Preferences pane.

Figure 9-2 illustrates an example login that I created.

Figure 9-2:
The .Mac pane within System Preferences keeps track of your login information.

Like the convenient operating system that it is, Tiger handles all your .Mac login chores automatically from this point on.

If you're a dialup Internet user, you were dreading this moment. Here it is. I'm truly sorry, but in my opinion, a high-speed broadband connection is a real requirement in order to take full advantage of a .Mac subscription. You can certainly still use all the functionality of .Mac with any type of Internet connection, but you're going to spend from now until the next Democratic presidency waiting for files to copy and things to happen.

If you decide to sign up for a full year's .Mac membership, I salute you for your discerning taste in online services. However, you can opt for a 60-day trial subscription at this point, which is only fair because Apple wants you to check out things at your leisure. Table 9-1 shows the major differences between a free trial subscription and a full $100 yearly subscription to .Mac.

Table 9-1	What a Ben Franklin Buys with .Mac				
Status	*iDisk/E-Mail Storage*	*Publish iCalendars*	*HomePage Web Site*	*Virex Backup*	*Antivirus*
Trial	50MB total	No	No	iDisk only	No
Subscriber	250MB total	Yes	Yes	iDisk/CD/DVD	Yes

A .Mac subscription also allows you to synchronize your e-mail, Address Book contact information, and your Safari bookmarks between multiple Macs. What a real boon if you spend time on the road with an iBook or a PowerBook laptop!

As a trial member to .Mac, you're limited to reading your .Mac e-mail through the Web-based browser offered on the .Mac Web site, as shown in Figure 9-3. That's neat, certainly, and you can use Web mail from any computer with an Internet connection. However, as a full subscriber, you can also send and receive .Mac email seamlessly from Tiger's Mail application, which is the preferred method of checking your messages.

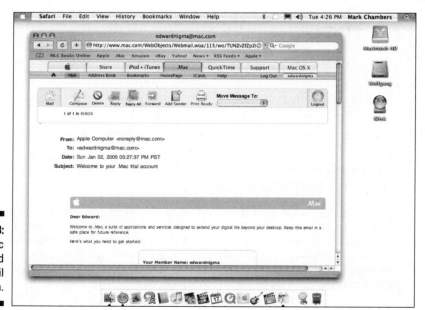

Figure 9-3:
The .Mac Web-based e-mail system.

Is .Mac an ISP?

.Mac is many things, but it isn't an ISP. You need to join an ISP first because you need an existing Internet connection to use the services and features included in .Mac membership. This makes a lot of sense, considering that most of us already have Internet access. (Plus, Apple doesn't have to worry with all the support and hardware headaches that an ISP has to deal with.)

.Mac works with the ISP that you already have, so you don't have to worry about AOL or EarthLink conflicting with .Mac. (However, I can't guarantee that your system administrator at work will allow .Mac traffic across his or her pristine network. Perhaps a steak dinner would help your argument.)

If you decide that you want the extra functionality of a .Mac subscription, upgrading is easy. When you open the .Mac pane within System Preferences and click the iDisk button, Tiger displays a countdown reminder telling you how many days remain on your trial period. Just click Join Now to upgrade. You can also visit the .Mac Web site at any time and click Join Now to access the same Web-based subscription system.

iDisk . . . iGetIt!

So how do you open your iDisk? Tiger gives you a number of different avenues:

- ✔ **Choose Go⇨iDisk from the Finder menu and then choose My iDisk from the submenu.**

  Keyboard types can press ⌘+Shift+I instead.

- ✔ **Click the iDisk icon in the Finder window Sidebar.**

- ✔ **Click the iDisk button on your Finder toolbar.**

  It's easy to add an iDisk button. Open a Finder window, click View, and then click Customize Toolbar. Drag the iDisk icon up to the toolbar and click Done.

After you open your iDisk, an iDisk volume icon also pops up on your Desktop. You can open the little scamp later in your computing session by simply double-clicking the Desktop icon. The Desktop iDisk icon hangs around until you log out, restart, or shut down your iMac.

It's all in the folders

Your iDisk contains a number of different folders. Some of them are similar to the subfolders in your Home folder, and others are unique to the structure of your iDisk. In this section, I provide the details on the iDisk folder family.

You can't store files or create folders in the root (or top level) of an iDisk.

Storage folders

Everything that you copy to or create on your iDisk must be stored in one of these six folders (refer to Figure 9-1 to see them):

- ✓ **Documents:** Store the documents that you create with your applications in this folder, which only you can access.

- ✓ **Movies:** This folder stores your QuickTime movies (including any that you might use in your .Mac Web pages).

- ✓ **Music:** iTunes music and playlists go here.

- ✓ **Pictures:** The JPEG and GIF digital images that you store in this folder can be used with other .Mac services (like your Web pages) or within iPhoto.

- ✓ **Public:** The files that you store in this folder are meant to be shared with other people (as well as offered on your .Mac Web pages). You can also allow others to copy and save files to your Public folder as well (more on this later in this section).

- ✓ **Sites:** You can use HomePage to create Web pages in this folder, or you can add Web pages that you've created with your own applications.

These folders can be opened in a Finder window just like any typical folder on your iMac's internal hard drive, and you can open and save documents to your iDisk folders, using all your applications. In other words, these six iDisk folders act just like normal, everyday folders. Pretty doggone neat!

Funky specialized folders

Your iDisk contains three folders that you *can't* use to store stuff (directly, anyway):

- ✓ **Backup:** This is the storage vault for the backup files created with the .Mac Backup application.

  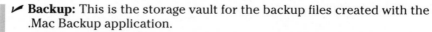

  Because you have read access to the Backup folder, you can copy the backup files from this folder to a CD, DVD, or removable drive on your iMac. (I cover backing up later in this chapter.)

✔ **Library:** Like the Library folders that you find in the root of your hard drive (and in your Home folder), this folder stores all sorts of configuration settings for the .Mac features that you're using, like your Backup settings.

✔ **Software:** This read-only folder is a special case. Apple stuffs this folder full of a wide variety of the latest in freeware and shareware as well as commercial demo software. You can copy whatever you like from the Software folder to your iMac's Desktop and then install your new toy from that local copy. (Oh, and the contents of the Software folder don't count against your total storage space limit.) Enjoy!

Mirror, mirror, on your drive . . .

You can use your iDisk even if you aren't connected to the Internet. This magic is accomplished through a *mirror,* or local copy of your iDisk, that's stored on your local hard drive. ("Hey, wasn't I supposed to be getting *away* from storing things locally?") If you choose to use a mirror — you can disable this feature if you like — Tiger automatically synchronizes any files that you've created or changed on your local iDisk copy the next time you connect to the Internet. This is a great feature if you have more than one Mac in different locations because you can update and synchronize your iDisk files from any of your computers — all automatically!

Without a mirror, you *must* have an active Internet connection to use your iDisk.

To enable (or disable) the mirror feature, open System Preferences, click the .Mac icon, and then click the iDisk tab to display the settings you see in Figure 9-4. Click the Start button, and — after a moment of preparation, complete with its own dialog — the text above the button reads iDisk Syncing On.

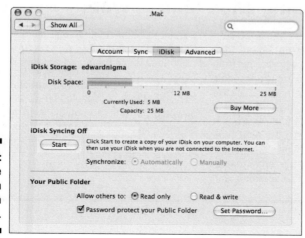

Figure 9-4:
Configure iDisk within System Preferences.

If you use a local copy of your iDisk — and I recommend it — choose to synchronize automatically. This ensures that your files get updated even if you're somewhat forgetful, like I am.

A mirror makes things much faster when you browse your iDisk or when you save and load documents from your iDisk. Tiger actually uses your local copy from your hard drive, and then updates your remote iDisk files in the background while you work. (Tiger is updating your iDisk whenever you see that silly animated circular-yin-yang-thinglet rotating next to your iDisk icon in the Finder window. You'll know it when you see it.)

Monitoring and configuring your iDisk

The iDisk pane in System Preferences groups together all the configuration settings you can make to your iDisk and your .Mac account. In this section, I review the controls that you can find here.

Disk space

Concerned about how much of your 25MB (for trial users) or 250MB (for subscribers) remains? The iDisk pane (refer to Figure 9-4) includes the Disk Space bar graph, which always displays how much of your iDisk space is free.

Public folder

The Finder Go menu includes a shortcut to access another .Mac member's Public folder.

Putting .Mac Mail to work

If you decide to take advantage of a .Mac subscription, you can easily set up Tiger's Mail application to send and receive messages from your .Mac address. Launch the Mail application, click Mail, and then click Preferences. Click the Accounts button in the toolbar and then click the Add button (which sports a plus sign) at the bottom of the window. Click the Account Type pop-up menu and click .Mac. Type a description and press Tab to complete the other fields, including your full name, your .Mac name, and password. When everything's filled in, click the Close button on the Preferences window; then click Save when prompted by Mail.

That's it! You created a new account for your .Mac messages, and you can now retrieve them on your iMac and through the Web mail system at www.mac.com. In fact, Mail is probably pulling down at least two messages from Apple as you read this.

Password

I strongly recommend that you set a password to protect the contents of your Public folder.

This password must be entered by anyone trying to open your Public folder. If you haven't supplied that person with the proper password, he can't open your Public folder. Just that simple. (There's nothing more embarrassing than discovering the bikini shots from your vacation are available for every .Mac user to peruse.)

Here's one drawback to this extra level of security: If you password-protect your Public folder, it can't be used to store anything that you offer on your .Mac Web pages.

Settings

While you're in the iDisk pane, you can configure your Public folder security settings. You can decide whether others should be able to

- Only read the contents of your Public folder.

  By default, the Public folder is set to read-only.

- Copy documents to your Public folder.

  To give others the ability to save and copy, click Read & Write.

Backing Up Your Treasured Stuff

My editors have heard me drone on and on long enough about how important it is to back up your hard drive. They probably rub their eyes when they encounter yet another instance of my preaching about *the wages of backup sloth* and *losing everything but hindsight.*

Well, you're lucky, because I was just about to launch into another round of backup warnings. .Mac subscribers get a great utility application called Backup when they join the club. Backup is a great application that saves a copy of your treasured data on just about any media on the planet, including

- Your iDisk (using the Backup folder that I discuss earlier in this chapter)
- An external USB or FireWire hard drive
- Recordable CD or DVD media
- Network servers
- Your iPod

Before you get too enthusiastic about backing up to your iPod, heed this: You can indeed back up to your iPod (or I wouldn't have listed it as an option), but your iPod's tiny hard drive isn't meant to handle the same serious thrashing as a full-size external hard drive. Personally, I've never used my iPod as a backup destination, and I don't recommend that you do either (unless no other recording media is handy and you absolutely have to have a backup).

Installing Backup

Backup isn't built into Tiger; you have to download it from the .Mac site at www.mac.com. After the image file is mounted on your Desktop, you see the Backup installation folder. Double-click the Backup.pkg file to begin the installation. After installation is complete, you can find Backup in your Applications folder.

Saving your stuff

Nothing is more important to a proud iMac owner than a secure backup; in this section, I demonstrate how you can produce both *manual* backups (produced whenever you like) and *automated* backups (which are scheduled at regular intervals). ***Do it!***

Manual backups

Beginning a backup is as easy as marking the check boxes next to the items that you want to safeguard.

Manual backup options depend on whether you're subscribed to .Mac:

 ✔ **After you subscribe to .Mac, the Back Up To pop-up menu allows you to choose from a CD, DVD, or drive destination.**

 ✔ **Trial members can select only the Back Up to iDisk option.**

   Figure 9-5 shows the default backup options for a trial .Mac member.

Follow these steps to add items (folders or files) to your backup that aren't in the default list:

 1. **Click the Add button — which bears a plus sign — at the bottom of the Backup window.**

   Backup opens a standard file/folder selection sheet.

Figure 9-5:
Backup
represents
online
peace of
mind.

2. **Navigate to the file or folder that you want to back up and click it to select it; then click Choose.**

   The new item appears in the list, already enabled. The total space requirement in the lower-right corner of the window is updated.

   You're limited to 25MB with a trial membership.

3. **Click Backup.**

   The rest is cake as your irreplaceable stuff is saved to your iDisk.

If you ever need to restore from your backup, click the pop-up menu at the top of the Backup window and click Restore from iDisk (or CD/DVD, or Drive, whichever is appropriate). Backup leads you through the restore process with the same aplomb.

Scheduled automatic backups

You can schedule unattended backups with Backup. Follow these steps:

1. **Click the Schedule Automatic Backups button at the bottom of the window.**

   You see the options shown in Figure 9-6.

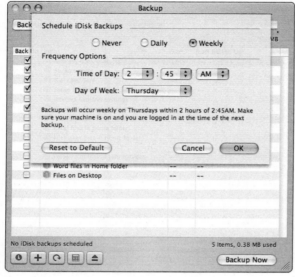

Figure 9-6:
Preparing to
schedule an
automated
backup.

2. **Click the pop-up menus next to the options:**

   - Select the Daily or the Weekly radio button (depending on how often your files are changed).
   - Set the backup time of day (and day of the week, if necessary).

3. **When you're ready to accept your settings and the schedule, click OK.**

   Your next scheduled backup time appears at the bottom of the Backup window.

The Backup application itself doesn't need to be running for the automated backup to kick off.

Scheduled backups require that

✔ **Your iMac remains awake.** Make sure that

   - You're logged in.
   - Sleep mode is completely disabled on the Energy Saver pane within System Preferences.

✔ **Your iMac has something to write on:**

   - *If you're saving to iDisk,* your computer needs to make an Internet connection.
   - *If you're saving to CD or DVD,* blank media must be loaded.
   - *If you're saving to an external drive,* your external hard drive must be connected and turned on.

Publishing a Web Site with HomePage

HomePage is a very popular feature for .Mac members. Most iMac owners aren't Web page designers, after all, and HomePage is extremely easy to use. Apple is smart enough to let trial .Mac members use a limited version of HomePage; you can try it before you decide to invest in a .Mac subscription.

Follow these steps to create a new Web page on your .Mac site with HomePage:

1. **Launch Safari and visit** www.mac.com.

2. **Click the HomePage link at the top of the .Mac Welcome page.**

   Tiger prompts you for your .Mac member name and password, and then displays the HomePage top-level page that you see in Figure 9-7.

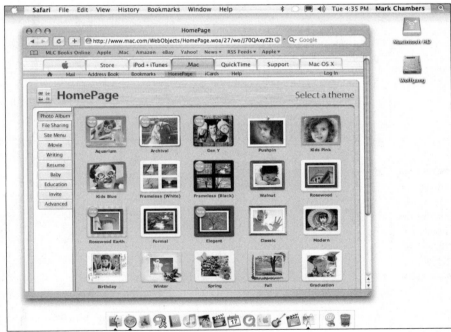

Figure 9-7: Good call — you're about to create a .Mac Web page.

3. **Choose a theme for your page from the tabbed display at the left of the screen.**

   Some of the categories are specially designed for certain chores. For example, the Photo Album theme collection is perfect for showing off your digital photographs online, and the File Sharing category presents an easy downloading format for your visitors. Each of these different categories displays different onscreen instructions that are specific to their use.

The Advanced tab allows you to use your own HTML files that you've copied to your iDisk Sites folder.

Say you want an elegant site to show off your best photography online. Click the Formal frame in the Photo Album category.

4. **Choose the folder with the photos you want to include on the page.**

This can be either your iDisk Pictures folder or a subfolder that you created within it.

5. **Click Choose.**

HomePage loads all the images in the selected folder. You see a new screen that looks something like Figure 9-8.

Figure 9-8: Designing an online art gallery is easy with HomePage.

6. **Mark the Show check box for each image that you want to appear.**

7. **Drag the image thumbnails to the order that you want.**

8. **Click in the text boxes to change**

- The Web page title

- An introductory sentence (or two)

- The titles for each photo

You can show a *counter* (of many visitors have been to your new page) and an e-mail button (so your visitors can send a message to your .Mac e-mail account). To use either of these features, just mark the corresponding Show check box to enable it.

9. **Click Preview in the toolbar at the top of the page to see what your page will look like.**

   If the page you see in Preview mode isn't up to snuff, click the Back button in the Safari toolbar to edit it.

10. **If you like what you see, click the Publish button.**

    Huzzah — *you're a Web page designer!* (Insert sound of champagne cork popping here.)

    HomePage displays your new Web page address, which you can click to jump directly to your new work of art. (Mine is shown in Figure 9-9.)

Figure 9-9: And it was so very hard to produce — thanks, Apple!

The steps to create a page vary by category. However, the only category that really requires any rocket science is the Advanced tab. Not to worry, though: Just follow the onscreen instructions for creating a Web site with your own HTML files, and you'll be fine.

Chapter 10

Hooking Up with Handy Helpers

*T*his chapter is all about getting interesting things into — and out of — your iMac. Some are more common (almost mundane these days) and pretty easy to take care of, like scanners and printers. Then I might surprise you with something new to you, like the iSight video camera that's the perfect companion to iChat AV.

I also show you how to send and receive faxes, without hiding anything up your sleeve, and how you can pull that fancy satellite or cable TV signal into your iMac.

It's perfectly okay to tell everyone else that you're watching the financial channel. But watching a little football never hurt anyone. . . .

Connecting Printers

All hail the USB port! It's the primary connection point for all sorts of goodies. In this section, I concentrate on adding a USB printer and a typical USB scanner to your system.

If you're itching to connect a USB digital camera for use with iPhoto, let me redirect you to Chapter 12, where I cover the iPhoto experience in depth.

USB printers

Connecting a USB printer to your iMac is duck soup. Don't you wish all things in life were this easy? You might very well be able to skip most of the steps in this section entirely, depending on whether your printer came with an installation disc. (Virtually all do, of course, but you might have bought yours used from eBay.)

Your printer needs to be fully supported within Mac OS X:

✔ If the software is designed for earlier versions of Mac OS X (like 10.2 or 10.3), it probably works with Tiger.

✔ I always recommend visiting the manufacturer's Web site to download the latest printer driver and support software after you install your printer. That way, you know that you're up-to-date.

Save and close your files before installing your printer. You might have to restart your iMac to complete the installation.

The physical connections for your printer are pretty simple:

✔ Make sure that your printer's USB cable is plugged in to both your iMac and the printer itself.

✔ The printer should be plugged in to an AC wall socket and turned on (after the USB connection has been made).

✔ Don't forget to add the paper!

The finishing printer installation steps depend on whether you have a manufacturer's installation CD for your printer.

Sure, I've got the install disc

If your printer comes with the manufacturer's installation disc, follow these steps when everything is connected and powered on:

1. **Insert the installation disc in the iMac.**

   The disc contents usually appear in a Finder window. If they don't, double-click the installation disc icon on the Desktop to open the window.

2. **Double-click the installation application to start the ball rolling.**

3. **Follow the onscreen instructions.**

   Files get copied to your hard drive.

   You might have to restart your iMac.

You're ready to print!

Don't forget to visit your printer manufacturer's Web site to check whether any driver updates are available for your particular model.

Whoops, I've got diddly-squat (Software-wise)

Didn't get an installation CD? Try installing the printer without software or downloading the software from the manufacturer's Web site.

Installing without software

If you didn't get an installation CD with your printer, you might be lucky enough that your printer's driver was included in your installation of Mac OS X. Here's how to check for that pesky driver after you connect the printer and switch it on:

1. **Open a Finder window and navigate to the Utilities folder.**

   It's usually inside your Applications folder.

2. **Double-click the Printer Setup Utility icon.**

3. **Check the Printer list in the Printer Setup Utility window to see whether your printer has already been added automatically within Tiger.**

   Figure 10-1 shows an example. If your printer appears here, dance a celebratory jig. You can close the Utility window and choose that printer from the Print dialog in your applications.

Figure 10-1: If Mac OS X recognizes your printer, you're ready to go.

If you don't have installation software and your iMac doesn't automatically match the printer with a driver, adding the printer manually is your last installation option. Follow these steps:

1. **Open a Finder window and navigate to the Utilities folder.**

2. **Double-click the Printer Setup Utility icon.**

3. **Click the Add icon on the Printer Setup Utility toolbar.**

4. **Click the Print Using pop-up menu.**

   The list of supported printer models appears.

5. **Click the closest match to your printer in the Print Using list.**

Figure 10-2 shows an example of some of the printer models recognized within Tiger. If you don't find an exact match for your printer, you have a couple of options:

- *Look for just the brand name, like EPSON.*
- *Try the generic USB setting.*

  If you pick USB, Tiger defaults to Auto Select for the printer model. You can manually change this if the automatic selection wasn't right.

6. **Click Add.**

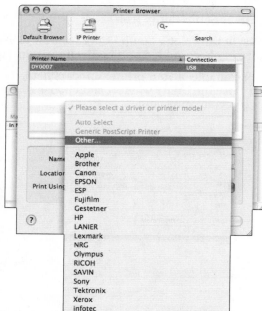

Figure 10-2: Choosing my printer from the Add sheet's pop-up menu.

Downloading software

Check the manufacturer's Web site for your printer's software. Look for

✔ **Special software drivers that the printer might need**

Install any drivers you find *before* you run an installation application. Otherwise, the installation app might not be able to recognize or configure the printer if the driver hasn't been installed first.

✔ **Installation application**

If the manufacturer offers an installation application for your printer, download the application and run it.

Networked printers

Need to access a shared or networked printer? Your iMac can use printers on

- ✔ **Ethernet wired networks**

    You can use a printer that's been shared on another computer on your network (or a printer with standalone network hardware).

- ✔ **AirPort and AirPort Extreme Wireless networks (if your iMac has an AirPort or AirPort Extreme card)**

    You can also use printers on wireless networks that don't use Apple hardware, as long as those networks are Wi-Fi certified 802.11b or 802.11g.

If you're printing over any network, you need these snippets of information for the printer:

- ✔ The shared printer name (ask the network administrator, or the person using the computer to which the shared printer is connected)
- ✔ The Workgroup name (for shared printers connected to a PC running Windows)

If the printer is connected to a Macintosh computer on your network, you don't have to configure anything on your iMac. When you want to use the printer, just select it from the Printer drop-down list box on the Print dialog.

If the printer is connected to a Windows PC, you have to set up the printer before you use it. Follow these steps:

1. **Run Printer Setup Utility.**

    "Hey, can't I reach the functionality that Printer Setup Utility offers from System Preferences?" Yep, indeed you can. Click Print & Fax, and then click the Add Printer button (which carries a plus sign). Tiger launches the Printer Setup Utility, and you're in business.

2. **Click Add.**

3. **Click the More Printers button.**

4. **Choose Windows Printing from the first pop-up menu.**

5. **Click the More Printers button.**

6. **Choose Windows Printing from the first pop-up menu.**

7. **Choose the Workgroup name from the second pop-up menu.**

    The available network printers appear in the Printer list.

8. **Click the desired printer name and click Add.**

Connecting Scanners

USB and FireWire scanners practically install themselves. As long as the model is listed as Mac OS X-compatible and it supports the TWAIN device standard (just about all scanners do), things really *are* plug-and-play. (By the way, TWAIN actually stands for either *Technology Without An Important Name* or *Technology Without An Interesting Name,* depending on whom you ask. Don't ever let anyone tell you that engineers don't have a sense of humor.)

If you have the scanner manufacturer's installation disc, go ahead and use it. However, most scanners don't require specialized drivers, so even that orphan model that you picked up from Uncle Milton last year should work (if it's recognized by Mac OS X). It doesn't hurt to check the manufacturer's Web site to see whether any of the software has been updated since the disc was produced.

If Mac OS X doesn't support your older scanner, a third-party application might be able to help. Get thee hence to Hamrick Software at `www.hamrick.com` and download a copy of the latest version of VueScan. This great scanning application supports over 350 scanner models, including a number that don't work with Tiger otherwise. At $60, it's a world-class bargain to boot.

Ready to go? Make sure that your scanner is powered on and connected to your iMac (and that you load a page or photograph to scan). If your scanner's installation disc provided you a proprietary scanning application, I recommend that you use that application to test your scanner. In fact, it's Mark's Maxim time!

If your printer or scanner includes bundled applications, *use them!*™

Sure, Mac OS X has the Printer Setup Utility for printers and the Image Capture application for scanners and digital cameras, but these are barebones tools compared with the print manager and image acquisition software that comes bundled with your hardware. I turn to Tiger's built-in hardware handling stuff only when I don't have anything better.

Hey, I'm not saying that anything's wrong with Image Capture (as shown in Figure 10-3), which is in your Applications folder, if you need to use it. However, don't expect Image Capture to support any specialized features offered by your scanner (like one-button e-mail or Web publishing). You have to use the application especially designed for your manufacturer and model to take advantage of any extras that it offers.

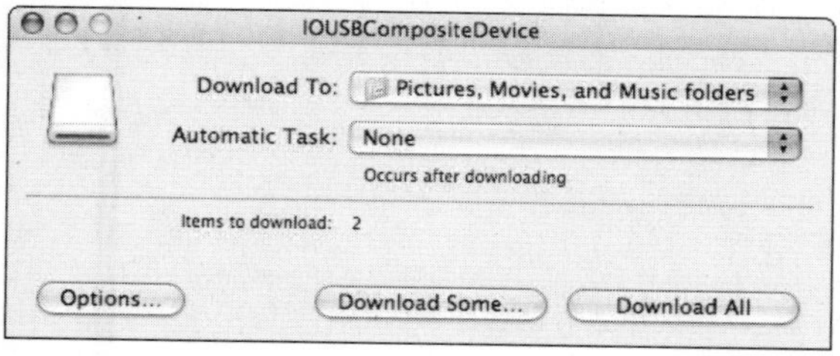

Figure 10-3:
Preparing
to inhale
images
with Image
Capture.

Have iSight, Will iChat

When I first got started in computers in the very early '80s, the very idea of chatting with someone in full-motion color video with sound was the stuff of dreams (or you were watching the TV show *Buck Rogers in the 25th Century.* Remember that one, with Gil Gerard and Erin Gray?) Your camera and your VCR were analog . . . *if* you could possibly afford such luxuries.

Ah, what a difference two decades make. Now you can use the Dynamic Duo of Apple's iSight camera (check it out in Figure 10-4) and Tiger's iChat AV to videoconference in style. All current Intel-based models have an iSight camera built-in, but if you have an older Mac without one, you can pick up an external iSight camera for about $150.

The external iSight camera sported by today's iMacs includes an impressive list of features:

- A built-in noise-suppressing microphone (perfect for offices with loud ambient noise)

- 640 x 480 resolution

- An auto-focus lens that can handle objects as close as 50mm

- Full-duplex audio (talk and listen at the same time) and up to three other video participants (or up to ten voice-only connections simultaneously)

- 30 frames per second (fps) at 24-bit color (techno-talk for high-quality, good-looking video)

Figure 10-4:
The external
iSight
camera
available for
older Macs
is a sight
to behold.

Connecting an external iSight camera is as simple as plugging the FireWire cable into your iMac. Like the internal model, the external iSight camera is automatically recognized by Mac OS X and iChat AV.

You should understand two caveats before embarking on the Voyage of Video Chat:

 ✔ **Speed is an issue.** To really take advantage of video within iChat AV, you need a fast Internet connection — at least high-speed DSL or cable Internet.

 If you're using your company's high-speed Internet at the office, you might notice a drop in video quality if network traffic is heavy.

 ✔ **All participants need a video camera.** Plenty of folks online have bought an iSight camera and then suddenly realized that most of their iChat AV buddies didn't have video capability! No need to worry since your iMac has a built-in microphone.

Even with an iSight camera available, you can still join in text-based and audio chats. iChat AV displays audio and video buttons next to each person on your Buddy List to help you keep track of who can communicate with you (and how they can do it).

And Then There's Your Fax Machine, 007

Dear reader, you've got an iMac. Meaning, as long as your machine is running in your home and you've bought an external USB modem for your computer, you simply don't need a dedicated fax machine! Your iMac can take care of sending and receiving faxes for a typical home office. (If your iMac hangs out at a larger office, you'd better keep that dedicated fax machine. Otherwise, you'd go crazy trying to handle a typical day's faxing.)

Before you set up fax send and receive, connect your iMac's external modem to your telephone jack. Just connect one end of the telephone cable to your USB modem's phone port and the other to the wall jack. (If your external modem is already connected to your telephone jack for your Internet connection, you're still fine and dandy; however, you won't be able to send or receive faxes whilst you're online. Makes sense, right?)

Receiving faxes automatically

After your modem is connected, follow these steps to set up your iMac to automatically receive incoming faxes:

1. **Click the System Preferences icon on the Dock.**
2. **Click Print & Fax.**
3. **Click the Faxing tab to display the settings that you see in Figure 10-5.**

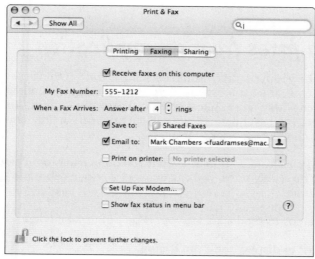

Figure 10-5: These settings control fax reception.

4. **Mark the Receive Faxes on This Computer check box to enable it.**

   Like magic, all the other settings are suddenly active.

5. **Type your Fax number into the My Fax Number text box (area code first).**

   This is required by law.

6. **In the Answer After field, specify how many rings are required to get your iMac modem's attention.**

   The default is four rings. Click the up and down arrows next to the number to change the number to what you need.

7. **Select the incoming fax options that you want:**

   • *If you don't want to save faxes, disable (clear) the Save To check box.*

     By default, received faxes are saved to the Shared Faxes folder.

   • *If you want your iMac to send a copy of every received fax to an e-mail address, mark the Email To check box to enable it.*

     You can select the address by either typing the e-mail address directly into the text box or clicking the silhouette button to open your Address Book. From the Address Book window, double-click the contact card with the desired e-mail.

   • *If you want the e-mail automatically printed, mark the Print on Printer check box to enable it, click the drop-down list box, and choose the desired printer.*

8. **Click the Close button on the System Preferences window.**

   You're set!

Sending faxes from an application

Now this, as the youth of today would exclaim, is *trick*. (I think that means outrageously cool, at least for the next year or so.) Mac OS X allows you to send faxes from within any application that allows you to print. No extra software is needed, you don't have to run a client application first, and everything is easily configured. Trick indeed!

You can send faxes from your iMac even if you don't want to receive faxes. If you want to do it only once, you can connect a phone cable and unplug it when you're done.

Follow these steps to send a fax via your iMac's internal modem:

1. **Press ⌘+P to display the Print dialog.**

2. **Click PDF.**

3. **Click the Fax PDF menu item to display the dialog that you see in Figure 10-6.**

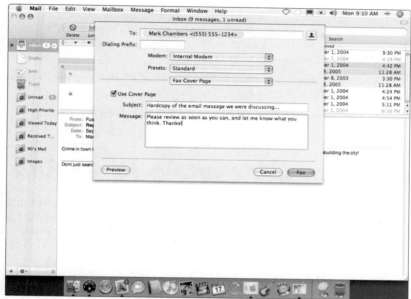

Figure 10-6:
Preparing
to ship
some-
thing out,
fax-style.

4. **Select a phone number to receive the fax.**

   You can either

   - *Type the recipient's fax number directly into the To text box* (including the area code, if necessary).

   - *Click the silhouette button to open your Address Book.* From the Address Book window, double-click the contact card with the desired fax number.

5. **Use the Dialing Prefix box to add any necessary prefix to the actual fax number.**

   You can use this if

   - *Your office phone line needs a prefix to dial an outside line.*

   - *You need to invoke an all-powerful calling card.*

6. **If you want a cover page, set it up.**

   Select the Use Cover Page check box and then type a subject line for the top of the fax. You can also type a short note containing any information that you want to appear there.

Tiger automatically prints the number of pages, the date and time the fax is sent, and the From/To information on the cover sheet.

7. **Click the Fax Cover Page drop-down list box to configure the layout and modem settings that you want.**

   For instance, you would choose Copies & Pages to type a range of pages if necessary, or Modem to choose between your iMac's internal modem or an external USB modem.

8. **To double-check what you're sending, click Preview to display a preview of the document.**

9. **Click Fax and listen while your modem does the rest.**

Turning Your iMac into a TV — And More

Your iMac's beautiful LCD screen would seem to be the perfect artist's canvas for watching cable or satellite TV broadcasts, but there's no coax input on the back of your computer. Therefore, unless you invest in some additional hardware, you're restricted to watching DVD movies.

Such an obvious need is going to be filled quickly, and a number of different hardware manufacturers have produced external devices that can merge your iMac and your TV signal. Most are USB or FireWire peripherals, and many have all the features of today's TiVo and digital video recorders.

My favorite example is the EyeTV 200, from Elgato Systems (www.elgato.com), which uses a FireWire connection. Check out what this superstar includes for your investment of $330:

- A 124-channel cable-ready TV tuner
- The ability to pause, fast-forward, record, or even edit the video you've stored on your iMac's hard drive
- Real-time MPEG-2 encoding, for DVD-quality recordings
- Analog-to-digital conversion, allowing you to back up your old VHS recordings to digital video
- Full-screen TV display or in a window anywhere on your desktop
- Its own wireless remote control

I really love the ability to fast-forward through commercials, and I can take anything that I record on my iMac and use it in iDVD and iMovie. The addition of TV under your control sorta finalizes the whole digital hub thing, now doesn't it?

Part IV
Living the iLife

The 5th Wave   By Rich Tennant

©RICHTENNANT

THE LEVINES EDIT THEIR AFRICAN SAFARI VIDEO

"Do you think the 'Hidden Rhino' clip should come before or after the 'Waving Hello' video clip?"

In this part . . .

Here they are, the applications that everyone craves: This part covers iTunes, iPhoto, iMovie HD, iDVD, and GarageBand like your Grandma's best quilt. You find out how to share your images, music, and video clips between the iLife '05 applications on your iMac, and how to create everything from your own DVDs to a truly awesome hardcover photo album!

Chapter 11

The Musical Joy of iTunes

Sometimes, words just aren't enough. iTunes is that kind of perfection.

To envision how iTunes changes your iMac, you have to paint the picture with *music* — music that's easy to play, easy to search, and easy to transfer from place to place. Whether it be classical, alternative, jazz, rock, hip-hop, or folk, I can guarantee you that you won't find a better application than iTunes to fill your life with your music.

In this chapter, I lead you through all the features of my absolute favorite member of the iLife suite . . . and it's going to be pretty doggone obvious how much I appreciate this one piece of software.

Boy, Check Out That iTunes Window!

Indeed, Figure 11-1 shows off the iTunes window like the jewel that it is. I complete the roll call of switches and controls in Figure 11-2; there are just too many neat WUDs (Wonderful User Devices) to list them all in one pass.

This isn't the only face of the iTunes window. It morphs into something different when you're browsing music from the Apple Music Store, and you can also decide to watch animation while you listen. More on these different looks later.

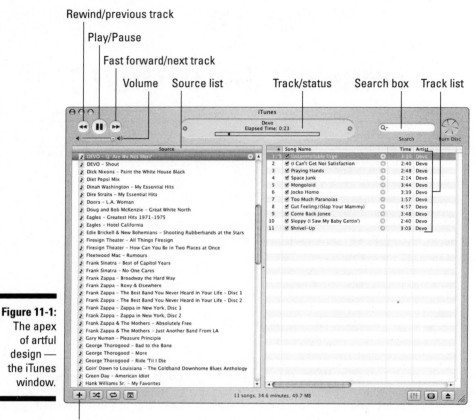

Rewind/previous track

Play/Pause

Fast forward/next track

Volume   Source list   Track/status   Search box   Track list

Figure 11-1:
The apex
of artful
design —
the iTunes
window.

Create a playlist

Before I dive into a discussion of how to use all this good stuff, let me introduce
you to the controls that you'll use most often within the iTunes window:

- **Source list:** Imagine all your albums listed alphabetically — or, even
  better, playlists of your favorite songs that you create to match your particular mood. You find both in the Source list, along with a handful of
  special categories called Library, Party Shuffle, Radio, and Music Store.
  (As you can tell from Figure 11-1, I listen to a *very* wide range of musical
  genres.)

- **Rewind/Previous Track:** Click and hold down this button to move backward quickly through the song that's currently playing. Clicking returns
  you to the beginning of the track, and double-clicking this button takes
  you to the previous track in the list.

- **Play:** Recognize it from your old cassette deck? Click Play, and iTunes
  begins playing the selected music from the Track list. (I tell you more
  about selecting your favorite hits in the following section.) While your

music is playing, this bad boy turns into a Pause button, which you can click to pause your music. To begin playing again where you paused, click the Play button again.

✔ **Forward/Next Track:** Click and hold this button down to move forward through a song at a fast clip, or click it normally to jump directly to the next track in the list.

✔ **Volume:** Drag this unassuming control to raise or lower the volume within iTunes. Go figure.

✔ **Track list:** Ah, you knew I'd get to this sooner or later. The track list displays all the songs, radio stations, and assorted whatnot that you can play within iTunes. Double-clicking an item in the track list starts it playing immediately.

✔ **Track/Status display:** A cool-looking LCD display in the middle of brushed chrome . . . oh, yes. The display usually shows you the progress of the current song and also rotates to inform you of the track name and artist. iTunes also uses the display show prompts and messages about things like burning discs and importing music.

Note those two tiny icons at both sides of the track display:

- Click the *Play icon* at the left side, and the track display transforms into a graphic bar display like those on the finest stereo systems. (Click the icon again to return to the normal display.)

- Click the *circular icon* at the right side of the display, and iTunes immediately returns the selection highlight in the track list to the song that's currently playing.

✔ **Search box:** This works much like the Search box in the Finder window toolbar. You can type artist, album, and song names here. Then press Return, and iTunes presents you with items that match in the track list.

✔ **Create a Playlist:** Click this button to add a new empty playlist to your Source list, ready to be filled with whatever songs or items you crave.

That's the cheap tour. Simple, elegant, and powerful as a Ferrari. Time to get started playing music!

The Lazy iTunes Guide

In this section, I show you how to take care of business: how to play your music (in all its many forms), how to create playlists, how to organize your collection, and how to watch your music. (No, that last one wasn't a typo. Just wait.)

Listening to song files, playlists, Internet radio, and audio CDs

iTunes recognizes a number of different audio file formats, and you can listen to any of them:

- **MP3:** Unless you've been hiding under a rock for the last few years, you'll recognize this popular format. MP3 files produce excellent quality at a small size, but a discerning ear can hear the effects of the compression used to shrink an MP3 file. (Oh, and these files aren't copy-protected.)

- **AAC:** Apple's AAC format offers better compression than MP3, so your songs are smaller and sound better. However, AAC files might be copy-protected, so they can't be shared among more than a handful of Macs. When you buy and download music from the Apple Music Store (which I crow about later in this chapter), the songs that you get are in AAC format.

- **AIFF:** AIFF was the original high-quality format for audio files on the Mac, but they're uncompressed and just too doggone big, so most folks have left them behind in favor of MP3 and AAC.

- **WAV:** Microsoft's original Windows audio format is quite similar to AIFF. WAV format songs can reach the highest quality possible, but they're so honking huge that practically no one uses WAV format any longer.

- **Apple Lossless:** Audiophiles love this new format from Apple because the compression doesn't affect the sound quality (as it does with MP3 and AAC files), yet Apple Lossless files are much smaller than AIFF and WAV files and sound as good. Is this the perfect audio format? Stay tuned, friends: Only time will tell. (Oh, and yes, copy protection is included at no extra charge.)

Okay, enough techno-info. Back to the music! iTunes makes it easy to listen to a song:

- **From a Finder window:** Double-click the song icon (as shown in Figure 11-2) or drag the song file from the window to the iTunes icon in the Dock.

  iTunes launches automatically, if necessary, and the song appears in the track list while it plays. You can also drag a song file from a Finder window directly to the iTunes track list.

- **From the iTunes track list:** Double-click the track entry.

That's all there is to it! A tiny "playing" speaker appears next to the song that's playing in the track list. If you pause iTunes, the speaker goes silent, but it remains next to the track to indicate what you're going to hear if you press Play again. Although the highlight cursor might be on another song or playlist, that tiny speaker icon always sticks next to whatever's playing right then.

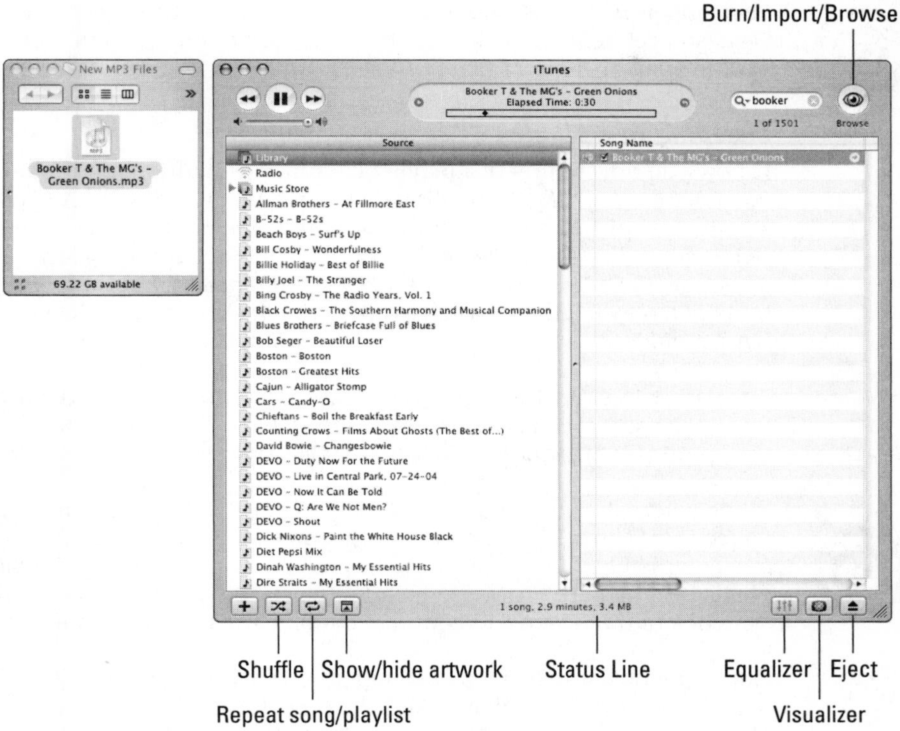

Burn/Import/Browse

Figure 11-2:
Listen to an
MP3 song
by clicking it
in the Finder
window.

Shuffle | Show/hide artwork | Status Line | Equalizer | Eject

Repeat song/playlist | Visualizer

Speaking of the Play button, you really don't have to press it. Instead, you can press the space bar to play or pause a song in iTunes. In fact, pressing the right-arrow key works the same as clicking the iTunes Next Track button, and pressing the left-arrow key works just like clicking the Previous Track button.

While you're listening to a song, notice the cursor as it moves along the progress bar in the Status display. Feel free to click and drag that cursor to the left and right, which works the same as using the Rewind and Fast Forward controls. (In fact, I use this method exclusively because it lets you cover a lot of musical ground when you're listening to a 24-minute track from Frank Zappa.)

If you get tired of hearing an album in the same order that you memorized years ago, make use of the Shuffle button. Click a playlist and then click the Shuffle button that you see in Figure 11-2. The button turns blue, and iTunes mixes the order of your music automatically. To exit shuffle mode, click the Shuffle button again. (If you click the Library entry at the top of the Source list and click Shuffle, you get a wild mix taken from every song that you've collected.) Note that Shuffle doesn't actually change the order of the songs in the track list.

You can specify whether iTunes should shuffle by songs or albums. Choose iTunes⇨Preferences, click the Advanced toolbar button, and then click either Shuffle Song or Album.

Listening to a playlist

I show you how to create a playlist later in the chapter, but for now, you can consider it a unit, like a traditional vinyl album or audio CD. A *playlist* can be a collection of songs that you choose yourself and organize by genre (like *Boudreaux's Favorite Zydeco Hits*), or it can include the songs that appear in an actual album (such as Fleetwood Mac's *Rumours*). In other words, the contents of a playlist are completely up to you. It's a container, like a folder in the Finder window.

Listening to a playlist is simplicity itself: Just click the desired playlist in the Source list and click Play or press the spacebar. iTunes immediately shows you the contents of the playlist in the track list and starts to play the first track.

While you're listening to a playlist, feel free to browse other music in your collection; iTunes keeps track of what song is due next, even if you're looking at a completely different playlist. To jump to a specific track in a different playlist that you're browsing, just double-click it. iTunes immediately switches to that track and continues to play the rest of the new playlist.

Out of the box, iTunes stops playing after it reaches the end of the last song in a playlist. Don't like that? Then you'll be ecstatic to discover that a single click of the Repeat Song/Repeat Playlist button (as shown in Figure 11-2) repeats all the songs in the playlist. (The button turns blue when Repeat is on.) If you click the same button again, a tiny 1 icon appears, and only the current song repeats. A third and final press of the Repeat button turns the feature off, and you're back to Start. (Click the Library icon at the top of your Source list, click Repeat, and the tunes keep on coming until you choose to stop them. For my collection, that takes almost *four solid **days!***)

Tuning in to streaming Internet radio

Here's another neat Internet technology that you might not have heard of: a *streaming radio* station plays music that iTunes can receive and play for you in real time. The music sounds just as if the broadcast were traveling across the airwaves rather than across that expensive cable modem. (Well, except for the fadeouts and static, but you won't miss those.)

To display the variety of Internet radio stations provided by Apple, click the Radio icon in the Source list. Figure 11-3 illustrates the wide selection, categorized by genre. I guess the folks in Cupertino enjoy their music, too!

Figure 11-3:
Suddenly
the Internet
means more
than e-mail
and the
Web.

Recognize those triangle icons from the Finder window's list mode? Yep, just click a triangle to expand or collapse that category to see the entries it contains. To start playing, double-click a station entry.

A station's *bit rate* means a lot, especially if you're using a dialup modem connection. The higher the bit rate, the better the sound. In fact, a bit rate of 128 Kbps gives you CD-quality sound, but it takes a high-speed Internet connection (like a DSL or cable modem connection) to move all that data fast enough to provide uninterrupted music. Therefore, if you're using a dialup connection, I recommend that you stick with stations offering music at around FM quality, at 56 Kbps or less. (You'll know this is the problem if iTunes keeps pausing during play so that it can catch up to the station's data.)

You can also tune in to an Internet radio station by entering that station's Web address directly into iTunes. Press ⌘+U (or, for the keyboard-wary, click Advanced and click Open Stream) to display a text box in which you can type or paste the station's Web address. Click OK, and sit back.

Giving your audio CDs the treatment

To play a music CD, load the disc into your iMac. By default, iTunes launches automatically whenever you load a music CD. Click the CD icon in the Source list to select it, and then click the Play button and start enjoying yourself.

Hey, do *you* remember the '70s?

You know, Farrah Fawcett, disco balls, and the AMC Javelin? Now, do you yearn for the incomparable music that dates from 1970–1979? Then, my friend, have I got an Internet radio station for you! It's called *MLC Radio Online* (I bet you saw that coming, didn't you?), and it features the absolute best from the Decade that Shall Never Come Again. Rock, folk, disco, soul, and even the beginnings of New Wave and Alternative. (And yes, it does include *Kung Fu Fighting* by Carl Douglas. After all, the song was *hot*.)

MLC Radio Online requires a high-speed connection (DSL, cable modem, or satellite) because all those hits are 128 Kbps, CD quality! It isn't in Apple's default list — are you listening, Mr. Jobs? — but the station address is on my Web site, MLC Books Online, at www.mlc books.com. See you there, *Starsky & Hutch* fans!

The Rewind and Forward buttons also function as Previous Track and Next Track when you're listening to a CD. Click the Previous Track button once, and iTunes returns to the beginning of the track that's currently playing. (If you've used home or car CD systems, you'll immediately recognize this behavior.) To make the move to the previous track, you must double-click the button.

If you'd rather not have iTunes launch all by itself when you load an audio CD, open System Preferences and click the CDs & DVDs icon. Click the When You Insert a Music CD drop-down list box and choose the action that you prefer, or choose Ignore if you want nothing to happen.

To specify what action iTunes should take after it's launched by loading a CD, choose iTunes➪Preferences and then click the General toolbar button. Click the On CD Insert pop-up menu and choose your weapon.

To eject the disc, you can simply click the Eject button, (refer to Figure 11-2). iTunes immediately sends the disc packing.

Organizing, sorting, and searching (The right way)

What good is having the world's largest music collection if you can't find anything? In this section, I help you get organized by creating playlists, sorting stuff, and rearranging tracks as you see fit.

Creating playlists and moving your music

The Library category in the Source list is the Big Kahuna. Click Library, and you see literally every song in your collection, all in one huge list. The playlist is the other side of the coin because it allows you to compartmentalize your music any way you please.

You can create a playlist in several different ways:

- ✔ **Click the Create New Playlist button (which bears a plus sign) at the bottom of the iTunes window.**
- ✔ **Choose File⇨New Playlist.**
- ✔ **Press ⌘+N.**

No matter which method you choose, a new entry named `untitled playlist` appears in the Source list. The entry is actually a text entry box, ready for you to type a more descriptive name. Do so, and press Return. Bam! You've created an empty playlist.

Change your mind about a playlist name? No problem! You can rename a playlist just like you rename a file in the Finder window: Click the file to select it, pause for a second, and then click again. The edit box reappears, and you can type the new name that you really want.

As you can tell from the figures in this chapter, I prefer to name most of my playlists with artist or band name first, followed by a dash, and then followed by the album name. (This helps keep things organized alphabetically in the Source list. When you have almost 1,500 songs in your Library, the alphabet becomes a truly handy tool.) Most of my playlists are actually albums, so this makes sense. You, on the other hand, might prefer to build every one of your playlists song by song, so *My Favorite Swedish Rock Ballads* might work better as a name. It's all up to you!

After you create your new playlist, you can drag songs from your Library and drop them on top of the playlist entry in the Source list. Alternatively, you

---

Doing the iPod dance

If you're the proud owner of an iPod, I salute you. My old 15GB model is still chugging away and still has a little room left for a few more songs. Each time you plug your iPod into its cradle, iTunes automatically updates your iPod's hard drive with any changes, additions, or deletions that you've made to your Library. It's all pretty automatic.

I wish I had more space to go into more detail on advanced settings for the iPod within iTunes,

but this is a book dedicated to the iMac, and my editors tell me that I must concentrate on that glamorous piece of Apple hardware. If you'd like a comprehensive guide to *everything* that you can do with iTunes and iPod, *iPod & iTunes For Dummies,* 2nd Edition (by Tony Bove and Cheryl Rhodes; Wiley) devotes a full 384 pages to the dynamic duo.

can click the playlist name in the Source list and then drag the songs into the track list. To choose multiple files at once, hold down ⌘ while you click.

To delete a track from a playlist, click it to highlight the song and then press the Delete key. Note, however, that the song *isn't* deleted from your actual collection unless you click the Library entry in the Source list and delete the song there as well. Deleting a playlist works the same way: Click the playlist to select it, and then press Delete.

You can also select songs in the track list and create a playlist that contains those tracks. Click the desired tracks to select 'em and then choose File↪ New Playlist from Selection. You still get the playlist name edit box, but the playlist already contains the files that you chose.

After the songs that you want are in your new playlist — however they got there — they don't have to remain in the order that you first see them. For example, to move a song from the Track 2 position to the Track 3 position, click the song and drag it to the desired spot. (iTunes creates a ghost entry to help you keep track of where that track is going. Sorry, bad pun.)

This same drag-and-drop functionality works throughout most of iTunes. Drag tracks here and there to organize your music into the playlists that you create. It's just plain fun.

Searching for every artist named Elvis

(Don't laugh, I've done it.) You can use the Search box in the iTunes toolbar to locate a specific string of text. Follow these steps to find whether Elvis is in the building:

1. **Click the Library entry in the Source list to select it.**

   In most cases, you want to click the Library entry so that your search encompasses your entire music collection. However, if you've got a really *huge* playlist to search, you can select the individual playlist instead.

2. **Click the magnifying glass icon.**

   This displays a short pop-up menu from which you can choose to search through just one data field — the Artist, Album, Composer, or Song Name. The default is All, which doesn't limit the search to any one field; any match of any of the four criteria counts.

3. **Click in the Search box and type the text that you want to match.**

   iTunes immediately goes to work and displays the matches (within the criteria that you select) in the track list.

4. **Click the X icon at the right side of the Search box.**

   iTunes erases the search text, and the rest of your collection reappears. Now you can try another search, if you like.

By the way, the search for Elvis returned just two songs: *Elvis Has Just Left the Building* (Frank Zappa) and *Hound Dog* (the King himself). (Note to self: Get more Elvis.)

Sorting your music every which way

Check out those buttons atop each column in the track list. They work just like the buttons at the top of each column in a Finder window when you're using list mode. Click Song Name, for example, and your selected playlist or your entire Library is sorted by song name.

The ability to sort by Artist, Album, and Genre can provide interesting pickings for new playlists. Never before has it been so easy to compose your own greatest-hits collection from your favorite band or from a specific musical style.

Oh, and if the artist name, album name, or genre doesn't appear for songs in your track list, don't worry — that just means you need to add the information, and that's the next topic.

Adding or editing song information

Many of the MP3 and AAC files that you add to your collection already have *tags* — that's the techno-nerd name for the information that's embedded in a song file, which iTunes displays in the track list, like the year the song was released and the album name.

But what if a track (or an entire playlist) has no tags, or the tags are wrong? You can add or edit them yourself. Follow these steps:

1. **Click the desired songs to select them.**

   To select every song in the playlist, click the first track and then press ⌘+A.

2. **Press ⌘+I.**

   Mac fanatics everywhere can immediately identify what appears as the Get Info keyboard shortcut. The Info dialog for the selected tracks appears; Figure 11-4 illustrates the dialog that you see. (If you're adding information for just one song, click the Info button to get to the same spot. Personally, I usually find myself adding song information for every song in a playlist, so I usually see the Multiple Song version.)

3. **Click in each field that you want to add or edit and then enter the new tag information.**

   Remember, the same information that you add is embedded in every song that you select, so it needs to apply equally. For example, if you select songs from AC/DC, Louis Armstrong, and Hank Williams, Sr., you probably wouldn't want to apply the Genre tag *Rock* to all of them!

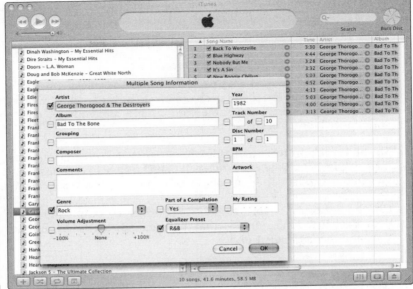

Figure 11-4:
Add
information
for multiple
songs.

4. **After you're finished, click OK.**

iTunes displays a progress bar as it embeds the tag data within the songs.

If you're wondering about that square marked Artwork, you can indeed drag an image of the album cover to the square to embed it as well. (This trick works exceptionally well with thumbnails dragged from the Amazon Web site.) To display album art while a song is playing, press ⌘+G to toggle the Artwork pane on and off.

Visualization — It's music for your eyes

Speaking of artwork, iTunes can display a kaleidoscopic animated light show right out of Woodstock for your visual pleasure. Click the Visualization button (Figure 11-2 yet again) to enter the light show or press ⌘+T. Figure 11-5 gives you an idea of the beautiful patterns that you might see.

To switch your iMac into mind-blowing full-screen mode, press ⌘+F. You even get an MTV-style song information block in the lower-left corner!

To exit visualization mode and get back to work — like I should right now — press ⌘+T again or click your mouse button.

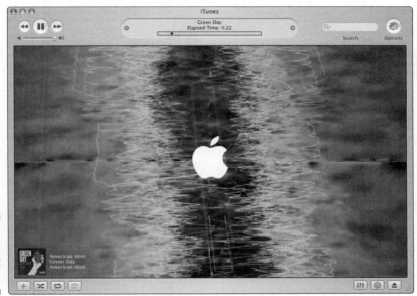

Pulling in Songs and Spitting 'Em Out

In this final section, I cover three very important tasks: two involve getting songs into iTunes (by importing them and buying them), and the last instructs you on how to get music out of iTunes (by burning your own audio CDs). I trust you'll be paying attention.

Importing songs from CD and hard drive

It's very easy to import — or, as the process is more popularly called, *rip* — music from music CDs that you own. First, however, it's a good idea to first set up your encoder, so go ahead and launch the application by clicking the iTunes icon on the Dock. Then follow these steps:

1. **Choose iTunes➪Preferences to display the Preferences dialog.**

2. **Click the Importing button on the toolbar.**

3. **Click the Import Using pop-up menu and choose either**

   • *MP3 Encoder:* Gives the best compatibility with other computers and devices

TIP

If you choose MP3 encoder, click the Setting drop-down list box and choose Higher Quality (192 Kbps).

In my experience, this bit rate gives you the best combination of good audio quality and smaller file sizes.

or

- *Apple Lossless Encoder:* Gives the best sound with the smallest file sizes

4. Click OK.

That takes care of your encoder settings — a process that you need to perform only once — and now you're ready to do the deed. With iTunes running, follow these steps to add the songs to your Library:

1. Load a music CD into your Mac.

If you have an active Internet connection, iTunes attempts to identify the tracks and name them for you.

2. Mark the check boxes of any tracks that you don't want to disable.

Any track with an enabled check box will be imported.

3. Click the Import button at the right side of the iTunes window.

Figure 11-6 illustrates iTunes importing my favorites from a Ray Charles music CD.

Figure 11-6:
Add songs
to iTunes
from an
audio CD.

To import songs from files that you've downloaded or copied to your hard drive, follow these steps:

1. **Open a Finder window and navigate to the location where the songs are stored.**

2. **Create a new playlist to hold the songs, as I describe earlier in the chapter.**

   Of course, this is optional. You can also import the songs straight into your Library and organize them later.

3. **In the Finder window, select all the songs that you want to import.**

4. **Drag the song files into the iTunes window and drop them either on top of the desired playlist or into the track list itself.**

iTunes takes a second to verify the files and assign their tag information, and then your new tracks appear in your playlist or the Library.

Buying Billie Holiday from the Apple Music Store

As long as you have an active Internet connection — and I fervently hope that it's a high-speed DSL or cable modem connection — the Apple Music Store is ready to server your needs, with well over a million tracks for you to choose from! Most single tracks are only $0.99 each, and most full albums are $9.99 at the time of this writing.

The first time that you access the Music Store, you provide your credit card and e-mail account information over a secure connection, and the Music Store remembers them and logs you in automatically from that point onward. There are no subscription or fees. You buy the tracks and albums you want, with no silly strings attached.

To browse or buy, click the Music Store entry in the Source list. After a moment or two, you see the entrance to the Store (as shown in Figure 11-7). To browse, simply

- Click an album cover from the entrance page.
- Click a link to one of the day's top songs or albums.
- Click the Choose Genre pop-up menu and pick your passion.
- Click the Power Search link to perform an advanced search for just that one artist or album.

Figure 11-7:
Browse the
shelves of
the Apple
Music
Store.

As you drill deeper into your favorite music, notice the Back and Forward arrows and the Home icon right under the iTunes track display. These controls work just like a Web browser, moving you to previous and next pages, or returning you to the top-level entrance page (respectively). *Nice.*

Oh, and those little arrows next to the album and artist names in the iTunes track list? If you already clicked one to experiment, you know that they automatically take you to the Music Store so that you can purchase more music by the same (or similar) artists.

If you decide to buy a track or album, just click the corresponding Add Song or Add Album button. The tracks that you marked are saved in the Shopping Cart subentry (under the Music Store entry in your iTunes Source list). After you're done shopping, click the Shopping Cart entry and click the Buy Now button. iTunes immediately begins downloading your new music, and the tracks are saved to the Purchased Music playlist (again, immediately underneath the Music Store entry in the Source list).

Now you can move the music you bought to anywhere in your collection, building a new playlist or distributing them amongst your existing playlists. Enjoy!

Burning like a true techno

Are you ready to record your own music and MP3 CDs? Sure you are! You can play the music CDs that you burn in just about any audio CD player or computer these days, but MP3 discs are a little more specialized. Because they are actually data discs that contain your music in MP3 format, you can store a lot more music on a single disc. (Luckily, more and more audio CD players, boom boxes, and computers can now recognize and play an MP3 disc.) Still, here's the Mark's Maxim to live by:

If it's the broadest compatibility ye desire, then burn a standard audio CD.™

To specify which type of disc you want to create, launch iTunes and follow these steps:

1. **Choose iTunes⇨Preferences to display the Preferences dialog.**
2. **Click the Burning button on the toolbar.**
3. **Select either the Audio CD or the MP3 CD radio button.**

Don't burn a Data CD unless you'll only read the disc on a computer. If you're burning a disc for your car or home audio CD player, choosing Data CD is a good definition of a *bad idea*.

4. **Click OK.**

After you configure the type of disc that you want to burn, follow these steps to burn the contents of a playlist to an audio or MP3 CD:

1. **In the iTunes Source list, select the playlist that you want to burn.**
2. **Click the Burn Disc icon at the upper right of the iTunes window.**

The icon changes into a truly neat burning symbol, and you're prompted to load a blank CD-R.

Never use a CD-RW to record an audio CD unless you're sure that your audio player supports rewriteable media — again, for the best compatibility, use a CD-R.

3. **Load the blank disc.**

iTunes displays the total songs and time for the recording.

4. **Click the Burn Disc icon again, and await your new music or MP3 CD with a smile on your face!**

Chapter 12

The Masterpiece That Is iPhoto

*i*Photo, my favorite image cataloging-editing-sharing tool, is probably right up at the top of the popularity ratings when it comes to the iLife suite because virtually every Mac owner is likely to have a digital camera or a scanner. Digital video (DV) camcorders have certainly grown more plentiful over the past three or four years, and the iPod is the hottest piece of music hardware on the planet at the time of this writing. The digital camera, however, has reached what those funny (strange) marketing people refer to as *saturation*.

With this in mind, I'm willing to bet that iPhoto is either the first or the second iLife application that you fall in love with (running neck and neck with iTunes). In this chapter, I show you how you can organize, print, share, and display your digital photographs with true Apple panache!

Touring the Glorious iPhoto Window

In Figure 12-1, you can see most of the major controls offered in iPhoto. (Other controls automagically appear when you enter different modes — I cover them in upcoming sections of this chapter.)

Source list   Viewer

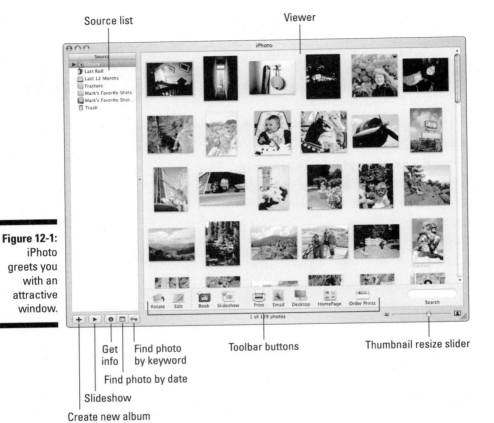

Figure 12-1:
iPhoto
greets you
with an
attractive
window.

Get info   Find photo by keyword   Toolbar buttons   Thumbnail resize slider

Find photo by date

Slideshow

Create new album

Although these controls and sections of the window are covered in more detail in the following sections, here's a quick rundown of what you're looking at:

✔ **Source list:** This list of image locations determines which photos iPhoto displays.

    • You can choose to display either your entire image library, or just the last "roll" of digital images that you downloaded from your camera.

    • You can create new *albums* of your own that appear in the source list; albums make it much easier to organize your photos.

✔ **Viewer:** This pane displays the images from the currently selected photo source.

You can drag or click to select photos in the Viewer for further tricks, like assigning keywords and image editing.

- **Create New Album button:** Click this button to add a new blank album, book, or slideshow to your source list.

- **Display a Slideshow button:** Click here to start an automated slideshow using the images that you select from the Viewer.

- **Get Info button:** Click this button to display information on the currently selected photos.

- **Find Photos by Date button:** Click this button to view photos that were added in a specific month or date. While you're viewing the calendar, click the tiny Date toggle button at the top left of the Calendar display to switch between month and date displays. (A month or date that appears in bold indicates that it will display at least one image.)

- **Find Photos by Keyword button:** Click this button to view photos that you've marked with one or more keywords. (More on this later in the chapter.)

- **Toolbar buttons:** This group of buttons selects an operation you want to perform on the images you've selected in the Viewer.

- **Thumbnail Resize slider:** Drag this slider to the left to reduce the size of the thumbnails in the Viewer (which allows you to see more thumbnails at once, which is a great boon for quick visual searches). Drag the slider to the right to expand the size of the thumbnails, which makes it easier to differentiate details between similar photos in the Viewer.

Handling Photos Like da Vinci

Even a superbly designed image display and editing application like iPhoto would look overwhelming if everything were jammed into one window. Thus, Apple's developers provide different operation modes (like editing and book creation) that you can use in the one iPhoto window. Each of these modes allows you to perform different tasks, and you can switch modes at just about any time by clicking the corresponding toolbar buttons.

In this section, I discuss three of these modes and what you can do when you're in them. Then I conclude the chapter with sections on publishing and sharing your images.

Import mode: Herding photos from your camera

In *Import* mode, you're ready to download the images that you've taken directly from your digital camera (as long as your specific camera model is supported within iPhoto). You can find out which cameras are supported by visiting the Apple iPhoto support page at

```
www.apple.com/macosx/upgrade/cameras.html
```

Follow these steps to import images:

1. **Connect your digital camera to your Macintosh.**

   Plug one end of a USB cable into your camera and the other end into your Macintosh's USB port.

2. **Launch iPhoto.**

   Launch iPhoto by clicking its icon on the Dock (or in your Applications folder).

   The first time that you launch iPhoto, you have the option of setting its autolaunch feature. I recommend using this feature because when you turn it on, iPhoto starts automatically whenever you connect a camera to your Mac.

3. **Type a roll name for the imported photos.**

4. **Type a description for the roll.**

   If you don't expect to download these images again to another computer or another device, you can select the Delete Items from Camera after Importing check box to enable it. iPhoto automatically deletes all the images after they're downloaded from the camera. This saves you a step and helps eliminate the guilt that can crop up when you nix your pix. (Sorry, I couldn't resist.)

Importing images from your hard drive

If you have a folder of images that you've already collected on your hard drive, a CD or DVD, an external drive, or a USB Flash drive, adding them to your library is easy. Just drag the folder from a Finder window and drop it into the Source list in the iPhoto window. iPhoto automatically creates a new album using the folder name, and you can sit back while the images are imported right into that new album. iPhoto recognizes images in several formats: JPEG, GIF, RAW, PNG, PICT, and TIFF.

If you have individual images, you can drag them as well. Select the images in a Finder window and drag them into the desired album in the Source list. To add them to the album that's currently displayed in the Viewer, drag the selected photos and drop them in the Viewer instead.

If you'd rather import images by using a standard Mac Open dialog, choose File➪Import. Simplicity strikes again!

5. **Click the Import button to import your photographs from the camera.**

   The images are added to your Photo Library, where you can organize them later into individual albums, as well as in a separate "virtual" film roll in the Source list.

"What's that about a roll, Mark? I thought I was finally getting away from that!" Well, you are — at least a physical roll of film — but after you download the contents of your digital camera, those contents count as a virtual "roll" of film in iPhoto. You can always display those images by clicking Last Roll or by choosing a specific roll (find both in the Source list). Think about that . . . it's pretty tough to arrange old-fashioned film prints by the roll in which they originally appeared, but iPhoto makes it easy for you to see just which photos were part of the same download group!

Organize mode: Organizing and sorting snapshots

In the days of film prints, you could always stuff another shoebox with your latest photos or buy another sticky album to expand your library. Your digital camera, though, stores images as files instead, and many folks don't print their digital photographs at all. Instead, you can keep your entire collection of digital photographs and scanned images well ordered and easily retrieved by using iPhoto's *Organize* mode. Then you can display them as a slideshow, print them to your system printer, use them as desktop backgrounds, or burn them to an archive disc.

A new kind of photo album

The key to organizing images within iPhoto is the *album*. Each album can represent any division you like, be it a year, a vacation, your daughter, or your daughter's ex-boyfriends. Follow these steps:

1. **Create a new album.**

   You can either

   - Choose File⇨New Album.

     or

   - Click the plus (+) button at the bottom of the Source list.

   The New Album sheet appears, as illustrated in Figure 12-2.

2. **Type the name for your new photo album.**

3. **Click OK.**

Figure 12-2:
Add a new
album within
iPhoto.

iPhoto also offers a special type of album called a *Smart Album,* which you can create from the File menu. A Smart Album contains only photos that match certain criteria that you choose, using the keywords and rating that you assign your images. Other criteria include recent film rolls, text contained in the photo filenames, dates the images were added to iPhoto, and any comments you might have added. Now here's the really nifty angle: iPhoto *automatically* builds and maintains Smart Albums for you, adding new photos that match the criteria (and deleting those that you remove from your Photo Library)! Smart Albums carry a gear icon in the Source list.

You can always display information about the currently selected item in the Information panel under the Source list — just click the Show Information button at the bottom of the iPhoto window, which sports the familiar "*i*-in-a-circle" logo. You can also type a short note or description in the comment box. For more in-depth information, select the desired item and then press ⌘+I.

You can rename an image by selecting it in the Viewer. The Title and Date fields below the Source list turn into text edit boxes, so you can simply click in either box to type a new name or alter the photo's date stamp. The same method works when you select a photo album in the source list — you can change the Album name from the Album text box.

You can drag images from the Viewer into any album you choose. If an album is displayed in the Viewer, you can drag an image and drop it in another album in the list to move that image from album to album. To copy an image, you can use Duplicate, just like in a Finder window.

To remove a photo that has fallen out of favor, follow these steps:

1. **Select the desired album from the source list.**

2. **In the Viewer, select the photo (click it) that you want to remove.**

3. **Press Delete.**

Even though a photo can be removed from an album, that doesn't remove it from your collection (which is represented by the Library entry in the Source list). That's because an album is actually just a group of links to the images in your collection. To completely remove the offending photo, click the Library entry to display your entire collection of images and delete the picture there, too.

To remove an entire album from the Source list, just click it in the Source list to select it — in the Viewer, you can see the images that it contains — and then press Delete.

Change your mind? Daughter's ex is back in the picture, so to speak? iPhoto comes complete with a handy-dandy Undo feature; just press ⌘+Z, and it's like your last action never happened. (A great trick for those moments when you realize you just deleted your only image of your first car from your Library.)

Organizing things with keywords

"Okay, Mark, iPhoto albums are a great idea, but do you really expect me to look through 20 albums just to locate pictures with specific functions?" Never fear, good iMac owner. You can also assign descriptive *keywords* to images to help you organize your collection and locate certain pictures fast. iPhoto comes with a number of standard keywords, and you can create your own as well.

To illustrate, suppose you'd like to identify your images according to special events in your family. Birthday photos should have their own keyword, and anniversaries deserve another. By assigning keywords, you can search for Elsie's 6th birthday or your silver wedding anniversary, and all related photos with those keywords appear like magic! (Well, *almost* like magic. You need to choose View➪Keywords, which toggles the Keyword display on and off in the Viewer.)

iPhoto includes a number of keywords that are already available:

- ✔ Favorite
- ✔ Family
- ✔ Kids
- ✔ Vacation
- ✔ Birthday
- ✔ Grayscale
- ✔ Widescreen
- ✔ Checkmark

What's the Checkmark all about, you ask? It's a special case — adding this keyword displays a tiny check-mark-in-a-circle icon in the bottom right-hand corner of the image. Checkmarks come in handy for temporarily identifying specific images because you can search for just your check-marked photos.

To assign keywords to images (or remove keywords that have already been assigned), select one or more photos in the Viewer. Choose Photos⇨Get Info and click the Keywords tab to display the Keywords pane, as shown in Figure 12-3.

Figure 12-3:
Time to add keywords to these selected images.

Mark the check box next to the keywords that you want to attach to the selected images. Or, click the marked check boxes next to the keywords that you want to remove from the selected images to disable them.

You're gonna need your own keywords

I'll bet you take photos of other things besides just kids and vacations — and that's why iPhoto allows you to create your own keywords as well. Display the iPhoto Preferences dialog by pressing ⌘+, (comma), click the Keywords button in the toolbar, and then click Add. iPhoto adds a new unnamed keyword to the list as an edit box, ready for you to type its name.

You can rename an existing keyword from this same dialog, too. Click a keyword to select it

and click Rename. Remember, however, that renaming a keyword affects *all the images that were tagged with that keyword* . . . and it might be confusing when photos that were originally tagged as Family suddenly appear with the keyword Foodstuffs.

To remove an existing keyword from the list, click the keyword to select it and then click Delete.

Digging throughout your library with keywords

Behold the power of keywords! To sift through your entire collection of images by using keywords, click the Find Photos by Keyword button at the bottom of the iPhoto window. iPhoto displays the Keywords panel, and you can click one or more keyword buttons to display just the photos that carry those keywords.

The images that remain in the Viewer after a search must have *all* the keywords that you specified. If an image is identified by only three of the four keywords that you chose, it won't be a match and it won't appear in the Viewer.

Playing favorites by assigning ratings

Be your own critic! iPhoto allows you to assign any photo a rating of anywhere from 0 to 5 stars. I use this system to help me keep track of the images that I feel are the best in my library. Select one (or more) images selected and then assign a rating with one of these steps:

- ✔ Choose Photos⇨My Rating and then pick the desired rating from the pop-up submenu.

  or

- ✔ Use the ⌘+0 through ⌘+5 shortcuts.

Sorting your images just so

The View menu provides an easy way to arrange your images in the Viewer by a number of different criteria. Choose View⇨Arrange Photos, and then click the desired sort criteria from the pop-up submenu. You can arrange the display by film roll, date, title, or rating. If you select an album in the Source list, you can also choose to arrange photos manually, which means that you can drag and drop thumbnails in the Viewer to place them in the precise order you want them.

Naturally, iPhoto allows you to print selected images, but you can also publish photos on your .Mac Web site. Click the HomePage button on the toolbar, and iPhoto automatically uploads the selected images and leads you through the process of creating a new Web page by using the HomePage online wizard.

Edit mode: Removing Uncle Milton's head

Not every digital image is perfect — just look at my collection if you need proof. For those shots that need a pixel massage, iPhoto includes a number of editing tools that you can use to fix common problems.

The first step in any editing job is to select, in the Viewer, the image that you want to fix. After you select the photo, click the Edit button on the iPhoto toolbar to switch to the Edit panel controls, as illustrated in Figure 12-4.

Now you're ready to fix problems, using the tools that I discuss in the rest of this section.

Figure 12-4: iPhoto is now in Edit mode — watch out, image problems!

Rotating those tipped-over shots

If an image is in the wrong orientation and needs to be turned to display correctly, click the Rotate button to turn it once in a counterclockwise direction.

Hold down the Option key while you click the Rotate button to rotate in a clockwise direction.

Crop 'til you drop

Does that photo have an intruder hovering around the edges of the subject? You can remove some of the border by *cropping* an image, just as folks once did with film prints and a pair of scissors. (We've come a long way.) With iPhoto, you can remove unwanted portions of an image — it's a great way to get Uncle Milton's stray head (complete with toupee) out of an otherwise perfect holiday snapshot.

Follow these steps to crop an image:

1. **Select the portion of the image that you want to keep.**

   In the Viewer, click and drag on the part that you want. When you drag, a semi-opaque rectangle appears to help you keep track of what you're claiming. (Check it out in Figure 12-5.) Remember, whatever's outside of this rectangle will disappear after the crop is completed.

Figure 12-5: Select the stuff that you want to keep in your photo.

2. **Choose a preset size.**

   If you would like to force your cropped selection to a specific size — like 4 x 3 for an iDVD project — select that size from the Constrain drop-down list box (to the left of the Crop button).

3. **Click the Crop button in the Edit panel.**

   Oh, and don't forget that you can use iPhoto's Undo feature if you mess up and you need to try again — just press ⌘+Z.

iPhoto features multiple Undo levels, so you can press ⌘+Z several times to travel back through your last several changes.

Enhancing images to add pizzazz

If a photo looks washed out, click the Enhance button to automatically increase (or decrease) the color saturation and automatically improve the contrast within the photo. Enhance is automatic, so you don't have to set anything, but keep in mind that Enhance isn't available if any part of the image is selected. (If the selection rectangle appears in the Viewer, click anywhere outside the selected area to banish the rectangle before you click Enhance.)

To compare the enhanced version with the original photo, press Control to display the original image. When you release the Control key, the enhanced image returns. (This way, if you aren't satisfied, you can press ⌘+Z and undo the enhancement immediately.)

Removing rampant red-eye

Unfortunately, today's digital cameras can still produce the same "zombies with red eyeballs" as traditional film cameras. *Red-eye* is caused by a camera's flash reflecting off the retinas of a subject's eyes, and it can occur with both humans and pets.

iPhoto can remove that red-eye and turn frightening zombies back into your family and friends! Click the Red-Eye button and select a demonized eyeball by clicking in the center of it. To complete the process, click the X in the button that appears in the image.

Retouching like the stars

iPhoto's Retouch feature is perfect for removing minor flecks or lines in an image (especially those you've scanned from prints). Click Retouch, and you'll notice that the mouse cursor turns into a crosshair — just drag the cursor across the imperfection. Like the Enhance feature, you can compare the retouched and the original versions of the image by holding down and releasing the Control key.

Switching to black and white or sepia

Ever wonder whether a particular photo in your library would look better as a black-and-white (or *grayscale*) print? Or perhaps an old-fashioned *sepia* tone in shades of copper and brown? Just click the B & W or the Sepia button to convert an image from color to shades of gray or brown, respectively.

Adjusting brightness and contrast manually

Click Adjust to perform manual adjustments on brightness and contrast (the light levels in your image). To adjust the brightness and contrast, make sure that nothing's selected in the image, and then drag the Brightness/Contrast sliders until the image looks the way that you want.

While you're editing, you can use the Next and Prev buttons to move to the next image in the current album (or back to the previous image).

Publishing Your Own Art Gallery

Book mode unleashes what I think is probably the coolest feature of iPhoto: the chance to design and print a high-quality bound photo book! After you complete an album — all the images have been edited just the way you want, and the album contains all the photos you want to include in your book — iPhoto can send your images as data over the Internet to a company that will print and bind your finished book for you. (No, they don't publish *For Dummies* titles, but then again, I don't get high-resolution color plates in most of my books, either.)

At the time of this writing, you can choose from many different sizes and bindings, including a 6"-x-8" soft-cover book with 20 pages for about $15, and a hard-bound 8.5"-x-11" keepsake album with 20 pages for about $35 (shipping included in both prices). Extra pages can be added at a dollar a pop.

If you're going to create a photo book, make sure that the album you use includes only the highest quality (and highest resolution) images that you have available. The higher the resolution, the better the photos will look in the finished book.

To create a photo book, follow these steps:

1. **Click the desired album in the Source list to select it.**

2. **Click the Book toolbar button.**

   iPhoto prompts you to select the size of the book and a theme.

Your choices determine the number of pages and layout scheme, as well as the background graphics for each page.

 3. Click Choose Theme.

iPhoto displays a dialog asking whether you want to lay out your photos manually or allow iPhoto to do everything automatically. Although automatic mode is fine, I'm a thorough guy, so the rest of this example shows how to do a manual layout.

 4. Click Manually to display the controls shown in Figure 12-6.

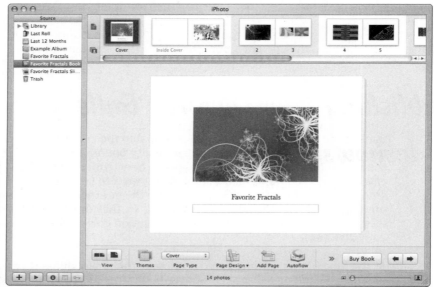

Figure 12-6:
Preparing to publish my own coffee-table masterpiece.

In Book mode, the Viewer changes in subtle ways. It displays the current page at the bottom of the display and adds a scrolling row of thumbnail images above it. This row of images represents the remaining images from the selected album that you can add to your book. You can drag any image thumbnail into one of the photo placeholders to add it to the page. You can also click the Page button at the left of the thumbnail strip — it looks like a page with a turned-down corner — to display thumbnails of each page in your book. (To return to the album image strip, click the Photos button under the Page button.)

 5. Rearrange the page order to suit you by dragging the thumbnail of any page from one location to another in the strip.

6. **In the Book panel below the Toolbar, you can adjust a variety of settings for the final book, including the book's theme, page numbers, and comments.**

   At this point, you can also add captions and short descriptions to the pages of your photo album. Click any one of the text boxes and begin typing to add text to that page.

7. **Click the Buy Book button when you're ready to publish your book.**

   In a series of dialogs that appear, iPhoto guides you through the final steps to order a bound book — you'll be asked for credit card information.

I wouldn't attempt to order a book via a dialup modem connection. Unfortunately, the images that you're sending are likely far too large to make it successfully. If possible, use a broadband or network connection to the Internet while you're ordering. If your only connection to the Internet is through a dialup modem, I recommend saving your book in PDF format and having it printed at a copy shop or printing service instead. (Choose File➪Print, and then click the Save as PDF button.)

Slideshows

At the ready, you can use iPhoto to create a slideshow:

1. **Click the album you want to display.**

2. **Click the Slideshow button on the toolbar (bottom left).**

   iPhoto adds a Slideshow item in the Source list. The same scrolling thumbnail strip appears at the top of the Viewer, this time displaying the images in the album.

3. **Click and drag the thumbnails to your desired order.**

To choose the background music for your slideshow, follow these steps:

1. **Click the Music button on the Slideshow toolbar to display the tracks from your iTunes library.**

2. **Drag the individual songs you want to the song list at the bottom of the sheet.**

   Drag them to rearrange their order in the list.

3. **Click OK to accept your song list.**

To configure your slideshow, follow these steps:

1. **Click the Settings button on the Slideshow toolbar.**

2. **From the sheet that appears, specify the amount of time that each slide remains onscreen, as well as an optional title and rating displays.**

   I recommend the Automatic Ken Burns effect (the same one in iMovie) that lends an animated movement to each image.

3. **If you want a 16:9 widescreen display for your slideshow, choose it from the Slideshow Format pop-up menu.**

4. **Click the Adjust button to modify the settings for a specific slide.**

   This is useful for keeping a slide onscreen for a longer period of time or for setting a different transition than the default transition you choose from the Slideshow toolbar.

To display a preview of a single slide and its transitions, follow these steps:

1. **Click the desired slide and then click Preview.**

   This is a handy way of determining whether your delay and transition settings are really what you want for a particular slide.

2. **To play your slideshow, click Play.**

   iPhoto switches to full-screen mode.

To share your completed slideshow, follow these steps:

1. **Click Share in the iPhoto menu.**

2. **Choose from either**

   • Sending the slideshow to iDVD (for later burning onto a DVD)

   • Exporting the slideshow as a QuickTime movie

   • Sending the slideshow through e-mail

Sending Photos through E-Mail

iPhoto can help you send your images through e-mail by automating the process. The application can actually prepare your image and embed it automatically within a new message.

To send an image through e-mail, select it and then click the Email button in the toolbar. The dialog that you see in Figure 12-7 appears, allowing you to choose the size of the images and whether you want to include their titles and comments as well.

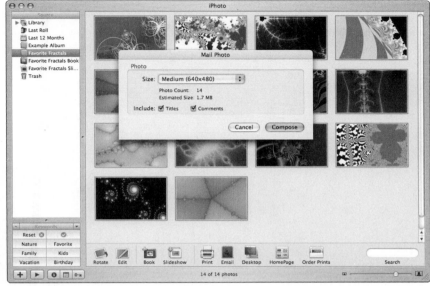

Figure 12-7:
Preparing
to send
an image
through
Apple Mail.

Keep in mind that most ISP (Internet service provider) e-mail servers won't accept an e-mail message that's over 1 or 2MB in size, so watch that Size display. If you're trying to send a number of images at Large or Full Size, you might have to click the Size drop-down list box to reduce the image resolution in order to get them all embedded in a single message.

When you're satisfied with the total file size and you're ready to create your message, click the Compose button. iPhoto automatically launches Apple Mail (or whatever e-mail application you specify) and creates a new message containing the images, ready for you to click Send!

Chapter 13

Making Film History with iMovie HD

*R*emember those home movies that kids used to make in high school? They were entertaining and fun to create, and your friends were impressed. In fact, some kids are so downright inspired that you're not surprised when you discover at your high school reunion that they turn out to be graphic artists, or they're involved in video or TV production.

iMovie HD, part of the iLife '05 suite, makes movie making as easy as those homemade movies. Apple has simplified all the technical stuff, like importing video and adding audio, so you can concentrate on your creative ideas. In fact, you won't find techy terms like *codecs* or *keyframes* in this chapter at all. I guarantee that you'll understand what's going on at all times. (How often do you get a promise like that with video editing software?)

With iMovie HD, your digital video (DV) camcorder, and the other parts of the iLife suite, you can soon produce and share professional-looking movies, with some of the same creative effects and transitions used by Those Hollywood Types every single day.

If you turn out to be a world-famous Hollywood Type Director in a decade or so, don't forget the little people along the way!

Shaking Hands with the iMovie HD Window

If you've ever tried a professional-level video editing application, you probably felt like you were suddenly dropped in the cockpit of a jumbo jet. In iMovie HD, though, all the controls you need are easy to use and logically placed.

Video editing takes up quite a bit of desktop space. In fact, you can't run iMovie HD at resolutions less than 1024 x 768, nor would you want to.

To launch iMovie HD, click the iMovie HD icon on the Dock. (It looks like a director's clapboard.) You can also click the Application folder in any Finder window Sidebar and then double-click the iMovie HD icon.

When you first launch iMovie HD, the application displays a top-level dialog, as shown in Figure 13-1. From here, you can create a new iMovie HD project, open an existing project, or let iMovie HD do things automatically via Magic iMovie. (I cover Magic iMovie later in the section, "Doing iMovie Things iMagically.")

Figure 13-1: You see this top-level dialog when you first launch iMovie HD.

To follow the examples I show you here, follow these strenuous steps:

1. **Click the Create a New Project button.**
2. **When iMovie HD prompts you to type a name for your project, do so.**
3. **Click Create.**

   You're on your way!

Check out Figure 13-2: I'm not kidding when I say that iMovie HD is a lean, mean, video-producing machine. This is the whole enchilada, in one window:

The controls and displays here that you'll use most often include

- ✔ **Monitor:** Think of this just like your TV or computer monitor. Your video clips, still images, and finished movie play here.

- ✔ **Tool palette:** This row of buttons allows you to switch between your media clips (video clips, photos, and audio) and the various tools that you use to make your film. For example, Figure 13-2 illustrates the Clips pane, which appears when you click the Clips button (go figure).

  Hint: All the video clips that you use to create your movie are stored in the Clips pane. I show you what each of the other panes looks like in the Tool palette as you tackle different tasks in this chapter.

Monitor

Figure 13-2: If da Vinci had designed a computer application, it would look like iMovie HD.

Clips/Timeline Viewer switch

Import/Editing switch

Video controls

Scrubber bar

Tool palette

Viewer

✔ **Viewer:** iMovie HD switches between two views — the Clips viewer and the Timeline viewer — and I cover 'em both later in this chapter. The buttons that you use to toggle between the two views are shown in Figure 13-2.

✔ **Playhead:** The vertical line that you see in the viewer is the *playhead,* which indicates the current editing point while you're creating your movie. When you're playing your movie, the playhead moves to follow your progress through the movie.

✔ **Scrubber bar:** This bar makes it easy to crop, trim, or split a selected clip. The entire length of a clip that you select is covered by the scrubber bar so you can drag the playback handle at the top of the bar to quickly move throughout the clip.

✔ **Playback controls:** If these look familiar, it's no accident: These controls are used to play your movie (in window and full-screen mode) and to return the playhead to the beginning of the movie. A different set of controls appears when you import digital video from your DV camcorder.

✔ **Import/Editing switch:** Click this switch to toggle between importing DV clips from your DV camcorder and editing your movie.

Those are the major highlights of the iMovie HD window. A director's chair and megaphone are optional, of course, but they do add to the mood.

A Bird's-Eye View of Movie-Making

I don't want to box in your creative skills here — after all, you can attack the movie-making process from a number of different angles. (Pun unfortunately intended.) However, I've found that my movies turn out the best when I follow a linear process, so before I dive into specifics, allow me to provide you with an overview of movie making with iMovie HD.

Here's my take on the process, reduced to seven steps:

1. Import your video clips either directly from your DV camcorder or from your hard drive.

2. Drag your new selection of clips from the Clips pane to the Viewer and arrange them in the desired order.

3. Import or record audio clips (from iTunes, GarageBand, or external sources like audio CDs or audio files that you record yourself) and add them to your movie.

4. Import your photos (either directly from iPhoto or from your hard drive) and place them where needed in your movie.

5. Add professional niceties such as transitions, effects, and text to the project.

6. Preview your film and edit it further if necessary.

7. Share your finished film with others through the Web, e-mail, or a DVD that you create and burn with iDVD 5. (Read all about iDVD 5 in Chapter 14.)

That's the first step-by-step procedure in this chapter. I doubt that you'll even need to refer back to it, however, because you'll soon see just how easy it is to use iMovie HD.

Importing the Building Blocks

Sure, you need video clips to create a movie of your own, but don't panic if you have but a short supply. You can certainly turn to the other iLife applications for additional raw material. (See, I told you that integration thing would come in handy.)

Along with video clips you import from your DV camcorder, iSight camera, and hard drive, you can also call on iPhoto for still images (think credits) and iTunes for background audio and effects. In this section, I show you how.

Pulling in video clips

Your iMac is already equipped with the two extras that come in handy for video editing: namely, a large hard drive and a FireWire port. Because virtually all DV camcorders today use a FireWire connection to transfer clips, you're set to go. (And even if your snazzy new DV camcorder uses a USB 2.0 connection, you're still in the zone — but make sure you use one of the USB 2.0 ports on your iMac, which are on the back of the computer!) Here's the drill if your clips are on your DV camcorder:

1. **Plug the proper cable into your iMac.**

2. **Set the DV camcorder to VTR (or VCR) mode.**

   Some camcorders call this Play mode.

3. **Slide the Import/Editing switch (refer to Figure 13-2) to the Camera position.**

   The playback controls under the monitor subtly change, now mirroring the controls on your DV camcorder, allowing you to control the unit from within iMovie HD. *Keen!*

   You also get an Import button as a bonus.

4. **Locate the section of video that you want to import by using the play-back controls.**

5. **Click Stop and rewind to a spot a few seconds prior to the good stuff.**

6. **Click the Play button again.**

   This might not be necessary on all cameras.

7. **Click the Import button at the bottom of the monitor.**

   iMovie HD begins transferring the footage to your iMac.

8. **When the desired footage is over, click the Import button again to stop the transfer.**

   iMovie HD automatically adds the imported clip to your Clips pane.

9. **Click Stop to end the playback and admire your handiwork.**

If your clips are already on your hard drive, rest assured that iMovie HD can import them, including *high-definition* (HD) format. iMovie HD also recognizes a number of other video formats, as shown in Table 13-1.

To import a video file, follow this bouncing ball:

1. **Click the Clips button on the Tool palette to display the Clips pane.**

2. **Choose File⇨Import.**

3. **Double-click the clip to add it to the Clips pane.**

   Alternatively, you can also drag a video clip from a Finder window and drop it in the Clips pane.

Table 13-1	Video Formats Supported by iMovie HD
File Type	*Description*
DV	Standard digital video
iSight	Live video from your iSight camera
HDV	High-definition (popularly called *widescreen*) digital video
MPEG-4	A popular format for streaming Internet and wireless digital video

Making use of still images

Still images come in very handy as impressive-looking titles or as ending credits to your movie. (Make sure you list a gaffer and a best boy to be truly professional.) However, you can also use still images to introduce scenes or to separate clips according to your whim. For example, I use stills when delineating the days of a vacation within a movie or different Christmas celebrations over time.

Here are two methods of adding stills to your movie:

✔ **Adding images from iPhoto:**

    a. Click the Photos button in the Tool palette.

    Experience the thrill that is your iPhoto library, right from within iMovie HD (as shown in Figure 13-3).

    b. Click the pop-up menu in the center of the Photo pane to display your entire iPhoto library or more selective picks like specific albums or film rolls.

    c. When you find the image you want to add, just drag it to the right spot within the viewer.

✔ **Importing images from your hard drive:**

    a. Choose File⇨Import to add images in any format supported by iPhoto, including TIFF, JPEG, GIF, PICT, PNG, and PSD.

    These images show up in the Clips pane.

Figure 13-3:
Pulling still images from iPhoto is child's play.

b. Drag them to the viewer just like they were video clips.

If you're a member of the International Drag-and-Drop Society, you can drag images directly from a Finder window and drop them into the viewer as well.

Importing and adding audio from all sorts of places

You can pull in everything from Wagner to Weezer as both background music and sound effects for your movie. In this section, I focus on how to get those notes into iMovie HD, and then how to add them to your movie by dragging them to the Timeline viewer.

You can add audio from a number of different sources:

✔ **Adding songs from iTunes:**

a. Click the Audio button in the Tool palette to display the contents of your iTunes library.

b. Click the pop-up menu at the top of the pane and choose playlists to view, like the Dinah Washington playlist I selected in Figure 13-4.

Figure 13-4:
Call on your iTunes library to add music to your iMovie.

Digging for music gold

If you have several gigabytes of music in your iTunes library, it might be more of a challenge to locate "Me and Bobby McGee" by Janis Joplin, especially if she's included in a compilation. Let your iMac do the digging for you! Click in the Search box below the track list and begin typing a song name. iMovie HD immediately narrows down the song titles displayed to those that match the characters you type. To reset the search field and display all your songs in the library or selected playlist, click the X icon that appears at the right of the field.

Naturally, if you've exported any original music you compose in GarageBand to your iTunes Library, you can use those songs in your own movie!

You can add a track at the current location of the playhead in the Timeline viewer by clicking the song to select it and then clicking the Place at Playhead button.

✔ **Adding sound effects:**

- *If you need a sound effect — like the sound of a horse galloping for your Rocky Mountain vacation clips — click the pop-up menu at the top of the pane and choose iMovie Sound Effects.*

 iMovie HD includes a number of top-shelf audio effects from Skywalker Studios that you can use in the second audio track on the Timeline viewer. This way, you can add sound effects even when you've already added a background song.

- *To add a sound effect at the current location of the playhead in the Timeline viewer, click the effect to select it and then click Place at Playhead.*

✔ **Ripping songs from an audio CD:**

- a. *Load an audio CD.*

- b. *Click the pop-up menu at the top of the Audio pane.*

- c. *Choose Audio CD from the very bottom of the menu.*

 iMovie HD displays the tracks from the CD, and you can add them at the current playhead position the same way as iTunes songs.

Narration the easy way

Ready to create that award-winning nature documentary? You can add voice-over narration to your iMovie HD project that would make Jacques Cousteau proud. In fact, you can actually record your voice as you watch your movie playing, allowing perfect synchronization with the action! To add narration, follow these steps:

1. **If you're not already using the Timeline viewer, click the Clips/Timeline viewer button to switch to the Timeline viewer.**

2. **Drag the playhead in the Timeline viewer to the point where the narration should begin.**

3. **Click the Audio button on the Tools palette.**

4. **Click the Play button on the playback controls.**

5. **Click the Record button in the Audio pane.**

   You can monitor the volume level of your voice with the Microphone meter.

6. **Watch the video while you narrate so you can coordinate your narration track with the action.**

7. **Click Stop in the Audio pane.**

   iMovie HD adds your recorded audio within the Timeline viewer. If you need to try again, press Delete to remove the audio clip and repeat the steps.

   ✔ **Recording directly from a microphone:** Yep, if you're thinking voice-over narration, you've hit the nail on the head. Check out the sidebar, "Narration the easy way" for the scoop.

   ✔ **Importing audio from your hard drive:**

   a. *Choose File⇨Import to import digital audio in any format recognized by QuickTime.*

   The big players are MP3, AAC, Apple Lossless, WAV, and AIFF. The audio you import is inserted in the viewer at the current playhead location.

   b. *(Optional) Of course, you're also welcome to drag audio files from a Finder window and drop them into the viewer.*

iMovie HD displays all the audio for your movie in two tracks in the Timeline viewer, so you won't see your audio in the Clips viewer.

Building the Cinematic Basics

Time to dive in and add the building blocks to create your movie. Along with video clips, audio tracks, and still images, you can also add Hollywood-quality transitions, optical effects, and animated text titles. In this section, I demonstrate how to elevate your collection of video clips into a real-life furshlugginer movie.

Adding clips to your movie

You can add clips to your movie, using either the Clip viewer or the Timeline viewer. The Dynamic Duo work like this:

- ✔ **Clip viewer:** This displays your clips and still images. Each clip that you add occupies the same space. This is a great view for rearranging the clips and still images in your movie.

- ✔ **Timeline viewer:** This displays clips with relative sizes: The length of each clip in the Timeline viewer is relative to the duration of the scene. (In plain English, a 60-second clip that you add to the Timeline viewer appears half the length of a 120-second clip.)

To add a clip to your movie

1. **Click the Clips button on the Tool palette to display the Clips pane.**

2. **Drag the desired clip from the Clips pane to the spot where it belongs in either viewer.**

Do this several times, and you've got a movie, just like the editors of old used to do with actual film clips. This is a good point to mention a movie-making Mark's Maxim:

> ***Preview your work — and do it often.***™

Use the View Fullscreen playback button under the monitor to watch your project while you add content. If you've ever watched directors at work on today's movie sets, they're constantly watching a monitor to see what things will look like for the audience. You have the same option in iMovie HD!

Removing clips from your movie

Don't like a clip? Cake. To banish a clip from your movie

1. **Click the clip in the viewer to select it.**

2. **Press Delete.**

   The clip disappears, and iMovie HD automatically rearranges the remaining clips and still images in your movie.

If you remove the wrong clip, don't panic. Instead, use iMovie HD's Undo (press ⌘+Z) feature to restore it.

Deleting clips for good

iMovie HD has its own separate Trash system (different from the Mac OS X Trash). It's located at the bottom of the application window. If you decide that you don't need a clip or still image and you want to delete it from your iMovie HD project completely, drag the media item from either the Clips pane or from either viewer and drop it on top of the Trash icon. (Note, however, that deleting a clip or still image from iMovie HD does not delete it from your hard drive.)

To delete the contents of the iMovie HD Trash, choose File⇨Empty Trash. To display the contents of the iMovie HD Trash, click the Trash icon; to retrieve an item that you suddenly decide you still need, drag the item back into the Viewer.

Reordering clips in your movie

If Day One of your vacation appears after Day Two, you can easily reorder your clips and stills by dragging them to the proper space in the Clip viewer. When you release the mouse, iMovie HD automatically moves the rest of your movie aside with a minimum of fuss and bother.

Editing clips within iMovie HD

If a clip has extra seconds of footage at the beginning or end, you don't want that superfluous stuff in your masterpiece. Our favorite video editor gives you the ability to crop, split, and trim. These editing functions include

- ✔ **Crop:** Deletes everything from the clip except a selected region
- ✔ **Split:** Breaks a single clip into multiple clips
- ✔ **Trim:** Deletes a selected region from the clip

Before you can edit, however, you have to select a section of a clip:

1. **Click a clip in the Clips pane to display it in the Monitor.**

2. **Drag the playback head on the *scrubber bar* (that blue bar underneath the monitor) to the beginning of the section that you want to select.**

3. **Shift-click anywhere on the scrubber bar to the right of the starting point.**

   The selected region turns yellow when you select it.

   You're ready to edit that selected part of the clip.

Note the handles that appear at the beginning or ending of the selection. You can make fine changes to the selected section by dragging them.

   ✔ **To crop:** Choose Edit➪Crop. Everything but the selected region is removed.

   ✔ **To split:** Choose Edit➪Split Video Clip at Playhead. The clip is divided into two clips.

   ✔ **To trim:** Choose Edit➪Clear. The selected section disappears.

Adding transitions

Many iMovie HD owners approach transitions as *visual bookends:* They merely act as placeholders that appear between video clips. Nothing could be farther from the truth because judicious use of transitions can make or break a scene. For example, which would you prefer after a wedding cere-mony — an abrupt, jarring cut to the reception, or a gradual fadeout to the reception?

Today's audiences are sensitive to the transitions between scenes. Try not to overuse the same transition, weighing the visual impact of a transition carefully.

iMovie HD includes a surprising array of transitions, including old favorites (like Fade In and Dissolve) and some nifty stuff you might not be familiar with (like Billow and Disintegrate). To display your transition collection, click the Trans (transitions) button on the Tool palette, as shown in Figure 13-5.

To see what a particular transition looks like, click it in the list to see a short preview of the transition in the preview window at the top of the pane. (If things move too fast, slow down the preview with the Speed slider.) Click the Preview button to display the transition within the Monitor.

Adding a transition couldn't be any easier: Drag the transition that you choose from the list in the Transitions pane and drop it between clips or between a clip and a still image. Note that the transition takes a few seconds to render. iMovie HD displays a red progress bar in the viewer to indicate how much longer rendering will take.

Figure 13-5:
Add
transitions
for flow
between
clips in
iMovie HD.

Oh, we got effects!

iMovie HD also offers a number of fun visual effects that you can add to your clips and stills. Perhaps not the full-blown visual effects of the latest science-fiction blockbuster, but then again, your movie already stars Uncle Milton, and most people would consider him a special effect.

For example, to immediately change a clip (or your entire movie) into an old classic, you can choose the Aged Film or Sepia effects to add that antique look.

To view the effects, click the Effects button on the Tools palette. Click an effect from the list in the Effects pane (see Figure 13-6) to display the options you can customize for that particular effect. The settings you can change vary for each effect, but most of them include the Effect In and Effect Out sliders, which allow you to gradually add an effect over a certain amount of time from the beginning of the clip and then phase it out before the clip ends. When you make a change to the settings, you see the result in the preview window at the top of the Effects pane.

Figure 13-6:
Adding a
favorite
effect of
mine — the
iMovie HD
Aged Film
effect.

To add an effect to a clip or still image in the Timeline viewer

1. **Click the clip or image to select it.**

   The selection turns blue.

2. **Click the desired effect.**

3. **Click Preview to see what the effect will look like in the monitor.**

4. **Make any necessary adjustments to the settings for the effect.**

5. **When everything looks perfect, click Apply.**

Like transitions, effects take a few seconds to render. The faster your iMac, the shorter the time. Such is the life of a techno-wizard.

What's a masterpiece without titles?

The last stop on our iMovie HD Hollywood Features Tour is the Titles pane of the Tool palette, as shown in Figure 13-7. You can add a title with a still image, but iMovie HD also includes everything you need to add basic animated text to your movie.

Figure 13-7:
Add
subtitles for
your next
foreign
language
film.

Most of the controls you can adjust are the same for each animation style. You can change the speed of the animation, the font, the size of the text, and the color of the text. You can even add an optional black background; however, note that adding this background actually inserts a new clip into your movie in order to show the text, which might affect the timing of your sound effects or narration.

To add a title

1. **Select an animation style from the list.**

2. **Type one or two lines of text in the text boxes at the bottom of the Titles pane and make any changes to the settings specific to the animation style.**

   iMovie HD displays a preview of the effect with the settings that you choose.

3. **To view the text titles in the Monitor, click the Preview button.**

4. **Drag the animation style from the list to the Timeline.**

   The title appears in the Timeline viewer as a clip.

Doing iMovie Things iMagically

iMovie HD introduces *Magic iMovie,* which you can use to create your movie automatically from the settings you choose from just one dialog box. (I know, it sounds like a corny name, but the actual feature is truly cool.) If you're in a hurry or you want to produce something immediately after an event (and you can do without the creative extras that I discuss earlier in this chapter), a Magic iMovie is the perfect option.

In fact, the close integration of iMovie HD and iDVD 5 can automate the entire process of downloading video from your DV camcorder and producing a finished DVD. As you can read in Chapter 14, iDVD 5 has a similar new feature called *OneStep DVD* that can create a DVD-Video from your Magic iMovie!

Follow these steps to let iMovie HD take care of movie-making automatically:

1. **Connect your DV camcorder to your Mac with a FireWire cable.**

2. **Turn on the camcorder.**

3. **Set it to VCR (or VTR) mode.**

4. **Launch iMovie HD.**

   - *If you see the opening top-level dialog,* click Make a Magic iMovie.

   - *If you had a project open and that project appears instead,* choose File➪Make a Magic iMovie.

5. **Type a project name and choose a location.**

6. **Choose a video format.**

   Typically, you'll want to use DV, DV widescreen, or the proper HDV resolution format.

7. **Click Create.**

   iMovie HD displays the Magic iMovie dialog.

8. **Type a name for your movie in the Movie Title box.**

9. **(Optional) If you want transitions between scenes, select the Use Transitions check box to enable it and choose the transition you want from the pop-up menu.**

10. **(Optional) If you want a soundtrack, select the Play a Music Soundtrack check box and then click the click the Choose Music button to browse your iTunes music library or to select an audio CD that you've loaded.**

11. **To ship your finished movie directly to iDVD (which launches automatically), select the Send to iDVD check box.**

12. **Click Create.**

Sharing Your Finished Classic with Others

Your movie is complete, you've saved it to your hard drive, and now you're wondering where to go from here. iMovie HD can unleash your movie upon your unsuspecting family and friends (and even the entire world) in a number of different ways:

- ✔ **E-mail:** Send your movie to others as an e-mail attachment. iMovie HD even launches Apple's Mail application automatically!

- ✔ **HomePage:** Share your movie with the world at large by posting it on your .Mac Web site. (I provide more .Mac details to chew on in Chapter 9.)

- ✔ **Videocamera:** Transfer your finished movie back to your DV camcorder.

- ✔ **iDVD:** iMovie HD can export your movie into an iDVD project, where you can use it to create a DVD-Video.

- ✔ **QuickTime:** Any computer with an installed copy of QuickTime can display your movies, and you can use QuickTime movies in Keynote presentations as well.

- ✔ **Bluetooth:** If you have Bluetooth hardware installed on your iMac, you can transfer your movie to a Bluetooth device.

When you choose a sharing option, iMovie HD displays the video quality for the option. If you decide to send your movie through e-mail, for example, it's reduced as far as possible in file size, and the audio is reduced to mono rather than stereo. The Videocamera and Bluetooth options also give you onscreen instructions on readying the target device to receive your movie.

If you're worried about permanently reducing the quality of your project by sharing it through e-mail or your HomePage Web site, fear not! When you choose a sharing option to export your movie, your original project remains on your hard drive, unchanged, so you can share a better-quality version at any time in the future!

After you adjust any settings specific to the desired sharing option, click Share to start the ball rolling.

Chapter 14

iDVD — Your DVD Movie Factory

*H*ow does the old adage go? Oh, yes, it's like this:

> Any DVD movie must be a pain to create. You'll need a ton of money for software, too. And you'll have to take hours of training that will cause your brain to explode.

Funny thing is, *DVD authoring* — the process of designing and creating a DVD movie — really was like that for many years. Only video professionals could afford the software and tackle the training needed to master all the intricacies of DVD Menu design.

Take one guess as to the company that changed all that. (No, it wasn't Coca-Cola.) Apple's introduction of iDVD was (quite literally) a revolution in DVD authoring. Suddenly you, your kids, and Aunt Harriet could all design and burn DVD movies and picture slideshows. Dear reader, this iDVD thing is *huge*.

Plus, you'll quickly find out that iDVD 5 is tightly connected to all the other slices of your digital hub — in plain English, you can pull content from iTunes, iPhoto, and iMovie HD as easily as a politician makes promises.

In this chapter, I show you how your iMac can take on Hollywood as well as how you can produce a DVD movie with content that's as good as any you'd rent at the video store!

Hey, Where's the Complex Window?

Figure 14-1 shows the whole "kit and kaboodle." (Okay, Mark, drop it.) The same smart people who brought you the iMovie HD window designed the iDVD 5 window. You have to supply your own digital video clips, background audio, and digital photographs, of course.

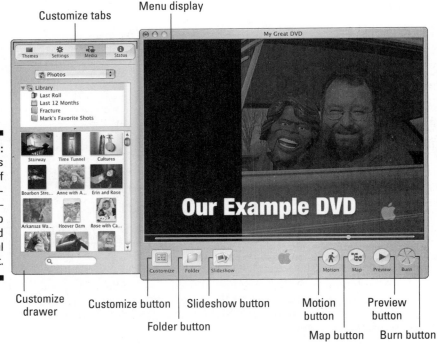

Customize tabs
Menu display

Figure 14-1:
iDVD 5 is a jewel of an application — easy to use and powerful to boot.

Customize drawer

Customize button

Folder button

Slideshow button

Motion button

Map button

Preview button

Burn button

Take a moment to appreciate iDVD — no secondary windows to fiddle with or silly palettes strung out everywhere. (Can you tell that I've had my fill of old-style DVD-authoring applications?) Allow me to list the highlights of the iDVD window:

- ✓ **Menu display:** This section takes up the largest part of the iDVD window, with good reason. You create your project here. In this case, *Menu* refers to your DVD Menu, not the menu at the top of your iMac's display.

- ✓ **Customize drawer:** Click the Customize button to display (or hide) this drawer. You tweak and fine-tune your project with the controls here.

- ✓ **Customize tab buttons:** The Customize drawer actually comprises four separate panes; to choose a new pane, click one of these tabs at the top of the drawer. The panes include

- *Themes:* You apply themes (such as Travel Cards, Wedding White, and Baby Mobile) to your DVD Menu to give it a certain look and feel.

- *Settings:* These options apply to the item currently selected, like drop shadows on your text titles or the appearance of your menu buttons.

- *Media:* From here, you can add media items, such as video clips and photos, to your menu.

- *Status:* This project status tab displays important stuff, such as the remaining space left on a blank DVD with your current menu design.

✔ **Folder:** Click Folder to add a new submenu button to your DVD Menu. The person using your DVD Menu can click a button to display a new submenu that can include additional movies or slideshows. (If that sounds like ancient Greek, hang on. All becomes clearer later in the chapter in the section, "Adding movies.")

In iDVD 5, a Menu can hold only 12 buttons, so submenus let you pack more content on your DVD. (Older versions of the application allowed only 6 buttons, so don't feel too cheated.) Anyway, each submenu that you create can hold another 12 buttons.

✔ **Slideshow:** If you want to add a slideshow to your DVD — say, using photos from your hard drive or pictures from your iPhoto library — click this button.

✔ **Motion:** Click this button to watch the animation cycle used with the current iDVD theme. Note that the animation *playhead* (the movie's time-line marker) moves underneath the Menu display to indicate where you are in the animation cycle. Like other playheads within the iLife suite, you can click and drag the round playhead button to move anywhere in the animation cycle. The animation repeats (just as it will on your finished DVD) until you click the Motion button again.

✔ **Map:** Click the Map button to display the organizational chart for your DVD Menu. Each button and submenu that you add to your top-level DVD Menu is displayed here, and you can jump directly to a particular item by double-clicking it. Use this road map to help design the layout of your DVD Menu system or use it to get to a particular item quickly. To return to the Menu display, click the Map button again.

✔ **Preview:** To see how your DVD Menu project looks when burned to a DVD, click Preview. You get a truly nifty onscreen remote control that you can use to navigate your DVD Menu, just as if you were watching your DVD on a standard DVD player. To exit Preview mode, click the Preview button again. Read more about this control in then upcoming section, "Previewing Your Next Hit."

✔ **Burn:** Oh, yeah, you know what this one is for — recording your completed DVD movie to a blank disc.

That's the lot! Time to get down to the step-by-step business of making movies.

Creating a New DVD Project

When you launch iDVD 5 for the first time, you see the opening dialog shown in Figure 14-2. From here, you can choose to create a new project the manual way, or you can throw caution to the wind and allow iDVD to create your latest epic for you!

Figure 14-2:
Produce
your movie
manually or
let iDVD do
the work.

✔ **Create a New Project:** Click this button to do things the old-fashioned, creative, and manual way. To follow the examples in this chapter, I recommend using that view as you read here. After you click this button, iDVD prompts you to type a name for your new DVD project and to also set a location where the project files should be saved. By default, the very reasonable choice is your Documents folder.

Manually creating a DVD involves four basic steps:

1. *Design the DVD Menu, adding a theme and any necessary buttons or links.*

2. *Add media.* You can drag movie files from iMovie HD, still images from iPhoto, and music from iTunes.

3. *Tweak, adjust, and fine-tune your DVD Menu settings.*

4. *Preview and burn your DVD.*

✔ **Open an Existing Project:** If you've used iDVD and had a DVD project open the last time you quit the application, iDVD automatically loads the DVD project you were working on. To choose a different existing project, click this button.

✔ **OneStep DVD:** To allow iDVD to help you create a movie, click the OneStep DVD button, and you choose the Dark Side (unless you're in a hurry and don't want to add your own creative touches, in which case OneStep DVD suddenly becomes the Light Side). iDVD does most of the work automatically, using the media clips and photos that you specify. I tell you more about the new OneStep DVD feature later, in the section, "A Word about OneStep DVD."

Choosing just the right theme

The first step to take when designing a new DVD Menu system is to add a theme. In the iDVD world, a *theme* is a preset package that helps determine the appearance and visual appeal of your DVD Menu, including a background image, menu animation, an audio track, and a group of settings for text fonts and button styles.

iDVD helps those of us who are graphically challenged by including a wide range of professionally designed themes for all sorts of occasions, ranging from old standbys like weddings, birthdays, and vacations to more generic themes with the accent on action, friendship, and technology. To view the included themes, click the Customize button in the lower-left corner of the iDVD window. A cool drawer slides out from the side of the window, and you can click the Themes tab (as illustrated in Figure 14-3).

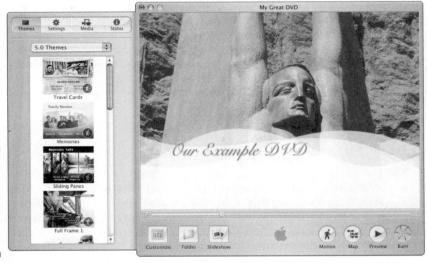

Figure 14-3: Select a new theme from the Customize drawer.

Taking advantage of drop zones

Most of Apple's animated themes include special bordered areas marked as drop zones. These locations have nothing to do with skydiving; rather, a *drop zone* is a placeholder within the Menu that can hold a single video clip or photograph. When you drag a video clip or image to a drop zone, that clip or picture is added to the animation within Apple's theme! Think about that for a moment; I know I did. You can actually personalize a Hollywood-quality animated DVD menu with *your own photos and video!*

Most of the themes included with iDVD 5 include at least one drop zone, and some are practically jampacked with drop zones. For example, the amazing Baby Mobile theme has a whopping six drop zones! If you think a menu looks just fine without anything in a drop zone, however, you don't have to put anything there.

The words Drop Zone disappear when you preview or burn your DVD.

To add a video clip or image to a drop zone, simply drag the clip or photo from a Finder window and drop it on the drop zone. You can also drag clips or photos from other sources, including the Movie and iPhoto panes within the iDVD drawer, the iMovie HD window, or the iPhoto window. (Remember, Apple is anything but strict on these matters.) Remember, drop zones don't act as links or buttons to other content — the stuff you add to a menu's drop zones appear only as part of the theme's animation cycle.

To delete the contents of a drop zone, Control-click (or right-click) the drop zone and choose Clear.

To choose a theme for your project — or to see what a theme looks like on your menu — click any thumbnail and watch iDVD update the Menu display.

If you decide while creating your DVD Menu that you need a different theme, you can change themes at any time. iDVD won't lose a single button or video clip that you add to your DVD Menu. You'll be amazed at how completely the look and sound of your DVD Menu changes with just the click of a theme thumbnail.

Adding movies

Drop zones and themes are cool, but most folks want to add video to their DVD. To accomplish this, iDVD uses *buttons* as links to your video clips. In fact, some iDVD Movie buttons actually display a preview of the video they will display! To play the video on a DVD player, the person selects the Movie button with the remote control, just like for a commercial DVD.

To add a Movie button, just drag a QuickTime movie file from the Finder and drop it onto your DVD Menu display. (Note that only MPEG-4 QuickTime movies are supported — older MPEG-1 and MPEG-2 movie clips may be rejected.) Alternatively, launch iMovie HD and drag a clip from the iMovie HD clip palette into the iDVD window.

iDVD and iMovie HD are soul mates, so you can also open the iDVD Customize drawer, click the Media tab, and then click Movies from the pop-up menu. Now you can drag clips from your Movies folder.

No matter the source of the clip, when you drop it onto your DVD menu, iDVD adds a Movie button, as you can see in Figure 14-4. Note that some buttons appear as text links rather than actual buttons. The appearance of a Movie button in your DVD menu is determined by the theme you choose.

Figure 14-4:
A new Movie button appears on your pristine DVD Menu.

A Movie button doesn't have to stay where iDVD places it! To move a Movie button to another location, click and drag it to the desired spot. By default, iDVD aligns buttons to invisible grid to keep your buttons aligned. If you don't want such order imposed on your life (and creativity), turn off this grid function by clicking the button to select it, clicking the Settings tab (in the Customize drawer), and selecting the Free Position radio button.

You can have up to 12 buttons on your iDVD Menu. To add more content than 12 buttons allows, add a folder by clicking the Folder button and drag another 12 movie files into the submenu that appears.

Keep in mind your target audience while you create your DVD. For example, will your finished DVD be shown on a standard TV or a high-definition (HD) TV? Standard TV sets have a different *aspect ratio* (height to width) and *resolution*

(the number of pixels onscreen) than a digital video clip, and a standard TV isn't as precise in focusing that image on The Tube. To make sure that your DVD content looks great on a standard TV screen, do the following:

1. **Click Advanced on the old-fashioned iDVD menu (the one at the top of the screen).**

2. **Choose the Show TV Safe Area command.**

   You can also press the convenient ⌘+T shortcut.

   If your entire family is blessed with a fleet of HD TVs, you can leave the Show TV Safe Area option off because these displays can handle just about any orientation.

   iDVD adds a smaller rectangle within the iDVD window that marks the screen dimensions of a standard TV.

If you take care that your menu buttons and (most of) your background image fit within this smaller rectangle, you're assured that folks with a standard television can enjoy your work. To turn off the Safe Area rectangle, press ⌘+T again.

Great, now my audience demands a slideshow

Many iMac owners don't realize that iDVD can use digital photos, as well as video clips, as content. In fact, you can add a group of images to your DVD Menu by using Slideshow buttons. Slideshow buttons allow the viewer to play back a series of digital photographs. iDVD handles everything for you, so there's no tricky timing to figure out or weird scripts to write. Just click the Slideshow button at the bottom of the iDVD window, and iDVD places a Slideshow button on your DVD Menu.

After the Slideshow button is on tap, you need to add the content — in this case, by choosing the images that iDVD adds to your DVD Menu. Follow these steps to select your slideshow images:

1. **Double-click the Slideshow Menu button — the one that you just added to the menu — to open the Slideshow window (see Figure 14-5).**

2. **Display the Customize drawer and click the Media pane.**

3. **Click the pop-up menu and choose Photos to display your iPhoto library and photo albums.**

Figure 14-5:
Who needs
a projector
anymore?
iDVD can
create a
great
slideshow.

4. **Drag your favorite image thumbnails from the Photos list and drop them into the My Slideshow window.**

   You can also drag images straight from a Finder window or the iPhoto window itself. (Those Apple folks are sooooo predictable.)

5. **Drag the photos in the My Slideshow window around to set their order of appearance in your slideshow.**

6. **To add audio with these pictures, drag your favorite audio file from the Finder and drop it in the Audio well (the box on the lower right, bearing the speaker icon) within the My Slideshow window.**

   Alternatively, click the pop-up menu in the Media pane and choose Audio to select an audio track from your iTunes library or playlists.

7. **Click the Return button to return to your DVD Menu.**

You can choose which image you want to appear on the Slideshow button. Click the Slideshow button that you added and see the slider that appears above the Slideshow button. Drag this slider to scroll through the images you added. When you find the image that you want to use for the Slideshow button in the DVD Menu, click the Slideshow button again to save your changes.

Now for the music . . .

Most of the Apple-supplied themes already have their own background music for your menu, so you might not even need to add music to your DVD Menu.

However, if you want to change the existing background music (or if your menu currently doesn't have any music at all), adding your own audio is child's play!

1. **Click the Customize button in the main iDVD window to open the Customize drawer.**

2. **Click the Settings tab to reveal the Shangri-La of the Settings pane (see Figure 14-6).**

Figure 14-6:
You'll do a lot of fine-tuning from the Settings pane.

3. **Drag an audio file from the Finder and drop it into the Audio well (that square sunken box beneath the Duration slider).**

   iDVD 5 accepts every sound format that you can use for importing (or *encoding*) in iTunes, including AIFF, MP3, AAC, Apple Lossless, and WAV audio files.

   To choose a background track from the Media pane, click the pop-up menu and choose Audio to display your iTunes library and playlists. Click the song you'd like to use and then click Apply.

4. **Click the Motion button at the bottom of the iDVD window to watch your DVD Menu animation cycle set to the new background audio.**

5. **Click the Motion button again to stop the animation and return to serious work.**

Who Needs Defaults?

You can easily make changes to the default settings provided with the theme you chose. iDVD offers all sorts of controls that allow you to change the appearance and the behavior of buttons, text, and the presentation of your content. In this section, I show you how to cast out iDVD's (perfectly good) defaults and then tweak things to perfection.

Using Uncle Morty for your DVD Menu background

Hey, Uncle Morty might not be a supermodel, but he has birthdays and anniversaries, and iDVD is more than happy to accommodate you in documenting those milestones! Follow these steps to change the background of your DVD Menu:

1. **Click the Customize button to open the Customize drawer.**
2. **Click the Settings tab; refer to Figure 14-6.**
3. **Drag an image from the Finder and drop it into the Background well in the Menu section.**

    iDVD updates the DVD Menu to reflect your new background choice.

Adding your own titles

The one tweak you'll probably have to perform within every iDVD project is fixing titles. Unfortunately, the default labels provided by iDVD are pretty lame, and they appear in two important places:

- ✔ **Menu title:** Your large main title usually appears at the top of the DVD Menu.
- ✔ **Button captions:** Each Movie and Slideshow button that you add to your menu has its own title.

To change the text within your Menu title or the titles below your buttons, follow these steps:

1. **Select the text by clicking it.**
2. **Click it again to edit it.**

    A rectangle with a cursor appears to indicate that you can now edit the text.

3. **Type the new text and press Return to save the change.**

Changing buttons like a highly paid professional

Customizing Movie buttons? You can do it with aplomb! Follow these steps:

1. **Click the Customize button to display the Customize drawer.**

2. **Click the Settings tab.**

3. **Click any Movie button from the DVD Menu to select it.**

   A slider appears above the button, which you can drag to set the thumbnail picture for that button in your DVD Menu. (Naturally, this is only for animated buttons, not text buttons.)

   Enable the Movie check box to animate the button.

4. **To create a Movie button with a still image, drag a picture from a Finder window or the Media pane and drop it on top of the button.**

5. **Adjust the properties for the button as desired with the controls in the Button section of the Settings panel.**

Table 14-1 describes the button properties:

Table 14-1	Button Settings You Can Customize
Movie Button Property	*What It Does*
Style	Changes the frame shape of the Movie button.
Snap to Grid	Forces placement of a Movie button on an imaginary grid.
Free Position	Unlike Snap to Grid, allows Movie buttons to be placed in a more freeform arrangement.
Transition	Determines the transition that occurs when the button is clicked (before the action occurs).
Size	Adjusts the size of the button and the caption text. Move the slider to the right to increase the button and caption size.

Give my creation motion!

I show you earlier in this chapter how to use a different image for your background, but what about an animated background? You can use any QuickTime movie from your iMovie HD library to animate your DVD Menu background! Didn't I tell you that this iDVD thing was *huge?*

Keep in mind that your background movie should be a short clip; 20–30 seconds is optimal. A clip with a fade-in at the beginning and a fade-out at the ending is the best choice because iDVD loops your background clip continuously, and your animated background flows seamlessly behind your menu.

I'm not talking drop zones; see the sidebar, "Taking advantage of drop zones." By using a movie clip as a background, you're actually replacing the entire animation sequence rather than just a single area of the background.

Follow these steps to add a new animated background:

1. **Click the Customize button to open the Customize drawer.**

2. **Click your old friend, the Settings tab.**

3. **Drag a movie from the Finder and drop it into the Background well.**

   You can click the Movies folder in the Finder window Sidebar to instantly display your iMovie collection.

4. **Click the Motion button in the iDVD window to try out your new background.**

5. **Click the Motion button again to stop the animation cycle.**

Previewing Your Next Hit

Figure 14-7 captures the elusive Preview remote control — truly an awesome sight. When you click Preview, the Customize drawer disappears, and your DVD Menu appears exactly as it will on the finished DVD.

Figure 14-7:
Preview mode — an incredible simulation indeed.

Ah, but appearances aren't everything: You can also use your DVD Menu! Click the buttons on the remote control to simulate the remote on your DVD player, or think outside the box and click a menu button directly with your mouse pointer. iDVD presents the video clip, runs the slideshow, or jumps to a submenu, just as it will within the completed disc.

This is a great time to test-drive a project before you burn it to disc. To make sure you don't waste a blank DVD, make certain that everything you expect to happen actually happens. Nothing worse than discovering that Aunt Edna's slideshow from her Hong Kong trip actually displays your family's summer trip to the zoo (whoops). If you made a mistake or something needs tweaking, click the Preview button again, and you're back to the iDVD window proper, where you can edit or fine-tune your project.

iDVD 5 allows you to save your project as a standard Mac OS X *disc image* rather than as a simple project file (or a physical DVD). This is a good idea for those folks who don't have a SuperDrive on board because you can use Apple's Disk Utility to open and mount the disc image just as if it were a burned disc. If you move the disc image to another Mac with a SuperDrive, you can use Disk Utility to burn it on that machine. To save an iDVD project as a disc image, choose File⇨Save a Disc Image (or press ⌘+Shift+R). For the complete word on disc images, visit Chapter 21 — hey, you didn't think I'd leave you out in the cold, did you?

A Word about OneStep DVD

At the beginning of the chapter, I mention the *OneStep DVD* feature that's been added to iDVD 5. If you're in a hurry to create a DVD from clips on your DV camcorder and you don't mind losing your creative input, OneStep DVD is just the ticket. In short, iDVD 5 allows you to plug in your DV camcorder, answer a question or two, and then sit back while the application does all the work. iDVD 5 imports the DV clips, creates a basic menu design, and burns the disc automatically!

Using OneStep DVD will appeal to any iMac owner with a SuperDrive. Why not produce a DVD right after a wedding or birthday that you can give as a gift? Photographers who cover those same special events might consider selling a DVD made with OneStep DVD. If you happen to capture something incredibly unique — like a UFO landing or an honest politician — you can use OneStep DVD to create an instant backup of the clips on your DV camcorder. You could even keep your friends and family up-to-date with the progress of your vacation by sending them a daily DVD of your exploits! (You gotta admit, even Grandma would consider that eminently *sassy!*)

Follow these steps to start the OneStep DVD process:

1. **Click the OneStep DVD button on the iDVD 5 top-level menu (refer to Figure 14-1).**

   iDVD displays the dialog you see in Figure 14-8.

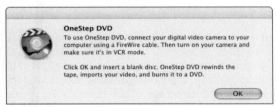

OneStep DVD

To use OneStep DVD, connect your digital video camera to your computer using a FireWire cable. Then turn on your camera and make sure it's in VCR mode.

Click OK and insert a blank disc. OneStep DVD rewinds the tape, imports your video, and burns it to a DVD.

OK

2. **Following the prompts, connect the FireWire cable from your DV camcorder; then turn on the camcorder and set it in VCR mode.**

3. **Click OK.**

4. **Load a blank DVD.**

A completed OneStep DVD plays automatically when you load it into a DVD player.

Burn That Movie, Baby!

When you're ready to record your next Oscar-winning documentary on family behaviors during vacation, just follow these simple words.

1. **Click the Burn button at the bottom of the iDVD window.**

   I have to admit, the Burn button that appears has to be my favorite single control in all my 20+ years of computing! It looks powerful, it looks sexy . . . it wants to *burn*. Harrumph. (Sorry about that.)

2. **After iDVD asks you to insert a blank DVD-R into the SuperDrive, iLoad a blank DVD-R, DVD-RW, DVD+R, or DVD+RW (depending on the media your iMac can handle).**

Your SuperDrive might be able to burn and read a DVD+R, DVD-RW, or DVD+RW, but what about your DVD player? Keep in mind that only DVD-Rs are likely to work in older DVD players. The latest generation of DVD players are likely DVD+R compatible as well, but I've seen only one or two DVD players that can handle rewriteable media. Therefore, remember the destination for the discs you burn and choose your media accordingly.

After a short pause, iDVD begins burning the DVD. The application keeps you updated with a progress bar.

Hey, while you're waiting, how about a timely book recommendation? If you want to discover how to burn all sorts of data, audio, and exotic CD and DVD formats, I can heartily recommend another of my books, *CD & DVD Recording For Dummies,* 2nd Edition (Wiley). It's a comprehensive manual for recording on the Mac. You'll find complete coverage of the popular Toast recording application from Roxio, too.

When the disc is finished, you're ready to load it into your favorite local DVD player, or you can load it back into your Mac and enjoy your work, using Apple's DVD Player.

Either way, it's all good!

Chapter 15

Recording Your Hits with GarageBand

Do you dream of making music? I've always wanted to join a band, but I never devoted the time nor learned to play the guitar. You know the drill: Those rock stars struggled for years to gain the upper hand over an instrument, practicing for untold hours, memorizing chords, and. . . . Wait a second. I almost forgot. You don't need to do *any* of that now!

Apple's GarageBand 2 (which is included in the iLife '05 suite) lets a musical wanna-be (like yours truly) make music with an iMac — complete with a driving bass line, funky horns, and a set of perfect drums that never miss a beat. In fact, the thousands of prerecorded loops on tap in GarageBand even allow you to *design* your music to match that melody running through your head, from techno to jazz to alternative rock.

This chapter explains everything you need to know to create your first song. I also show you how to import your hit record into iTunes so you can listen to it on your iPod with a big silly grin on your face (like I do) or add it to your next iMovie or iDVD project as a royalty-free soundtrack.

Oh, and don't be too smug when you think of all that practicing and hard work you missed out on. What a shame!

Let Me Introduce You to the Band

As you can see in Figure 15-1, the GarageBand window isn't complex at all, and that's good design so normal people like you and me won't be scared of using it. In this section, I list the most important controls so you know your Play button from your Loop Browser button.

Your music-making machine includes

- **Track list:** In GarageBand, a *track* is a discrete instrument that you set up to play one part of your song. For example, a track in a classical piece for string quartet could have four tracks — one each for violin, viola, cello, and bass. This list contains all the tracks in your song arranged so that you can easily see and modify them, like the rows in a spreadsheet. A track begins in the list, stretching out to the right all the way to the end of the song. As you can see in Figure 15-1, I already have one track defined — a Grand Piano (upper left).

- **Timeline:** This scrolling area holds the loops (see the following bullet) that you add or record, allowing you to move and edit them easily. As a song plays, the timeline scrolls to give you a visual look at your music. (Bear with me; you'll understand that rather cryptic statement within a page or two.)

- **Loop:** *Loops,* the building blocks of your song, are prerecorded clips of an instrument being played in a specific style and tempo. You can drag loops from the Loop Browser to a track and literally build a bass line or a guitar solo. (It's a little like adding video clips to the timeline in iMovie HD to build a film.)

- **Playhead:** This vertical line is a moving indicator that shows you the current position within your song as it scrolls by in the timeline. You can drag the playhead to a new location at any time. The playhead also acts like the insertion cursor in a word processing application: If you insert a section of a song or a loop from the Clipboard, it appears at the current location of the playhead. (More on copying and inserting loops later, so don't panic.)

- **Create a New Track:** Click this button to add a new track to your song.

- **Track Info:** If you need to display the instrument used in a track, click the track to select it and then click this button. You can also control settings like Echo and Reverb from the Track Info dialog (as shown in the upcoming Figure 15-11).

- **Open/Close the Loop Browser:** Click this to display the Loop Browser at the bottom of the window; click it again to close it. *Hint:* You can see more tracks at a time without scrolling by closing the Loop Browser.

- **Return to Beginning:** Clicking this button immediately moves the playhead back to the very beginning of the timeline.

Track list   Playhead   Timeline

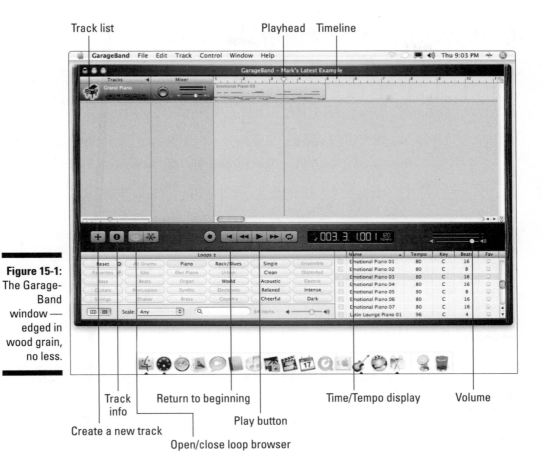

Figure 15-1:
The Garage-
Band
window —
edged in
wood grain,
no less.

Track
info   Return to beginning   Time/Tempo display   Volume

Create a new track   Play button

Open/close loop browser

- ✔ **Play:** Hey, old friend! At last, a control that you've probably used count-less times before — and it works just like the same control on your audio CD player. Click Play, and GarageBand begins playing your entire song. Notice that the Play button turns blue. To stop the music, click Play again; the button loses that sexy blue sheen, and the playhead stops immediately. (If playback is paused, it begins again at the playhead position when you click Play.)

- ✔ **Time/Tempo display:** This cool-looking LCD display shows you the cur-rent playhead position in seconds. You can also click the tempo indica-tor to change the tempo (or speed) of your song.

- ✔ **Volume:** Here's another familiar face. Just drag the slider to raise or lower the volume.

Of course, more controls are scattered around the GarageBand window, but these are the main controls to compose a song . . . which is the next stop!

Composing a Snappy Tune in GarageBand

In this section, I cover the basics of composition in GarageBand, working from the very beginning. Follow along with this running example:

1. **Press ⌘+N to create a new song.**

   GarageBand displays the New Project dialog that you see in Figure 15-2.

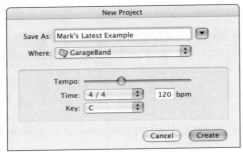

Figure 15-2: Start creating your new song here.

2. **Type a name for your new song and drag the Tempo slider to select the beats per minute (bpm).**

   A GarageBand song can have only one tempo (or speed) throughout, expressed as beats per minute.

3. **To adjust the settings for your song, you can select the**

   • Time signature. (See the Time box in Figure 15-2.)

   • Key (the Key box).

   If you're new to *music theory* (the rules/syntax by which music is created and written), just use the defaults. Most of the toe-tappin' tunes that you and I are familiar with fit right in with these settings.

4. **Click the Create button.**

   You see the window shown in Figure 15-1. (The Emotional Piano 03 loop in Figure 15-1 — which I show you how to add in the next section — is an example of a typical loop.)

Adding tracks

Although I'm not a musician, I am a music lover, and I know that many classical composers approached a new work in the same way you approach a new song in GarageBand — by envisioning the instruments that you want to hear. (Of course, I imagine that Mozart and Beethoven would have been thrilled to use GarageBand, but I think they did a decent job with pen and paper, too.)

If you've followed along to this point, you've noticed two problems with your GarageBand window:

✔ **The tiny keyboard in the middle of your GarageBand window:** You can record the contents of a software instrument track by "playing" the keyboard, clicking its keys with your mouse. (As you might imagine, this isn't the best solution.) If you're a musician, the best method of recording your own notes is with a MIDI instrument, which I discuss later in the chapter. For now, you can banish the keyboard window by clicking the window's Close button.

✔ **The example song has only one track.** If you want to write the next classical masterpiece for Grand Piano (the default track when you create a new song in GarageBand), that's fine. Otherwise, choose Track from the GarageBand menu and then choose Delete Track to start with a clean slate.

After your slate is clean, these are the two kinds of tracks that you can use in GarageBand:

✔ **Software instrument tracks:** These tracks aren't audio recordings. Rather, they're mathematically precise algorithms that are *rendered* (or built) by your iMac to fit your needs. If you have a MIDI instrument connected to your iMac, you can create your own software instrument tracks — more on MIDI instruments later in this chapter.

Within this chapter, I focus on software instrument tracks, which are easiest for a nonmusician to use.

✔ **Real instrument tracks:** A real instrument track is an actual audio recording, like your voice or a physical instrument without a MIDI connection.

Time to add a track of your very own. Follow these steps:

1. **Click the Create a New Track button (which carries a plus sign) at the bottom-left corner.**

   GarageBand displays the New Track dialog that you see in Figure 15-3.

2. **Click the Software Instrument tab.**

   See all those great instruments in the left column?

3. **Pick the general instrument category by clicking it.**

   I chose Drum Kits.

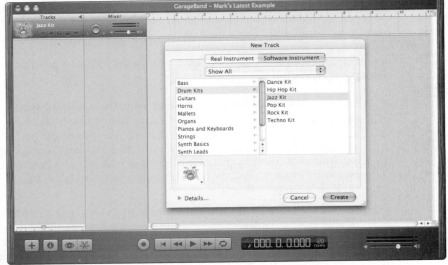

Figure 15-3:
Begin by
adding a
software
instrument
track.

4. **Choose your specific style of weapon from the right column, like Jazz
   Kit for a jazzy sound.**

5. **Click OK.**

Figure 15-4 illustrates the new track that appears in your list.

Figure 15-4:
The new
track
appears,
ready to
rock.

Choosing loops

When you have a new, empty track, you can add something that you can hear. You do that by adding loops to your track from the Loop Browser. (Apple provides you with thousands of different loops to choose from.) Click the Loop Browser button (which bears the All-Seeing Eye) to display your collection, as shown in Figure 15-5.

If your browser looks different from what you see in Figure 15-5, that's because of the view mode that you're using, just like the different view modes available for a Finder window. The two-icon button in the lower-left corner of the Loop Browser toggles the browser display between column and button view. Click the rightmost of the two buttons to switch to button mode.

Looking for just the right loop

The track in this running example uses a jazz drum kit, but I haven't added a loop yet. (Refer to Figure 15-4.) Follow these steps to search through your loop library for just the right rhythm:

1. **Click the button that corresponds to the instrument you're using.**

   In this example, this is the Kits button in the Loop Browser. Click it, and you see a list of different beats appear in the pane at the right of the browser window. (Jump down to Figure 15-6 for a sneak peek.)

Figure 15-5:
The Loop Browser, shown in button view.

Column/Button
View button

Search box

2. Click one of the loops with a green musical note icon.

Go ahead, this is where things get fun!

Because I use only software instruments in this track (and throughout this chapter), I am limited to choosing only software instrument loops, which are identified with a green musical note icon.

GarageBand begins playing the loop nonstop, allowing you to get a feel for how that particular loop sounds.

3. Click another entry in the list, and the application immediately switches to that loop.

Now you're beginning to understand why GarageBand is so cool for both musicians and the note-impaired: It's like having your own band, with members who never get tired and play whatever you want while you're composing. (Mozart would have *loved* this.)

If you want to search for a particular instrument, click in the Search box (shown at the bottom of Figure 15-5) and type the text to match. GarageBand returns the search results in the list.

Scroll down the list and continue to sample the different loops until you find one that fits like a glove. (For this reporter, it's Lounge Jazz Drums 01.)

4. Drag the entry to your Jazz Kit track and drop it at the very beginning of the timeline (as indicated by the playhead).

Your window should look like Figure 15-6.

Figure 15-6:
A track with
a loop
added.

If you want that same beat throughout the song, you don't need to add any more loops to that track (more on extending that beat in the next section). However, if you want the drum's beat to change later in the song, you add a second loop after the first one in the *same* track. For now, leave this track as-is.

Whoops! Did something that you'd rather not have done? Don't forget that you can undo most actions in GarageBand by pressing the old standby ⌘+Z immediately afterward.

Second verse, same as the first

As you compose, you can add additional tracks for each instrument that you want in your song:

- Each track can have more than one loop.
- Loops *don't* have to start at the beginning; you can drop a loop any-where in the timeline.

For example, in Figure 15-7, you can see that my drum kit kicks in first, but my bass line doesn't begin until some time later (for a funkier opening).

You put loops on separate tracks so they can play simultaneously on different instruments. If all your loops within a song are added on the same track, you hear only one loop at any one time, and all the loops use the same software instrument. By creating multiple tracks, you give yourself the elbowroom to bring the entire band at the same time. It's uber-convenient to compose your song when you can see each individual instrument's loops and where they fall in the song.

Between choosing instruments, click the Reset button in the Loop Browser to choose another instrument or genre category.

Figure 15-7 illustrates what my timeline looks like with a jazz organ and a smooth bass onboard. Cool, Daddy-o!

Resizing, repeating, adding, and moving loops

If you haven't already tried listening to your entire song, try it now. You can click Play at any time without wreaking havoc on your carefully created tracks. Sounds pretty good, doesn't it?

Figure 15-7:
The basics
of a song.

Join in and jam!

As I mention elsewhere in this chapter, GarageBand is even more fun if you happen to play an instrument! (And yes, I'm envious, no matter how much I enjoy the techno and jazz music that I create. After all, take away my iMac, and I'm back to playing the kazoo.)

Most musicians use MIDI instruments to play music on the computer. A definition of the pleasant-sounding acronym MIDI: *Musical Instrument Digital Interface.* There's a wide variety of MIDI instruments available these days, from traditional keyboards to more exotic fun, like MIDI saxophones. For example, Apple sells a 49-key MIDI keyboard from M-Audio for around $100 — it uses a USB connection to your iMac.

Most MIDI instruments on the market today use a USB connection, so connecting one is as simple as plugging it into your iMac's USB port. If you have an older instrument with traditional MIDI ports — they're round, and will never be confused with a USB connector — you need a

USB-to-MIDI converter (which might need a special software driver). You can find a converter like this on the Apple Web site from Edirol that sells for $50.

After your instrument is connected, you can record tracks with any software instrument. Create a new Software Instrument track as I demonstrate in this chapter, select it, and then play a few notes. Suddenly you're playing the instrument you picked! (If nothing happens, check the MIDI status light — which appears in the time display — to see whether it blinks with each note you play. If not, check the installation of your MIDI connection and make sure you've loaded any required drivers.)

Drag the playhead to a beat or two before the spot in the timeline where you want your recording to start. This gives you time to match the beat. Then click the Big Red Record Button and start jamming! When you're finished playing, click the Play button to stop recording.

But wait: I bet the song stopped after about five seconds, right? (You can watch the passing seconds, using either the Time/Tempo display or the second rule that appears at the very top of the timeline.) I'm sure that you want your song to last more than five seconds! After the playhead moves past the end of the last loop, your song is over. Click Play again to pause the playback; then click the Return to Beginning button to move the playhead back to the beginning of the song.

The music stops so soon because your loops are only so long. Most are five seconds in length, and others are even shorter. In order to keep the groove going, you've got to do one of three things:

- ✔ **Resize the loop.** Hover your mouse cursor over either the left or right edge of most loops, and a very interesting thing happens: Your cursor changes to a vertical line with an arrow pointing away from the loop. That's your cue to click and drag — and as you drag, most loops expand to fill the space you're making, repeating the beats in perfect time. By resizing a loop, you can literally drag the loop's edge as long as you like.

- ✔ **Repeat the loop.** Depending on the loop that you pick, you might find that resizing it won't repeat the measure. Instead, the new part of the loop is simply dead air. For example, in Figure 15-8, you can see that trying to resize my Upright Hip Hop Bass 05 loop didn't actually continue the music. (Look at the rhythm marks of that loop, indicated by a series of small horizontal lines at the bottom of the loop in the timeline. See how they appear for one second on the timeline and then disappear, much like an old-time piano roll for a player piano?)

Figure 15-8: Some software instrument loops must be repeated rather than resized.

The length of this particular loop is limited to a single second. However, if you move your cursor over the side of this loop, it turns into a vertical line with a circular arrow, which tells you that you can click and *repeat* the loop. GarageBand actually adds multiple copies of the same loop automatically, as shown in Figure 15-9, for as far as you drag the loop.

✔ **Add a new loop.** You can switch to a different loop to change the flow of the music. Naturally, the instrument stays the same, but there's no reason why you can't use a horn riff loop in your violin track (as long as it sounds good if played by a violin)! To GarageBand, a software instrument track is compatible with *any* software instrument loop that you add from the Loop Browser as long as that loop is marked with our old friend, the green musical note.

Figure 15-9: By repeating the bass loop, you can keep the thump flowing.

You can also use the familiar cut (⌘+C) and paste (⌘+V) editing keys to cut, copy, and paste loops from place to place — both on the timeline, and even from track to track. And, naturally, you can click a loop and drag it anywhere. After all, you are working under Mac OS X.

Each track can be adjusted so that you can listen to the interplay between two or more tracks or hear how your song sounds without a specific track:

✔ **Click the tiny speaker button under the track name in the list, and it turns blue to indicate that the track is muted.**

To turn off the mute, click the speaker icon again.

✓ **You can change the volume or balance of each individual track by using the mixer that appears next to the track name.**

This comes in handy if you want an instrument to sound louder or confine that instrument to the left or right speaker.

A track doesn't have to be filled for every second with one loop or another. As you can see in Figure 15-10, my first big hit — I call it *Turbo Techno* — has a number of repeating loops with empty space between them as different instruments perform solo. Not bad for a techno-wizard who can barely whistle. Listen for it soon at a rave near you!

Tweaking the settings for a track

You don't think that John Mayer or U2 just "play and walk away," do you? No, they spend hours after the recording session is over, tweaking their music in the studio and on the mixing board until every note sounds just like it should — and you can adjust the settings for a track, too. The tweaks that you can perform include adding effects (pull a Hendrix and add echo and reverb to your electric guitar track) and kicking in an equalizer (for fine-tuning the sound of your background horns).

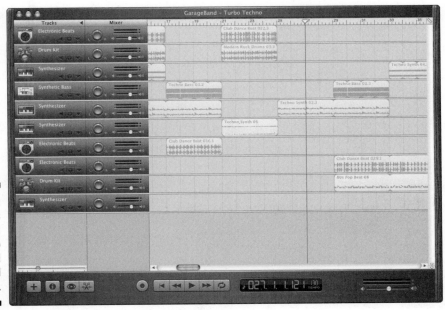

Figure 15-10: The author's upcoming techno hit — and produced on an iMac.

To make adjustments to a track, follow these steps:

1. **Click the desired track in the track list.**

2. **Click the Track Info button.**

3. **Click the Details triangle at the bottom to expand the dialog and show the settings in Figure 15-11.**

4. **Mark the check box of each effect you want to enable.**

    Each of the effects has a modifier setting. For example, you can adjust the amount of echo to add by dragging its slider.

5. **To save the instrument as a new custom instrument — so that you can choose it the next time you add a track — click the Save Instrument button.**

6. **Click the Close button to return to GarageBand.**

Time for a Mark's Maxim:

> *Save your work often* in GarageBand, just like the other iLife applications. One power blackout, and you'll never forgive yourself. Press ⌘+S, and enjoy the peace of mind.™

Figure 15-11:
Finesse your tune by tweaking the sound of a specific track.

Your Hit Is Ready for iTunes

After you finish your song, you can play it whenever you like through Garage-Band. But then again, that isn't really what you want, is it? You want to share your music with others with an audio CD, or download it to your iPod so that you can enjoy it yourself while walking through the mall!

iTunes to the rescue! Just like the other iLife applications that I cover in this book, GarageBand can share the music you make through the Digital Hub that is your iMac.

Setting preferences

The first step of the export process is to set the iTunes preferences within GarageBand:

1. **Choose GarageBand⇨Preferences and then click Export to display the settings that you see in Figure 15-12.**

2. **Click in each of the three text boxes to type the playlist, composer name, and album name for the tracks you create.**

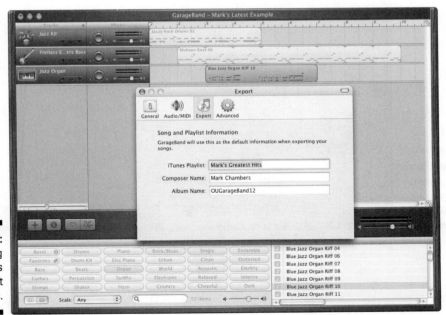

Figure 15-12:
Setting
iTunes
Export
preferences.

You can leave the defaults as-is, if you prefer.

Each track that you export is named after the song's name in GarageBand.

Creating MP3 files

After you set your Export preferences, you can create an MP3 file from your song in just a few simple steps:

1. **Open the song that you want to share.**

2. **Choose File⇨Export to iTunes.**

   After a second or two of hard work, your iMac opens the iTunes window and highlights the new (or existing) playlist that contains your new song, as shown in Figure 15-13.

Figure 15-13: Now you really *are* a rock star!

Part V
Sharing Access and Information

The 5th Wave   By Rich Tennant

" It all started when I began surfing the web for
'Baked Alaska' and frozen custards..."

In this part . . .

Ready to share your iMac among all the members of your family? If you want to synchronize your Bluetooth cell phone with your iMac, or you've decided to build a wireless home network, you've come to the right place. In this part, I show you how to provide others with access to your documents and data — securely, mind you, and with the least amount of hassle.

Chapter 16

Creating a Multiuser iMac

. . . .

In This Chapter

▶ Enjoying the advantages of a multiuser iMac

▶ Understanding access levels

▶ Adding, editing, and deleting user accounts

▶ Restricting access for managed accounts

▶ Configuring your login window

▶ Sharing files with other users

▶ Securing your stuff with FileVault

. . . .

*E*verybody wants a piece. (Of your iMac, that is.)

Perhaps you live in a busy household with kids, significant others, grandparents, and a wide selection of friends — all of them clamoring for a chance to spend time on the Internet, take care of homework, or enjoy a good game.

On the other hand, your iMac might occupy a classroom or a break room at your office — someplace public, yet everyone wants his own private iDaho on the iMac, complete with a reserved spot on the hard drive and his own hand-picked attractive desktop background.

Before you throw your hands up in the air in defeat, read this chapter and take heart! Here you find all the step-by-step procedures, explanations, and tips to help you build a multiuser iMac that's accessible to all.

(Oh, and you still get to use it, too. That's not being selfish.)

Once Upon a Time (An Access Fairy Tale)

Okay, so we don't need Cinderella, Snow White, or that porridge-loving kid with the trespassing problem. Instead, you have your brother Bob.

Every time Bob visits your place, it seems he needs to do "something" on the Internet, or he needs a moment with your iMac to bang out a quick message, using his Web-based email application. Unfortunately, Bob's forays onto your iMac always result in stuff getting changed, like your desktop settings, your Address Book, and your Safari bookmarks.

What you need, good reader, is a visit from the Account Fairy. Your problem is that you have but a single user account on your system, and Tiger thinks that Bob is *you*. By turning your iMac into a multiuser system and giving Bob his own account, Tiger can tell the difference between the two of you, keeping your druthers separate!

With a unique user account, Tiger can track all sorts of things for Bob, leaving your computing environment blissfully pristine. A user account keeps track of stuff such as

- Address Book contacts
- Safari bookmarks and settings
- Desktop settings (including background images, screen resolutions, and Finder tweaks)
- iTunes libraries, just in case Bob brings his own music (sigh)
- Web sites that Bob might ask you to host on your computer (resigned sigh)

Plus, Bob gets his own reserved Home folder on your iMac's hard drive, so he'll quit complaining about how he can't find his files. Oh, and did I mention how user accounts keep others from accessing *your* stuff? And how you can lock Bob out of things like applications, iChat, Mail, and Web sites (including that offshore Internet casino site that he's hooked on)?

Naturally, this is only the tip of the iceberg. User accounts affect just about everything you can do in Tiger. The moral of my little tale? A Mark's Maxim to the rescue:

> **Assign others their own user accounts, and let Tiger keep track of everything. You can share your iMac with others and live happily ever after!**™

Big-Shot Administrator Stuff

Get one thing straight right off the bat: *You* are the administrator of your iMac. In network-speak, an *administrator* (or *admin* for short) is the one with the power to Do Unto Others — creating new accounts, deciding who gets access to what, and generally running the multiuser show. In other words, think of yourself as the Monarch of Mac OS X. (The ruler, not the butterfly.)

I always recommend that there should be only one (or perhaps two) accounts with administrator-level access on any computer. This makes good sense because you can be assured that no one will monkey with your iMac while you're away from the keyboard. Why a second admin account? If you're often away on business, you might need to assign a second administrator account to a *trusted* individual who knows as much about Tiger as you do. (Tell 'em to buy a copy of this book.) That way, if something breaks or an account needs to be tweaked in some way, the other person can take care of it whilst you're gone.

In this section, I explain the typical duties of a first-class iMac administrator.

Deciding who needs what access

Tiger provides three levels of user accounts:

- **Admin (administrator):** See the beginning of this section.
- **Standard level:** Perfect for most users, these accounts allow access to just about everything but don't let the user make drastic changes to Tiger or create new accounts.
- **Managed level:** These are standard accounts with specific limits that are assigned either by you or by another admin account.

Another Mark's Maxim is in order:

> **Assign other folks standard level accounts and then decide whether each new account needs to be modified to restrict access as a managed account.** *Never* **assign an account admin-level access unless you deem it truly necessary.**™

Standard accounts are quick and easy to set up, and I think they provide the perfect compromise between access and security. You'll find that standard access allows your users to do just about anything they need to do, with a minimum of hassle.

Managed accounts are highly configurable so you can make sure that your users don't end up trashing the hard drive, sending junk mail, or engaging in unmonitored chatting. (***Note:*** Parents, teachers, and those folks designing a single public access account for a library or organization — this means *you*.)

Adding users

All right, Mark, enough pre-game jabbering — show this good reader how to set up new accounts! Your iMac already has one admin-level account set up for you (created during the initial Tiger set-up process). To add a new account, follow these steps:

1. **Click the System Preferences icon on the Dock and then click the Accounts icon to display the Accounts pane that you see in Figure 16-1.**

Figure 16-1:
Add new
user
accounts
here.

2. **Click the New User button — the one with the plus sign at the bottom of the accounts list — to display the new user sheet shown in Figure 16-2.**

If your New User button is grayed out, your Accounts pane is locked. Remember that you can toggle the padlock icon at the lower-left corner of most of the panes in System Preferences to lock changes. To gain access, do the following:

a. *Click the padlock icon to make changes to the Accounts pane.*

b. *When Tiger prompts you for your admin account password, enter it.*

c. *Click OK.*

Now you can click the New User button.

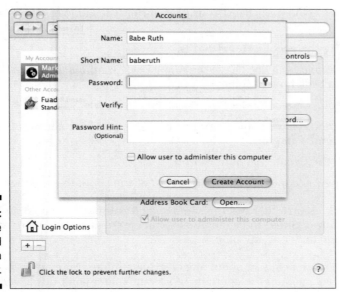

Figure 16-2:
Fill out those
fields, and
you have a
new user.

3. **Type the name that you want to display for this account in the Name text box. Press Tab to move to the next field.**

   Tiger displays this name on the Login screen, so behave!

4. **(Optional) Although Tiger automatically generates the user's *short name* (for use in iChat, and for naming the user's Home folder), you can type a new one. (No spaces, please.) Press Tab again.**

5. **In the Password text box, type the password for the new account. Press Tab to move to the next field.**

   Run out of password ideas? No problem! Click the key button to display the new Password Assistant, from which Tiger can automatically generate password suggestions of the length you specify. After you generate the password you want, press ⌘+C to copy the password, click in the Password text box on the new user sheet, and then press ⌘+V to paste it.

6. **In the Verify text box, retype the password you chose. Press Tab again to continue your quest.**

   (Optional) Tiger can provide a password hint after three unsuccessful login attempts. To offer a hint, type a short question in the Password Hint text box.

   From a security standpoint, password hints are taboo. (Personally, I **never** use 'em. If someone is having a problem logging in to a computer I administer, you better believe I want to know *why*.) Therefore, I strongly recommend that you skip this field — and if you *do* offer a hint, **keep it**

vague! Avoid hints like, "Your password is the name of the Wookie in Star Wars." Geez. . . .

7. **Decide the account level status.**

   - *Standard level:* Leave the Allow User to Administer This Computer check box disabled.

   - *Admin level:* Select the check box to enable it.

   You should have only one or two of these, and your account is already an admin account.

8. **Click the Create Account button.**

   The new account shows up in the list at the left of the Accounts pane.

Each user's Home folder has the same default subfolders, including Movies, Music, Pictures, Sites, and such. A user can create new subfolders within his or her Home folder at any time.

Here's one more neat fact about a user's Home folder: No matter what the account level, most of the contents of a Home folder can't be viewed by other users. (Yes, that includes admin-level users. This way, everyone using your iMac gets her own little area of privacy.) Within the Home folder, only the Sites and Public folders can be accessed by other users — and only in a limited fashion. More on these folders later in this chapter.

Modifying user accounts

Next, consider the basic modifications that you can make to a user account, such as changing existing information or selecting a new picture to represent that user's unique personality.

To edit an existing account, log in with your admin account, display the System Preferences window, and click Accounts to display the account list. Then follow these steps:

1. **Click the account that you want to change.**

   Don't forget to unlock the Accounts pane if necessary. See the earlier section, "Adding users," to read how.

2. **Edit the settings that you need to change.**

   For example, you can reset the user's password or (if absolutely necessary) upgrade the account to admin level.

3. **Click the Picture tab and then click a thumbnail image to represent this user (as shown in Figure 16-3).**

An easy way to get an image is to use one from your hard drive:

a. *Click Edit and drag a new image from a Finder window into the Images well.*

Alternatively, you could click the Snapshot button (which bears a tiny camera) to grab a picture from your iSight video camera.

b. *Click Set to return to the Accounts pane.*

Tiger displays this image in the Login list next to the account name.

4. **When everything is correct, press ⌘+Q to close the System Preferences dialog.**

Standard-level users have some control over their accounts — they're not helpless, y'know. Standard users can log in, open System Preferences, and click Accounts to change the account password or picture, as well as the card marked as theirs within the Address Book. All standard users can also set up Login Items, which I cover later in this chapter. Note, however, that managed users might not have access to System Preferences at all, so they can't make changes.

I banish thee, Mischievous User!

Not all user accounts last forever. Students graduate, co-workers quit, kids move out of the house (at last!), and Bob might even find a significant other who has a faster cable modem. We can only hope.

Anyway, no matter what the reason, you can delete a user account at any time. Log in with your admin account, display the Accounts pane in System Preferences, and then follow these steps to eradicate an account:

1. **Click the account that you want to delete.**

2. **Click the Delete User button (which bears the Minus Sign of Doom).**

   Tiger displays a confirmation sheet, as shown in Figure 16-4. By default, the contents of the user's Home folder are saved in a file in the Deleted Users folder when you click OK. (This safety is a good idea if the user might return in the future, allowing you to retrieve their old stuff. However, this option is available only if you have enough space on your hard drive to create the Home folder file.)

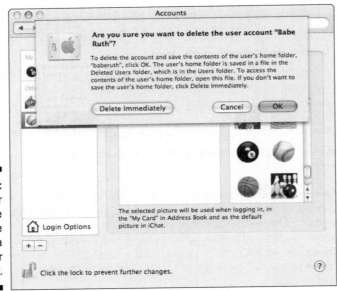

Figure 16-4:
This is your last chance to save the stuff from a deleted user account.

3. **To clean up completely, click the Delete Immediately button.**

   Tiger wipes everything connected with the user account off your hard drive.

4. **Press ⌘+Q to close the System Preferences dialog.**

Time once again for a Mark's Maxim:

> *Always* **delete unnecessary user accounts. Otherwise, you're leaving holes in your iMac's security.**™

Setting up Login Items and Parental Controls

Every account on your iMac can be customized. Understandably, some settings are accessible only to admin-level accounts, and others can be adjusted by standard-level accounts. In this section, I introduce you to the things that can be enabled (or disabled) within a user account.

Automating with Login Items

Login Items are applications or documents that can be set to launch or load automatically as soon as a specific user logs in — for example, Apple Mail or Address Book. In fact, a user must be logged in to add or remove Login Items. Even an admin-level account can't change the Login Items for another user.

A user must have access to the Accounts pane within the System Preferences window in order to use Login Items. As you can read in the following section, a user can be locked out of System Preferences, which makes it impossible for Login Items to be specified for that account. (Go figure.)

To set Login Items for your account, follow these steps:

1. **Click the System Preferences icon on the Dock and then click the Accounts icon.**

2. **Click the Login Items tab to display the settings that you see in Figure 16-5.**

Figure 16-5:
Add apps to
your Login
Items list.

3. **Click the Add button (with the plus sign) to display a file selection sheet.**

4. **Navigate to the application you want to launch each time you log in, click it to select it, and click Add.**

   If you're in the mood to drag and drop, just drag the applications you want to add from a Finder window and drop them directly into the list.

5. **Press ⌘+Q to quit System Preferences and save your changes.**

Login Items are launched in the order they appear in the list, so feel free to drag the items into any order you like.

Managing access settings for an account

A standard-level account with restrictions is a managed account. (You can read about these earlier in this chapter.) With these accounts, you can restrict access to many different places within Tiger and your iMac's applications via *Parental Controls.* (Naturally, admin-level accounts don't need Parental Controls because there are no restrictions on an admin account.)

In short, Parental Controls come in handy in preventing users — family members, students, co-workers, friends, or the public at large — from damaging your computer, your software, or Tiger itself. If an account has been restricted with Parental Controls, the account description changes from Standard to Managed in the Accounts list.

To display the Parental Controls for a standard account, log in with an admin-level account, open System Preferences, and click Accounts. Click the Standard account in the list and then click the Parental Controls tab to display the specific categories that you see in Figure 16-6:

- ✔ **Mail:** From this category, you can specify *good* (read that as *trusted* and *nice,* as defined by the admin) e-mail addresses that this user can exchange mail with.

- ✔ **Finder & System:** Choose this category to specify what operating system features the user can access (including the System Preferences window itself). You can also switch an account to use Simple Finder, which I explain in a moment.

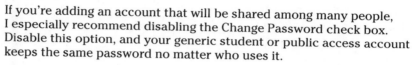

  If you're adding an account that will be shared among many people, I especially recommend disabling the Change Password check box. Disable this option, and your generic student or public access account keeps the same password no matter who uses it.

- ✔ **iChat:** Enable this category to specify the admin-approved instant messaging accounts that this user can chat with.

- ✔ **Safari:** Enabling this check box simply turns on site access controls within Safari. (To actually specify "good" sites that the user can visit, you have to log in as the user and launch Safari.)

Figure 16-6:
You don't have to be a parent to assign Parental Controls!

To restrict one or more features or functions in a category, mark the corresponding check box to enable it and then click the Configure button to select the restrictions. (Mail displays the Configure sheet automatically. There's always gotta be an exception.)

For the ultimate in restrictive Tiger environments — think public access or kiosk mode — you can assign the Simple Finder (shown in Figure 16-7) to an account. Even the Dock itself is restricted, sporting only the Finder icon, the Trash, Dashboard, and folders that allow the user to access their documents and applications.

Figure 16-7:
The Simple Finder is pretty doggone simple.

Multiuser Rules for Everyone

After you're hip on user accounts and the changes you can make to them, turn to a number of topics that affect all users of your iMac — things like how they'll log in, how a user can share information with everyone else on the computer, and how each user account can be protected from unscrupulous outsiders with state-of-the-art encryption. (Suddenly you're James Bond! I told you Tiger would open new doors for you.)

Logging on and off in Tiger For Dummies

Hey, how about the login screen itself? How do your users identify them-selves? Time for another of my "Shortest books in the *For Dummies* series" special editions. (The title's practically longer than the entire book.)

Tiger offers four methods of logging folks in to your multiuser iMac:

- ✔ **The username and password login:** This is the most secure type of login screen you'll see in Tiger because you have to actually type your account username and your password. (A typical hacker isn't going to know all the usernames on your iMac.) Press Return or click the Log In button to compete the process.

  When you enter your username and password, you see bullets rather than your password because Tiger displays bullet characters to ensure security. Otherwise, someone could simply look over your shoulder and see your password.

- ✔ **The list login:** This login screen offers a good middle of the road between security and convenience. Click your account username in the list and type your password when the login screen displays the pass-word prompt. Press Return or click the Log In button to continue.

- ✔ **Fast User Switching:** This feature allows another user to sit down and log in while the previous user's applications are still running in the back-ground. This is perfect for a fast e-mail check or a scan of your eBay bids without forcing someone else completely off the iMac. When you turn on Fast User Switching, Tiger displays the currently active user's name at the right side of the Finder menu bar (see Figure 16-8).

  To switch to another account

  a. *Click the current user's name in the Finder menu.*

  b. *Click the name of the user who wants to log in.*

  Tiger displays the login window, just as if the iMac had been rebooted.

  The previous user's stuff is still running, so you definitely shouldn't reboot or shut down the iMac!

  To switch back to the previous user

  a. *Click the username again in the Finder menu.*

  b. *Click the previous user's name.*

  For security, Tiger prompts you for that account's login password.

- ✔ **Auto login:** This is the most convenient method of logging in but offers no security whatsoever. Tiger automatically logs in the specified account when you start or reboot your iMac.

Figure 16-8:
The Fast
User
Switching
menu,
unfurled for
all to see.

I *strongly recommend* that you use auto login only if

- Your iMac is in a secure location.

- You are the only one using your Mac.

- You're setting up a public-access iMac, in which case you want your iMac to immediately log in with the public account.

Never set an admin-level account as the auto login account. This is the very definition of ASDI, or *A Supremely Dumb Idea*.

To set up a username/password or list login, open System Preferences, click the Accounts icon, and then display the Login Options settings (see Figure 16-9). Select the List of Users radio button for a list login screen, or select the Name and Password radio button to require your users to type their full username and password.

To enable Fast User Switching, mark the Enable Fast User Switching check box (as shown in Figure 16-9).

To set Auto Login, select the Automatically Log in As check box. Click the account name pop-up menu and choose the account that Tiger should use (as shown by the now-legendary Figure 16-9).

Figure 16-9:
Configure
your login
settings
from the
Login
Options
pane.

Logging out of Tiger all the way (without Fast User Switching) is a cinch. Just click the Apple menu (🍎) and then choose Log Out. (From the keyboard, press ⌘+Shift+Q.) A confirmation dialog appears that will automatically log you off in two minutes — but don't forget that if someone walks up and clicks Cancel, he'll be using your iMac with your account! Your iMac returns to the login screen, ready for its next victim. Heed this Mark's Maxim:

> *Always* click the Log Out button on the logout confirmation dialog before you leave your iMac.™

Interesting stuff about sharing stuff

You might wonder where shared documents and files reside on your iMac. That's a good question. Like just about everything in Tiger, there's a simple answer. The Users folder on your iMac has a *Shared* folder within it. To share a file or folder, it must be placed in the Shared folder for standard- and managed-level users to be able to open it.

You don't have to turn on Personal File Sharing in the Sharing pane of System Preferences to use Shared folders on your iMac. Personal File Sharing affects only network access to your machine by users of other computers.

Admin-level accounts have the advantage because they can access virtually any location on your iMac's hard drive. Therefore, if one admin-level user wants to save a document for another admin-level user, that document can reside in other folders on your system besides just the Shared folder. (Personally, I don't mind using the Shared folder because it guarantees that other users can access it, but privacy between admin users is a closely guarded perk.)

Each user account on your iMac also has a *Public* folder within that user's Home folder. This is a read-only folder that other users on your iMac can access: They can only open and copy the files that it contains. (Sorry, no changes to existing documents from other users, or new documents from other users.) Every user's Public folder contains a *Drop Box* folder, where other users can copy or save files but can't view the contents. Think of the Drop Box as a mailbox where you drop off stuff for the other user.

Encrypting your Home folder can be fun

Allowing others to use your iMac always incurs a risk — especially if you store sensitive information and documents on your computer. Although your login password should ensure that your Home folder is off limits to everyone else, consider an extra level of security to prevent even a dedicated hacker from accessing your stuff.

To this end, Tiger includes *FileVault,* which automatically encrypts the contents of your Home folder. Without the proper key (in this case, either your login password or your admin's master password), the data contained in your Home folder is impossible for just about anyone to read. (I guess the FBI or NSA would be able to decrypt it, but they're not likely a worry at your place!)

The nice thing about FileVault is that it's completely transparent to you and your users. In other words, when you log in, Tiger automatically takes care of decrypting and encrypting the stuff in your Home folder for you. You literally won't know that FileVault is working for you — which is how computers are *supposed* to work.

To turn on FileVault protection for a specific account, follow these steps:

1. **Click the System Preferences icon on the Dock and then click the Security icon.**

2. **If necessary, click Set Master Password to create a master password.**

You need to be logged in with an admin-level account to set a master password. However, this needs to be done only once, no matter how many accounts you're hosting on your iMac. Using this master password, any admin-level user can unlock any Home folder for any user.

Before you move to Step 3, note that you must be logged in using the account that requires the FileVault protection. (Therefore, if you had to log in using your admin-level account to set a master password, you have to log out and log in again using the account you want to protect. Arrgh.)

3. **Click the Turn on FileVault button.**

4. **Enter your account's login password when prompted (see Figure 16-10) and then click OK.**

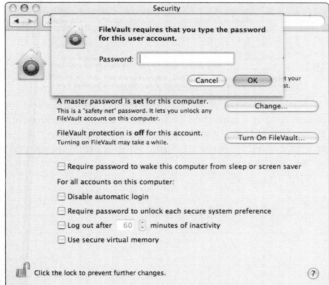

Figure 16-10: Your account password becomes your FileVault password.

5. **Click the Turn on FileVault button on the confirmation screen shown in Figure 16-11.**

6. **After Tiger encrypts your Home folder and logs you out, log in again normally.**

You're done!

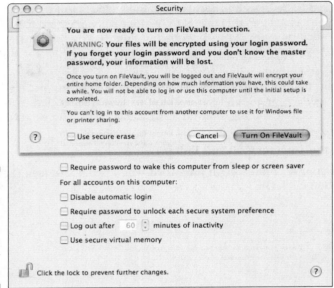

Figure 16-11:
Tiger wants
to be very,
very sure
that you're
ready for
FileVault.

Remember those passwords. Again, **do not forget** your account login password, and make doggone sure that your admin user never forgets the master
password! If you forget these passwords, you can't read anything in your
Home folder, and even the smartest Apple support technician will tell you
that nothing can be done.

Chapter 17

Building (Or Joining) a Network

*I*n my book (get it — *my book*), network access ranks right up there with air conditioning and the microwave oven. Like other "taken for granted, but I can't imagine life without them" kinds of technologies, it's hard to imagine sharing data from your iMac with others around you without a network. Sure, I've used a *sneakernet* (the old-fashioned term for running back and forth between computers with a floppy disk to copy files), but these days, Apple computers don't even *have* floppy drives. And what could you possibly fit on less than the meager floppy disk 2MB of space anyway?

Nope, networking is here to stay. Whether you use it to share an Internet connection, challenge your friends to a nice relaxing game of WWII battlefield action, or stream your MP3 collection to other computers that use iTunes, you'll wonder how you ever got along without one. In this chapter, I fill you in on all the details you need to know to get your iMac hooked up to a new (or an existing) network.

If you have just your iMac and an Internet connection (either through a dialup modem or a high-speed DSL/cable modem) and you have no plans to add another computer or a network printer, a network isn't necessary.

What exactly is the network advantage?

If you have other family members with computers or if your iMac is in an office with other computers, here's just a sample of what you can do with a network connection:

✔ **Share an Internet connection.** This is *the* major reason why many families and most small businesses install a network. Everyone can simultaneously use the same DSL (digital subscriber line) or cable Internet connection on every computer on the network.

✔ **Copy and move files of all sizes.** Need to get a 4GB iDVD project from one Mac to another? With a network connection, you can accomplish this task in just minutes. Otherwise — back to a sneakernet, but with an entire hard drive and not a floppy — you'd have to burn that file to a DVD-R or use an external hard drive. A network connection makes copying as simple as dragging the project folder from one Finder window to another.

✔ **Share documents across your network.** Talk about a wonderful collaboration tool. For example, you can drop a Word document or

Keynote presentation file in your Public folder and ask for comments and edits from others in your office.

✔ **Stream music.** With iTunes, you can share your MP3 collection on your iMac with other Macs and PCs on your network. Your ears can't tell the difference!

✔ **Play multiplayer games.** Invite your friends over and tell 'em that you're hosting a *LAN party* (the techno-nerd term for a large gathering of game players, connected through the same network, all playing the same multiplayer game. (Suddenly you'll see firsthand just how devious a human opponent can be.) Each participant needs to buy a copy of the same game, naturally, but the fun you'll have is worth every cent you spend. Don't forget the chips!

If your iMac isn't within shouting distance of an existing network and you don't plan on buying any more computers, a network isn't for you. Because the whole idea of a network is to share documents and applications with others, a lone iMac hanging out in your home with no other computers around it won't need a network.

The Great Debate: Wired versus Wireless

If you decide that you indeed need a network for your home or office, you have another decision to make: Should you install a *wired* network (which involves running cables between your computers) or a *wireless* network (which doesn't require any computer-connecting cables)?

Your first instinct is probably to choose a wireless network for convenience. After all, this option allows you to eliminate running cables behind furniture (or in the ceiling of your office building). Ah, but I must show you the advantages to a wired network as well. Table 17-1 shows the lowdown to help you make up your mind.

Table 17-1	Network Decision-making	
Function	*Wireless Networks*	*Wired Networks*
Speed	Moderate	Much Faster
Security	Moderate	Better
Convenience	Better	Worse
Compatibility	Confusing standards	Easier to understand
Cables	Few (or none)	Required

✔ **Wired:** A wired network offers two significant perks over a wireless network:

> • *Faster speeds:* Wired networks that are compatible with your iMac are up to twice as fast the fastest 802.11g wireless connections.
>
> The performance of a wireless connection is reduced by both interference (from structures like concrete walls and household appliances like some wireless phones and microwave ovens) and distance.
>
> • *Better security:* A wired network doesn't broadcast a signal that can be picked up outside your home or office, so it's more secure.
>
> Hackers can attack through your Internet connection. Hence the section, "USE YOUR FIREWALL!," later in this chapter.

✔ **Wireless:** A wireless connection really has only one advantage, but it's a big one: *convenience.*

Accessing your network anywhere within your home or office — without cables — is so easy. You can easily connect a wireless printer. (By using an AirPort Express mobile Base Station, even your home stereo can get connected to your MP3 collection on your iMac.)

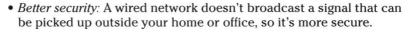

It's easy to graft wireless access to a wired network

Are you caught in the middle between wired and wireless networking? Or perhaps you're already using a wired network but would be absolutely thrilled by the idea of sitting on your deck in the sunshine whilst checking your e-mail on your laptop. By using both technologies, you can get the faster transfers of a wired network between all the computers in your office.

That is the configuration I use in my home office. My family gets all the convenience a wireless network offers, and everyone can connect to the Internet from anywhere in our house. On the other hand, my office computers have the faster performance and tighter security of a wired network. *Sassy* indeed!

Sharing Internet Access

Time to see what's necessary to share an Internet connection. In this section, I cover two methods of connecting your network to the Internet (And before you open your wallet, keep in mind that you might be able to use your iMac to share your broadband connection across your network!)

Using your iMac as a sharing device

Figure 17-1 illustrates how you can use your iMac to provide a shared Internet connection across your network, using either

✔ **A broadband DSL or cable connection**

✔ **A dialup modem**

You should try sharing a dialup modem Internet connection only if you have no other option. A dialup modem connection really can't handle the data transfer speeds for more than one computer to access the Internet comfortably at one time. (In plain English, your iMac's built-in modem just isn't fast enough for both you and your significant other to surf the Web at the same time.) Sharing a dialup connection just isn't practical.

In these configurations, the only hardware you need to buy for your wired network is an Ethernet hub or switch (more on these devices in the next section). Your iMac uses OS X Tiger's built-in Internet connection sharing feature to get the job done, but your iMac must remain turned on to allow Internet sharing. I show you how to do this in the upcoming section, "Internet connection," later in this chapter.

Using a separate Internet sharing device

Figure 17-2 illustrates how a broadband connection works if you use a dedicated Internet sharing device (often called an *Internet router*) to connect to your cable or DSL modem. You have to buy the additional hardware, but your iMac doesn't have to remain turned on just so everyone can get on the Internet.

Internet routers can include either wired or wireless network connections — many include both.

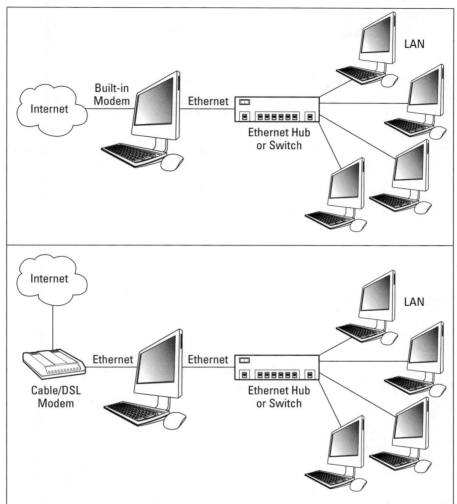

Figure 17-1:
Share an
Internet
connection
by using
your iMac.

Setting up an Internet router is a pretty simple matter, but the configuration depends on the device manufacturer and usually involves a number of different settings in System Preferences that vary according to the model of router you're installing. Grab a Diet Coke, sit down with the router's manual, and follow the installation instructions you'll find there.

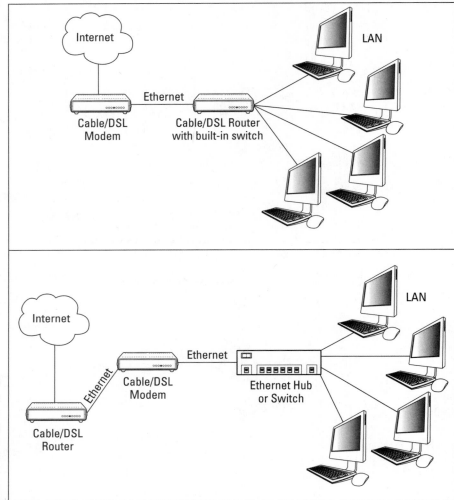

Figure 17-2:
Share an
Internet
connection
by using an
Internet
router.

Most Internet routers offer a DHCP server, which automatically assigns IP (Internet protocol) addresses, and I **strongly** recommend that you turn on this feature! (You can read more on DHCP later in the chapter, in the sidebar titled, "The little abbreviation that *definitely* could.")

What Do I Need to Connect?

Most *normal* folks — whom I define as those who have never met a network system administrator, and couldn't care less — think that connecting to a network probably involves all sorts of arcane chants and a mystical symbol or two. In this section, I provide you with the shopping list that you need to set up a network — or connect to a network that's already running.

Wireless connections

If you ordered your iMac with an AirPort Extreme wireless card installed and you already have an AirPort Extreme or Express Base Station, you're set to go. Otherwise, hold on tight as I lead you through the hardware requirements for wireless networking.

The maximum signal range of any wireless network can be reduced by intervening walls or by electrical devices like microwave ovens and wireless phones that can generate interference.

iMac hardware

Connecting an iMac to an existing wireless network requires only a single piece of hardware: an AirPort Extreme wireless card.

- All current iMac models sport built-in AirPort Extreme wireless hardware, so you don't need to buy any new toys.
- If you need to add wireless support to your iMac, you need an AirPort Extreme card. (Chapter 20 shows how to install it.)

After the card is safely ensconced within the confines of your iMac's sleek case, you can skip to the next section.

You can use some PC-compatible 802.11g cards in your iMac, but not all wireless cards are supported. Plus, you'll have to do a little additional configuration dancing to join an AirPort Extreme network. (Unfortunately, the passwords used by the two different types of hardware are incompatible.) For the whole story, visit `http://kbase.info.apple.com/index.jsp` and search for article number 106864, entitled *AirPort Extreme: Getting an equivalent network password.* (I bought an AirPort Extreme card, thus avoiding any additional work. Sounds like a Mark's Maxim!)

> **If you don't want the hassle of tweaking PC hardware to accommodate your iMac, buy Apple hardware and software.**™

Base stations

If you decide that you want to build your own network, you eschew cables, or you want to add wireless support to your existing wired network, you need a *base station.* The base station can act as a bridge between computers using wireless and your existing wired network, or a base station can simply act as a central switch for your wireless network.

You can use either a cool Apple Base Station or a boring 802.11g generic wireless base station; however, the Apple hardware requires less configuration and tweaking.

Apple base stations

As listed in Table 17-2, your iMac can work with three different Apple Base Station models for wireless networking:

✔ **AirPort Extreme**

I recommend AirPort Extreme if your network needs

- Faster 802.11g transfer speeds
- An enhanced antenna (which provides greater range)

✔ **AirPort Express (as shown in Figure 17-3)**

I recommend AirPort Extreme if you want to

- *Carry your wireless base station* with you (it's much smaller than Apple's other base stations)
- *Connect your home stereo* for wireless music streaming by using the AirTunes feature in iTunes

Figure 17-3:
The AirPort
Express
portable
Base
Station.

✔ **AirPort (discontinued)**

You might find the original AirPort Base Station on eBay or at a garage sale. Go ahead and pick it up if you want to save cash, unless you're considering multiplayer gaming or high-speed file transfers over your wireless network.

The 802.11g standard used by the AirPort Extreme and AirPort Express Base Stations delivers a connection that's several times faster than the old AirPort Base Station's 802.11b.

Table 17-2	Apple Wireless Network Base Stations		
Feature	**AirPort Extreme**	**AirPort Express**	**AirPort**
Price	$200	$130	$80 (used)
Users (maximum)	50	10	50
802.11g support	Yes	Yes	No
802.11b support	Yes	Yes	Yes
LAN Ethernet jack (high-speed Internet connection)	Yes	Yes	Yes
WAN Ethernet jack (wired computer network)	Yes	No	No
Stereo mini-jack	No	Yes	No
USB printer port	Yes	Yes	No
Maximum signal range (approximate)	150 feet (standard) 250 (with add-on antenna)	150 feet	100 feet
AC adapter	Separate	Built-in	Separate

The names of Apple's Base Stations are irritatingly similar; Apple usually does a better job differentiating their product names. Jot down the name of your model on a Stickie on your iMac's Desktop just so you don't get confused.

Installing an Apple Base Station is simple:

1. **If you have a DSL or cable modem, connect it to the Ethernet LAN jack on the Base Station.**

2. **If you have a wired Ethernet computer network, connect it to the WAN (wide area network) jack on the Base Station.**

3. **If you have a USB printer, connect it to the USB port on the Base Station.**

   I cover the steps to share a printer in the section, "Printers."

4. **Connect the power cable from the AC power adapter.**

   AirPort Express has a built-in AC adapter, so you just plug AirPort Express into the wall.

5. **Switch on your Base Station.**

6. **Run the installation software provided by Apple on your iMac.**

Non-Apple base stations and access points

If any company other than Apple manufactured your wireless base station or access point, the installation procedure is almost certainly the same. (Naturally, you should take a gander at the manufacturer's installation guide just to make sure, but I added many different brands of these devices and used the same steps for each one.)

However, I should note this extra hurdle to connecting to a non-Apple base station or access point via an AirPort or AirPort Extreme card. (More on this in the next section. For now, just remember that I recommend using Apple wireless hardware with your iMac whenever possible. It's just a little easier!)

Creating or joining a wireless network

As far as I'm concerned, the only two types of base stations on the planet are Apple and non-Apple (which includes all 802.11b and 802.11g Base Stations and access points). In these two sections, I relate what you need to know to get onboard using either type of hardware.

AirPort

To create or join a wireless network that's served by any flavor of Apple Base Station, follow these steps on each Mac with wireless support:

1. **Click the System Preferences icon on the Dock.**

2. **Click the Network icon.**

3. **From the Show pop-up menu, choose AirPort.**

4. **Mark the Show AirPort Status in Menu Bar check box.**

5. **Click the Apply Now button.**

6. **Click the AirPort status icon (looks like a fan) on the Finder menu bar.**

7. **From the AirPort menu, choose an existing network connection that you'd like to join.**

Some wireless networks might not appear in your AirPort menu list. These are *closed networks.* You can't join a closed unless you know the exact network name (which is far more secure than simply broadcasting the network name). To join a closed network, follow these steps:

1. **Select Other from the AirPort menu**

2. **Type the name of the network.**

3. **Enter the network password, if required.**

To disconnect from an AirPort Extreme network, click the AirPort menu and either

🟆 Choose Turn AirPort Off.

🟆 Connect to another AirPort network.

Non-Apple Base Stations and Access Points

If you're using an AirPort card to connect to a non-Apple base station or access point, you need to follow a specific procedure that takes care of the slightly different password functionality used by standard 802.11b/g hardware.

To read or print the latest version of this procedure, fire up Safari and visit http://kbase.info.apple.com/index.jsp, searching on the number 106250 (the Apple Knowledge Base article number). This article provides the details on how to convert a standard wireless encrypted password to a format that your AirPort card can understand.

Wired connections

If you're installing a wired network, your iMac already comes with most of what you need for joining your new cabled world. You just connect the hardware and configure the connection. Don't forget that you also need cables (check the sidebar, "Can I save money by making my own cables?") and an inexpensive Ethernet switch or hub. (If you're using an Internet router or other hardware sharing device, it likely has a built-in 4 or 8-port hub.)

iMac hardware

Your Ethernet 10/100 port (which looks like a slightly oversized modem port) is located in the line of ports on the back of your iMac, ready to accept a standard Ethernet Cat5 cable with RJ-45 connectors. If you're connecting to an existing wired network, you need a standard Cat5 Ethernet cable of the necessary length. I recommend a length of no more than 25 feet because cables longer than 25 feet are often subject to line interference (which can slow down or even cripple your connection). You'll also need a live Ethernet port from the network near your iMac. Plug the cable into your iMac, and then plug the other end into the network port.

Network hardware

If you don't know your hub from your NIC, don't worry — here I provide you with a description of the hardware that you need for your wired network.

Can I save money by making my own cables?

You can either purchase premade Cat5 cables, or you can (try) to make your own. However, you most definitely *don't* save money by making your own cables — at least, not if you're connecting computers that are located within 25 feet or so of one another. I strongly recommend that you buy premade Cat5 Ethernet cables (which come in a number of standard lengths) for two very important reasons:

✔ **You can be guaranteed that your cables work.**

✔ **You don't have to build the things yourself.**

Nothing is harder to troubleshoot than a shorted or faulty Ethernet cable — that's the voice of experience talking there.

If you're wiring multiple rooms in your house or office, you have to install your own cabling. That's when I suggest you either call your local computer store for help or enlist the aid of someone you know who has successfully installed Ethernet cable. If you're building a home, you can get your home wired for an Ethernet network at the same time as the AC wiring is installed. (This route is expensive, but if you're a computer maven, you'll budget that cost!)

Components

If you're building your own wired network, you need

✔ **A central connection gizmo:** You can use either

- A *hub*

- A *switch* (which is faster and slightly more expensive)

This gizmo's job is to provide more network ports for the other computers in your network. They typically come in 4- and 8-port configurations.

As I mention earlier in this chapter, most Internet routers (sometimes called *Internet sharing devices*) include a built-in hub or switch, so if you've already invested in an Internet router, make doggone sure that it doesn't come equipped with the ports you need before you go shopping for a hub or switch!

✔ **A number of Cat5 Ethernet cables** (determined by how many computers you're connecting).

Many companies sell *do-it-yourself networking kits* that contain everything you need for a small four-computer network, including cables and a hub. These kits are a great buy (typically selling for under $100), but most of these kits include a PC Ethernet NIC (network interface card) that your iMac doesn't need. (If you have a PC that doesn't have a network card, you can use the card in that computer.) If you don't need an Ethernet NIC for any of your computers, look for a do-it-yourself kit that comes with just the cables and the hub or switch (these usually go for $50 or a little less). I recommend Linksys kits (www.linksys.com).

Connections

After you assemble your cables and your hub or switch, connect the Ethernet cables from each of your computers to the hub or switch, and then turn on hub. (Most need AC power to work.) Check the manual that comes with your hub to make sure that the lights you're seeing on the front indicate normal operation. (Colors vary by manufacturer, but green is usually good.)

When your hub is powered on and operating normally, you're ready to configure Mac OS X for network operation. Just hop to the upcoming section, "Connecting to the Network." (How about that? Now you can add network technician to your rapidly growing computer résumé!)

Joining a wired Ethernet network

After all the cables have been connected and your central connection gizmo is plugged in and turned on, you've essentially created the hardware portion of your network. Congratulations! (Now you need a beard and suspenders.)

With the hardware in place, it's time to configure Tiger. In this section, I assume that you're connecting to a network with an Internet router, hub, or switch that includes a DHCP server. (Jump to the sidebar, "The little abbreviation that *definitely* could," for more on DHCP.)

Follow these steps on each Mac running Mac OS X that you want to connect to the network:

1. **Click the System Preferences icon on the Dock.**

2. **Click the Network icon (under Internet & Network).**

3. **From the Show pop-up menu, choose Built-in Ethernet.**

4. **From the Configure IPv4 pop-up menu on the TCP/IP tab (see Figure 17-4), choose Using DHCP.**

5. **Click the Apply Now button.**

   Enjoy the automatic goodness as Mac OS X connects to the DHCP server to obtain an IP address, a subnet mask, a gateway router IP (Internet protocol) address, and a Domain Name System (DNS) address. (Without a DHCP server, you'd have to add all this stuff manually. Ugh.)

   A few seconds after clicking the Apply Now button, you should see the information come up. You might also notice that the DNS Servers field is empty, but fear not because Mac OS X is really using DNS Server information provided by the DHCP server.

6. **Press ⌘+Q to quit System Preferences and save your settings.**

   You're on!

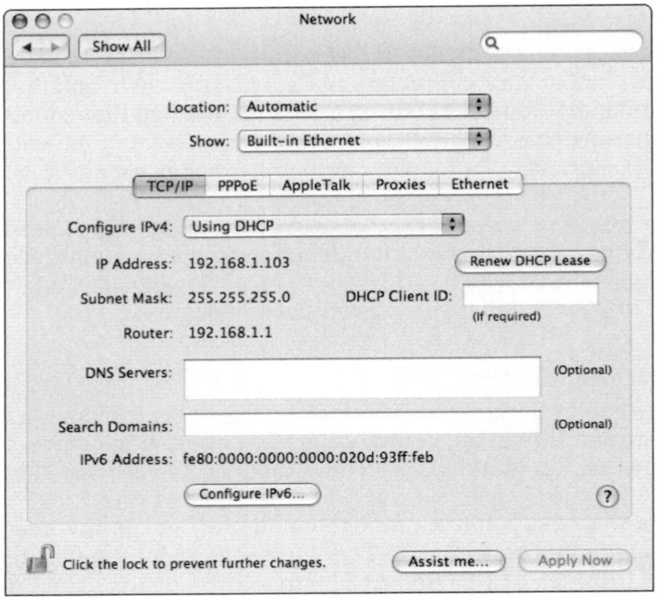

Figure 17-4:
All hail
DHCP, the
magical
networking
fairy!

Connecting to the Network

All right! Now the hardware is powered up, the cables (if any) are installed and connected and you've configured Tiger. You're ready to start (or join) the party. In this section, I show you how to verify that you're connected as well as how to share data and devices with others on your network.

Verifying that the contraption works

After you have at least two computers on a wired or wireless network, test whether they're talking to each other over the network by *pinging* them. (No, I didn't make up the term, honest.) Essentially, pinging another computer is like yelling, "Are you there?" across a crevasse.

To ping another computer on the same network from any Mac running Tiger, follow these steps:

1. **Open a Finder window, click Applications and then click Utilities.**

2. **Double-click the Network Utility icon to launch the application.**

3. **Click the Ping tab.**

4. **In the Please Enter the Network Address to Ping text field, enter the IP address of the computer that you want to ping.**

If you're pinging another Mac running Tiger, you can get the IP address of that machine by simply displaying the Network pane within System Preferences, which always displays the IP address.

If you're trying to ping a PC running Windows XP and you don't know the IP address of that machine

> a. *Click Start, right-click My Network Places, and choose Properties.*
>
> b. *From the Network Connections window, right-click your Local Area Network connection icon and choose Status.*
>
> c. *Click the Support tab.*
>
> The IP address of that PC is proudly displayed.

5. **Select the Send Only x Pings radio button and enter** 5 **in the text field.**

6. **Click the Ping button.**

Yay!: If everything is working, you should see results similar to those shown in Figure 17-5, in which I'm pinging my Windows server at IP address 192.168.1.106, across my wired Ethernet network.

The address 192.168.1.*xxx* is a common series of local network IP addresses provided by Internet routers, hubs and switches with DHCP servers, so don't freak if you have the same local IP address.

Nay: If you *don't* get a successful ping, check your cable connections, power cords, and Mac OS X settings. Folks using a wireless connection might have to move closer to the network base station to connect successfully, especially through walls.

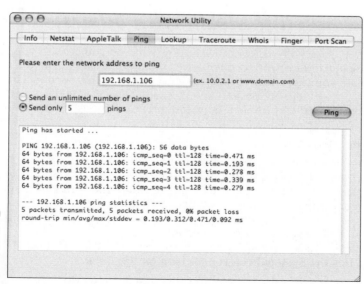

Figure 17-5:
Look, Ma,
I'm pinging!

The little abbreviation that *definitely* could

You know, some technologies are just *peachy*. (So much for my uber-tech image.) Anyway, these well-designed technologies work instantly, you don't have to fling settings around like wrapping paper on Christmas day, and every computer on the planet can use them: Mac, Windows, Linux, and even the laptops used by funny-looking folks from Roswell, New Mexico.

Dynamic Host Configuration Protocol, or DHCP for short, is about as peachy as it gets. This protocol enables a computer to automatically get all the technical information necessary to join a network. Let me hear you say, *"Oh yeah!"* Just about every network device on the planet can use DHCP these days, including Internet routers, hubs, switches, and (go figure) Mac OS X. Today's networking hardware and operating systems provide a *DHCP server,* which flings the proper settings at every computer on the network all by itself. Your Mac just accepts the settings and relaxes in a placid networking nirvana.

In this book, you can bet the farm that I assume you want to use DHCP and that your network hardware supports it as well. That way, I won't spend 30 pages of this book leading you through the twisting alleyways of manual network settings. (If you're really into such things, I spend those 30 pages and explain every single technowizard detail in my book *Mac OS X Tiger All-in-One Desk Reference For Dummies,* [Wiley]. It's about 800 pages long — hence the comprehensive angle.)

If you're connecting to an existing network, tell the network administrator that you're taking the easy route and using DHCP. One word of warning, however: Adding more than one DHCP server on a single network causes a civil war, and your system will lock up tight. Therefore, before adding hardware with a DHCP server to an existing network, ask that network administrator to make sure that you aren't making a mistake.

Sharing stuff nicely with others

It works . . . by golly, it works! Okay, now what do you *do* with your all-new shining chrome network connection? Ah, my friend, let me be the first to congratulate you, and the first to show you around! In this section, I cover the most popular network perks. (And the good news is that these perks work with both wired and wireless connections.)

Internet connection

If your DSL or cable modem plugs directly into your iMac (rather than a dedicated Internet sharing device or Internet router), you might ponder just how the other computers on your network can share that spiffy high-speed broadband connection. Your network comes to the rescue!

Follow these steps to share your connection:

1. **Click the System Preferences icon on the Dock.**
2. **Click the Sharing icon (under Internet & Network).**

3. **Click the Internet tab.**

4. **From the Share Your Connection From pop-up menu, choose Built-in Ethernet.**

5. **Mark the Built-in Ethernet check box (in the To Computers Using list).**

   Tiger displays a warning dialog stating that connection sharing could affect your ISP (Internet service provider) or violate your agreement with your ISP. I've never heard of this actually happening, but if you want to be sure, contact your ISP and ask the good folks there.

6. **Click OK in the warning dialog to continue.**

7. **Click Start to enable Internet sharing.**

8. **Click the Close button to exit System Preferences.**

Sharing an Internet connection (without an Internet router or dedicated hardware device) through Mac OS X requires your iMac to remain on continuously. This is no big deal if you're using your iMac as a Web server — and your iMac has absolutely no problem remaining on ad infinitum — but tell others in your office or your home that the svelte iMac must remain on, or they'll lose their Internet connection!

You can share a dialup modem Internet connection, but don't be surprised if you quickly decide to shelve the idea of sharing a 56 Kbps connection. Those dinosaurs are s-l-o-w beyond belief.

Files

You can swap all sorts of interesting files with other Macintosh computers on your network. When you turn on Personal File Sharing, Tiger lets all Macs on the network connect to your iMac and share the files in your Public folder.

Follow these steps to start sharing files and folders with others across your network:

1. **Click the System Preferences icon on the Dock.**

2. **Click the Sharing icon.**

3. **Click the Services tab.**

4. **Enable the connections for Mac and Windows sharing:**

   - *If you want to share files with other Macs on your network,* select the Personal File Sharing check box.

     Other Mac users can connect to your computer by clicking Go in the Finder menu and choosing the Network menu item. The Network window appears, and your iMac is among the choices.

   - *If you want to share files with networked PCs running Windows,* select the Windows Sharing check box.

Windows XP users should be able to connect to your Mac from their My Network Places window (or, with pre-XP versions of Windows, from the Network Neighborhood). Those lucky Windows folks also get to print to any shared printers you've set up. (The following section covers shared printers.)

5. **Click the Close button to exit System Preferences.**

Tiger conveniently reminds you of the network name for your iMac at the bottom of the Sharing pane.

Printers

Boy, howdy, do I love describing easy procedures, and sharing a printer on a Mac network ranks high on the list! You can share a printer that's connected to your iMac (or your AirPort Extreme or AirPort Express Base Station) by following these very simple steps:

1. **Click the System Preferences icon on the Dock.**

2. **Click the Print & Fax icon (under Hardware).**

3. **Click the Sharing tab.**

4. **Select the Share These Printers with Other Computers check box.**

5. **Click the printers that you want to share.**

6. **Click the Close button to exit System Preferences.**

A printer that you share automatically appears in the Print dialog on other computers connected to your network.

A Web site

Web jockeys tell you that Mac OS X is a great platform for running a Web site that you can access from either the Internet or your local network. In fact, it's ridiculously easy to engage the mind-boggling power of Tiger's Apache Web server. (Keep in mind, however, that your iMac must always be on and connected to the Internet, or your Web pages won't be available to your folks in Schenectady.)

To begin serving Web pages, follow these steps:

1. **Click the System Preferences icon on the Dock.**

2. **Click the Sharing icon.**

3. **Click the Services tab.**

4. **Select the Personal Web Sharing check box.**

5. **Click the Close button to exit System Preferences.**

To check out the default HTML page that ships with Apache, launch Safari and visit this URL, replacing *username* in the address with your username:

```
http://127.0.0.1/~username/
```

To add pages to your Web server, navigate to the Sites folder that resides in your Home folder. Because this is the root of your Apache Web server, the files that you add to this folder are accessible from your Web server.

Don't forget that folks connecting to your Web site across the Internet must use your public IP address! (The 127.0.0.1 IP address that I just mention is a special address that allows your iMac to connect with itself. Rather egocentric, but it works.) Your iMac's IP address appears in the Built-in Ethernet description on the Network pane in System Preferences. If you're using an Internet router or Internet connection sharing device, your *public* IP address might be different. Check the documentation for the device to determine how to find your actual public IP address.

USE YOUR FIREWALL!

The following Mark's Maxim, good reader, isn't a request, a strong recommendation, or even a regular Maxim — consider it an **absolute commandment** (right up there with *Get an antivirus application now*).

> **Turn on your firewall *now*.**™

By connecting your network to the Internet, you open a door to the outside world. As a consultant to several businesses and organizations in my hometown, I can tell you that the outside world is chock-full of malicious individuals who would *dearly love* to inflict damage on your data or take control of your iMac for their own purposes. Call 'em hackers, call 'em delinquents, or call 'em something I can't repeat, but *don't let them in!*

Tiger comes to the rescue again with the built-in firewall within Mac OS X. When you use this, you essentially build a virtual brick wall between you and the hackers out there (both on the Internet, and even within your local network). Follow these steps:

1. **Click the System Preferences icon on the Dock.**

2. **Click the Sharing icon.**

3. **Click the Firewall tab.**

4. **Click Start to activate your firewall.**

5. **Click the Close button to exit System Preferences.**

Tiger even keeps track of the Internet traffic that you *do* want to reach your iMac, such as Web page requests and file sharing. When you activate one of the network features that I demonstrate in the preceding section, Tiger automatically opens a tiny hole (called a *port* by net-types) in your firewall to allow just that type of communication to your iMac.

For example, if you decide to allow FTP (File Transfer Protocol) access on the Services pane (within System Preferences, on our old friend the Sharing pane), Tiger automatically enables the check box to allow FTP access on the Firewall panel. (You can also control which ports are active directly from the Firewall panel, just in case.)

You can also add ports for applications that aren't on the firewall's Allow list — this includes third-party Instant Messaging clients, multiplayer game servers, and the like.

 1. **Click New.**

 2. **Click the Port Name pop-up menu to display the default list of external network applications (which includes applications like ICQ, IRC, and Retrospect).**

    From here, you have two options:

    If the application is listed, you're in luck:

     a. *Click it.*

     b. *Click OK to open the default ports for that application.*

    If the application isn't listed

     a. *Click Other.*

     b. *Type the TCP Port and UDP port listed in the application's documentation.*

     c. *Click OK to open the ports you specified.*

Chapter 18

Communicating with Wireless Devices

*L*et's talk cordless. Your iMac is already pretty doggone all-inclusive because everything that most other computers string together with cords has been integrated into the iMac's case, including the monitor and speakers. Depending on the connection options that you choose when you buy your iMac (or what you've added since), the only cord that you absolutely need might be your AC power cord.

For most of us, this introduces an entirely new realm of possibilities . . . and that results in more questions. Exactly how do other wireless devices communicate with your iMac? Can you really share the data on your iMac with your cellphone or your PDA? Can you sit in the comfort of your overstuffed recliner and watch a DVD from 15 feet away?

In this chapter, I describe to you what's cooking in the world of wireless devices. I won't delve into wireless Ethernet networking between your Mac and other computers — that's covered in depth within the confines of Chapter 17 — but I cover the wireless Bluetooth connections that you can make with other devices besides computers.

Bluetooth Is Not a Pirate (Matey)

Originally, wireless computer connections were limited to *IR* (short for infrared) and 802.11b, or the original Wi-Fi specification, for wireless Ethernet networks. This was fine — after all, what were you gonna connect to your Mac besides other computers? Ah, but progress marches on.

A little Danish history

Enter the explosion in popularity of modern cellphones and personal digital assistants (PDAs). In 1998, a consortium of big-name cellphone, PDA, and computer laptop manufacturers decided that their products needed a method of communicating with each other. This new wireless standard needed to be inexpensive and consume as little battery power as possible, so designers decided to keep the operational distance limited to a maximum of about 30 feet. Plus, the idea was to keep this new wireless system as hassle-free as possible: Everyone agreed that you should simply be able to walk within range of another device, and the two would immediately link up automatically. Thus *Bluetooth* was born!

Bluetooth has been incorporated into a whole range of peripherals and devices, including

- ✔ Cellphones
- ✔ PDAs
- ✔ Laptops
- ✔ Wireless computer peripherals such as keyboards and mice
- ✔ Printers
- ✔ Music players
- ✔ Headphones

Does the name Bluetooth sound faintly like Viking-speak to you? It should. For some absolutely ridiculous reason, the companies that developed the Bluetooth standard decided to name their creation after the 10th century Danish king Harald Blatand, nicknamed Bluetooth, who succeeded in joining Denmark and Norway in a political alliance. Hence the rather Viking and runic-looking Bluetooth symbol. (Geez, these folks need to take a day off. Read comic books, or play with a Slinky. *Something.*)

Is your iMac Bluetooth-ready?

Danish royalty aside, you'll be happy to know that Apple includes Bluetooth as standard equipment on today's iMac models. However, if you're using an older iMac and you didn't order your computer with Bluetooth built in, you're currently out of the Bluetooth loop.

Yes, Virginia, you can broadcast your music

If you've been following the Apple scene for the last year or so, you might already know about another of Apple's wireless success stories: the AirPort Express Base Station. Okay, I'm guilty — the AirPort Express is actually covered in Chapter 17. However, I do also want to mention it here because you can use one of these neat devices to stream music to any room (and any standard stereo system) in your house, and that counts as wireless device-style magic to me.

Naturally, you need an existing AirPort Extreme wireless network (connected to your iMac) that's already operating in order to send your music across the airwaves. In essence, you're using the AirPort Express as a music receiver instead of a base station. All your iTunes playlists are sent over the wireless connection to the AirPort Express unit, which in turn sends it across a standard Audio Out cable to the Line In jack or optical digital connector on your stereo.

Here's how simple it is: You plug the AirPort Express into the AC wall socket next to your stereo or boom box (in fact, even a set of AC or battery-powered speakers will work) and connect an Audio Out cable from the Base Station to the sound system. Wait until the status light turns green to indicate that the unit is online. Then run the AirPort Express Assistant on your iMac, which leads you through the setup process with onscreen prompts.

iTunes recognizes your remote audio hookup automatically. All you have to do is click the remote unit in the pop-up menu at the bottom-right corner of the iTunes window, and you're suddenly Wolfman Jack!

However, you don't need to pitch your older iMac if it doesn't have the Bluetooth hardware you crave! You can add Bluetooth capability to your computer with a simple USB Bluetooth adapter. Figure 18-1 illustrates the USB Bluetooth adapter from Belkin (www.belkin.com), which sells online for about $30. It includes automatic data encryption, which is necessary only if there's a hacker within about 30 feet of your computer, but more security is always better in my book. The adapter can link up with up to seven other Bluetooth devices simultaneously. (Come to think of it, there were a lot of people within 30 feet of my iMac during my last LAN party bash. I guess this stuff really *is* important!)

Tiger and Bluetooth, together forever

You'd expect a modern, high-tech operating system like Mac OS X to come with Bluetooth drivers. You'd be right, but Apple has gone a step further: Tiger comes with a System Preferences pane and a utility application to help your iMac connect with the Bluetooth devices that are likely hanging out in your coat pockets.

Figure 18-1:
A wireless
Bluetooth
adapter
allows any
iMac to join
in the fun.

The Bluetooth pane in System Preferences allows you to

✔ **Set up new Bluetooth devices.** Click the Devices tab and then click Setup New Device to run the Bluetooth Setup Assistant, which configures Bluetooth devices for use with Tiger.

By following the device-specific onscreen instructions, you can choose to set up a number of common Bluetooth toys, including keyboards, mice, cellphones, and printers — or you can work with other types of devices by choosing Other. The Setup Assistant searches for your Bluetooth device and makes sure that it's ready to party with your iMac.

Make sure that your Bluetooth device is in range and *discoverable* (more on this in the next section) before you run the Bluetooth Setup Assistant.

✔ **Configure Bluetooth connections.** Click the Sharing tab to create, remove, enable, or disable your Bluetooth connections, using them as virtual serial ports (for the simple transfer of data) or virtual modems (for bidirectional transfers, like using an Internet connection through a Bluetooth cellphone). The two different types of data exchange that you can enable or disable from this panel are

  • **File transfers:** Bluetooth devices can browse the folder that you specify and receive files from your iMac.

  • **File exchanges:** Your iMac can browse and receive files from Bluetooth devices.

These openings to the outside world are presented as individual connections in the Service Name list, and you can toggle them on and off individually. You can also specify whether a Bluetooth port is encrypted. Figure 18-2 shows an active Bluetooth virtual modem that's set up to allow my iMac to sync up with my Palm Pilot, using the Bluetooth-PDA-Sync service.

Figure 18-2:
You can add, delete, enable or disable Bluetooth ports from the Sharing tab.

When you know that you won't be using Bluetooth devices — like while you're on the road — disable a Bluetooth service on a laptop to help conserve battery power.

The other Bluetooth resource that you can use is the standalone application *Bluetooth File Exchange*. (Yes, you can call it *BFE* if you like. I do whenever possible.) You have to launch BFE the old-fashioned way — it's located in your Utilities folder, inside your Applications folder. Much like a traditional FTP (File Transfer Protocol) application, double-clicking the Bluetooth File Exchange icon presents you with a file selection dialog — you're choosing the file(s) you want to send to the connected Bluetooth device! You can also elect to browse the files on a networked Bluetooth device so that you can see what the owner of that device is offering.

The Bluetooth icon appears in the System Preferences window only if your iMac has Bluetooth hardware.

You can also set up your defaults for file exchanges from the Bluetooth pane in System Preferences. Click the Sharing tab and then select the Bluetooth File Exchange check box to display the settings that you see in Figure 18-3. Here you can control what Tiger does when you receive files or Personal Information Manager (PIM) data with Bluetooth File Exchange. For instance, with these settings, Tiger can

➤ Prompt you for permission to receive each file or PIM item

➤ Accept all files and PIM items without restriction or prompting

➤ Save all incoming files and items to the folder that you specify

➤ Offer only the files and items in the folder that you specify when other Bluetooth items browse your iMac

Figure 18-3:
Configure
file
exchanges
within
System
Preferences.

Personally, I'm all for the defaults in Tiger for file exchanges because

- ✔ I want to know when someone's sending me something.
- ✔ I want anything I receive to be saved in my Documents folder.
- ✔ If I turn on File Transfer, I want to allow others to browse the contents of my Public folder.

However, feel free to adjust, enable, and disable to your heart's content.

Mr. Security speaks — yet again

From a security standpoint, several settings in the Bluetooth pane of System Preferences can really lock things down (or open things up) in Bluetooth networking.

The settings in question include

- ✔ **Your Discovery status (Settings tab):** Click the Settings tab to display the pane that you see in Figure 18-4. When the Discoverable check box is enabled, other Bluetooth devices in range can recognize that your computer has a Bluetooth port ready. Naturally, you usually want this enabled so that your devices can automatically connect to each other, but you can disable it and connect manually if you want to keep strange Bluetooth devices at arm's length.

✔ **Encryption (Sharing tab):** I *always* recommend that you force other Bluetooth devices to encrypt the connection because it once again helps ensure that others don't sidle up to your iMac and start pulling down files or your PIM data.

Each service in the Service Name list on the Sharing pane has a check box in the Encrypted column (denoted by the key icon). Leave this check box enabled on each service, and you'll be a happy puppy.

✔ **Require Pairing for Security (Sharing tab):** When this check box is enabled, the selected service has to be *paired* with your cellphone or Bluetooth device. A passkey is entered when you set up the device on your iMac, and that passkey must also be entered into your device. (This is a one-time deal, so you don't need to remember the passkey.) If a Bluetooth connection is attempted and the passkeys don't match, the link is disabled, and the connection is broken.

✔ **Show Bluetooth Status in the Menu Bar (Settings tab):** I recommend that you enable this feature. The Bluetooth menu lets you conveniently toggle your iMac's Discovery status as well as set up a device or send and browse files. (You can also see what devices are connected to your iMac with the click of a menu icon. 'Nuff said.)

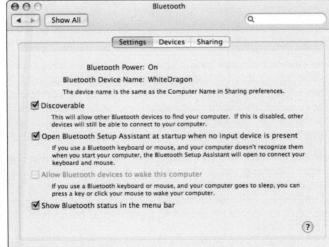

Figure 18-4: Keep tight control over Bluetooth connections from the Settings panel.

Concerning Wireless Keyboards and Mice

You can order your iMac in a fully wireless configuration — if you spend a little more, Apple throws in an internal Bluetooth adapter, a wireless Apple Pro keyboard, and a wireless Apple optical mouse. Everything's already included for you.

Then again, there are always the troublemakers (you talkin' to me?) who add Bluetooth separately using a USB adapter. Well, I've got good news for us bad boys and girls: A number of wireless Bluetooth keyboard/mouse packages are on the market, and any one of 'em should work fine with your iMac. In fact, you can buy Apple's wireless Bluetooth keyboard and mouse separately, for a total of about $120. Other offerings from Logitech (www.logitech.com) and our old buddy Microsoft run about the same amount.

When shopping for a Bluetooth keyboard/mouse desktop, keep these facts in mind:

✔ **Some keyboards are created more than equal.** Many of today's third-party keyboards are completely encrusted with extra function buttons that do everything from opening your e-mail application to searching your kitchen cabinets for another can of spray cheese.

I like these programmable function keys — they can bring up your favorite applications with a single keystroke while you're relaxing 20 feet away — so look for the keyboard that offers the most programmable keys in your price range.

✔ **Rodents crave energy.** Does the wireless mouse come with its own recharging stand? If so, that's a big plus. Depending on how much you use your iMac, a mouse that runs on standard batteries can go through a set in as little as a month's time! (Not surprisingly, many computer owners use rechargeable batteries in their wireless mice.) In fact, some wireless mice include an on/off switch to help conserve battery power.

✔ **Wireless doesn't always mean Bluetooth.** Just because a keyboard or mouse is wireless doesn't automatically make it a Bluetooth device. There are plenty of wireless RF (radio frequency) devices out there, too. These toys need their own transmitters, which are usually USB-based as well, so things can get kind of confusing. Therefore, read the box or technical specifications carefully to make sure you're buying Bluetooth.

✔ **Bluetooth stuff isn't self-cleaning.** Sure, your new wireless keyboard and mouse can hang out with you on the sofa, but that doesn't mean that they're happy sharing your nacho puffs and grape soda. Look for an optical mouse that doesn't use a ball, and check whether a prospective keyboard can be easily cleaned and maintained before you buy it.

Most Bluetooth devices are controlled through the Bluetooth pane in System Preferences. However, wireless keyboards and mice are a special case because they're monitored through the Bluetooth section of the Keyboard & Mouse pane, as shown in Figure 18-5. (You can even add a new wireless device from this panel — geez, those Apple designers give you a dozen roads to the same spot on the map, don't they?)

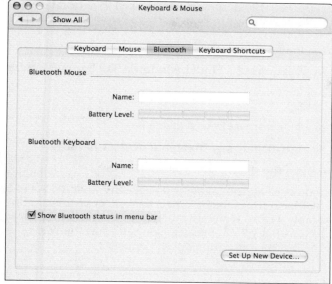

Figure 18-5:
Check your
Bluetooth
keyboard
and mouse
battery
levels.

Getting Everything in iSync

No jokes about boy bands, please. *iSync* is the data transfer and synchronizing utility application that ships with Tiger, and it works fine with both wired and wireless Bluetooth connections. The difference is between Bluetooth File Exchange and iSync is a matter of intelligence:

- BFE merely transfers files and dumps them in the folders that you specify.

- iSync actually copies and updates your Address Book, Safari, and iCal information between devices. iSync compares the information on both your iMac and your devices and makes sure that they end up the same.

iSync also allows you to synchronize data between multiple computers using your .Mac membership so that your contacts, bookmarks, and calendar data on your iBook matches the data on your iMac. You can control what gets sent from the .Mac pane in System Preferences. (For more on .Mac, visit the confines of Chapter 9.)

Just because your phone or PDF supports Bluetooth *doesn't* mean that iSync is guaranteed to work. I know a couple of Mac owners who are still seething over their incompatible devices. For a complete list of the Bluetooth phones, PDAs, and other devices that work with iSync, visit

```
www.apple.com/isync/devices.html
```

After your supported Bluetooth device is linked to your iMac, follow these steps to add the new device to iSync and synchronize your data:

1. **Click the Finder icon on the Dock.**

2. **Click Applications in a Finder window's Sidebar and double-click iSync.**

3. **Press ⌘+N.**

   iSync displays the Add Device dialog box.

4. **Click Scan to display any Bluetooth devices in range.**

5. **Double-click the device that you want to use.**

   The window expands to allow you to specify what data is to be synchronized. (Other settings might appear as well, depending on the device. For example, Figure 18-6 illustrates the available data that can be synchronized with my iPod. Because you can't surf the Web on an iPod — *yet* — the Bookmarks option doesn't appear.)

Figure 18-6:
Specify the stuff to sync with an iPod.

6. **Mark the check boxes for each data type that you want to exchange.**

7. **Click Sync Devices.**

Never disconnect a device while a synchronization is in progress — you risk corrupting the data being transferred, or your iMac could lock up.

Deleting a calendar event or a contact on either your iMac or the Bluetooth device deletes that same data from the other machine! For example, if you decide you no longer need your personal contacts on your iMac at work and you delete 'em willy-nilly, *they'll be deleted from your PDA when you synchronize.* When I say that iSync creates a mirror image on both sides of the connection, I'm not lying — additions appear, and deletions disappear.

The Magic of Wireless Printing

To your iMac, a wireless Bluetooth printer is just another Bluetooth connection — but to you, it's the very definition of convenience, especially if desk space is limited next to your iMac. Just set that paper-producing puppy up anywhere in the 30-foot range, plug it in, set up the printer in Tiger, and let 'er rip.

Not all printer manufacturers produce Bluetooth models that communicate properly with your iMac. Make sure that the Bluetooth printer you buy supports HCRP. (Another jawbreaker acronym. This time it stands for *Hardcopy Cable Replacement Protocol.*)

You have two options to install a Bluetooth printer:

- ✔ Whenever possible, use the printer manufacturer's software (a printer might require a driver that a typical Bluetooth device doesn't need).

- ✔ You can usually successfully set up a printer via the Bluetooth Setup Assistant, which you can run from the Devices pane in the Bluetooth pane of System Preferences:

  a. *Make sure your printer is set as discoverable.*

    Check your printer manual to determine how to switch your printer to discoverable mode.

  b. *Click the Set Up New Device button.*

  c. *Choose to install a printer.*

  d. *Follow the onscreen instructions.*

Luckily, after you successfully set up a Bluetooth printer, you can just press ⌘+P to open the Print dialog and choose that printer from the Printer pop-up menu. No big whoop . . . and that's the way it *should* be.

Part VI

The Necessary Evils: Troubleshooting, Upgrading, Maintaining

The 5th Wave   By Rich Tennant

TROUBLE ON THE SET

©RICHTENNANT

All the software in the world won't make this a great film. Only you can, Rusty. Only you have the guts and determination to be the finest Frisbee catching dog in this dirty little town. Now come on Rusty—it's magic time.

We're losing the light, Dad.

In this part . . .

No computer is *completely* trouble-free — and if your iMac starts acting strangely (like a Windows PC), the troubleshooting tips you find in this part can help you get your favorite machine back to normal. I also provide you with all the guidance you need to maintain your iMac properly, and step-by-step instructions for upgrading your computer with goodies like additional RAM or external devices.

Chapter 19

It Just . . . Sits . . . There

I wish you weren't reading this chapter.

Because you are, I can only surmise that you're having trouble with your iMac, and that it needs fixing. (The other possibility — that you just like reading about solving computer problems — is more attractive, but much more problematic.)

Consider this chapter a crash course in the logical puzzle that is computer *troubleshooting*: namely, the art of finding out What Needs Fixing. You also see what you can do when you just plain can't fix the problem by yourself.

Oh, and you're going to encounter a lot of Tips and Mark's Maxims in this chapter — all of them learned the hard way, so I recommend committing them to memory on the spot!

Can You Troubleshoot? Yes, You Can!

Anyone can troubleshoot. Put these common troubleshooting myths to rest:

✓ **It takes a college degree in computers to troubleshoot.** Tell that to my troubleshooting kids in junior high. They'll think it's a hoot because they have Apple computers of their own in the classroom. You can follow all the steps in this chapter without any special training.

✔ **I'm to blame.** Ever heard of viruses? Failing hardware? Buggy software? Any of those things can be causing the problem. Heck, even if you do something by accident, I'm willing to bet it wasn't on purpose. It's Mark's Maxim time:

Don't beat yourself up — your iMac can be fixed.™

✔ **I need to buy expensive utility software.** Nope. You can certainly invest in a commercial testing and repair utility if you like. My favorite is TechTool Pro from Micromat (www.micromat.com), but a third-party utility isn't a requirement for troubleshooting. (I would, however, consider an antivirus application as a must-have, and you should have one already. Hint, hint.)

✔ **There's no hope if I can't fix it.** Sure, parts fail, and computers crash, but your Apple Service Center can repair just about any problem. And (ahem) if you've backed up your iMac (like I preach throughout this book), you'll keep that important data (even if a new hard drive is in your future).

✔ **It takes forever.** Wait until you read the Number One Rule in the next section; the first step takes but 30 seconds and often solves the problem. Naturally, not all problems can be fixed so quickly, but if you follow the procedures in this chapter, you should fix your iMac (or at least know that the problem requires outside help) in a single afternoon.

With those myths banished for good, you can get down to business and start feeling better soon.

Basic Troubleshooting 101

In this section, I walk you through my Should-Be-Patented Troubleshooting Tree as well as Tiger's built-in troubleshooting application, Disk Utility. I also introduce you to a number of keystrokes that can make your iMac jump through hoops.

The Number One Rule: Reboot!

Yep, it sounds silly, but the fact is that rebooting your iMac can often solve a number of problems. If you're encountering these types of strange behavior with your iMac, a reboot might be all you need to heal

✔ Intermittent problems communicating over a network

✔ A garbled screen, strange colors, or screwed-up fonts

✔ The Swirling Beach Ball of Doom that won't go away after several minutes

✔ An application that locks up

✔ An external device that seems to disappear or can't be opened

To put it succinctly, here's a modest Mark's Maxim:

Always try a reboot before beginning to worry. *Always.*™

If you're in the middle of a document, try to save all your open documents before you reboot. That might not be possible, but try to save what you can.

If you need to force an application to quit so you can reboot, follow these steps to squash that locked application:

1. Click the Apple (🍎) menu and choose Force Quit.

The dialog that you see in Figure 19-1 appears on your screen.

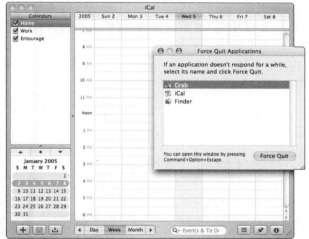

Figure 19-1:
Force a recalcitrant application to take off.

2. Click the offending application and then click the Force Quit button.

If you can get everything to quit, you should be able to click the Apple menu and choose Shut Down without a problem.

If your iMac simply won't shut down (or you can't get the offending application to quit), then do what must be done:

1. Press and hold your iMac's Power button until it shuts itself off.

You have to wait about four seconds for your iMac to turn itself off.

2. Press the Power button again to restart the computer.

Why is rebooting so darned effective?

Rebooting fixes problems because it resets everything. Your network connection, for example, might be acting up or have timed out, and rebooting restores it. Rebooting also fixes problems due to brownouts or those notorious AC power flickerings that we all notice from time to time. Such interruptions in constant juice might not bother you or me (or your less-intelligent toaster), but they can play tricks on your iMac that rebooting will fix.

After everything is back up, check whether the problem is still apparent. If you use your iMac for an hour or two and the problem doesn't reoccur, you've likely fixed it!

Special keys that can come in handy

A number of keys have special powers over your iMac. No, I'm not kidding! These keys affect how your iMac starts up, and they can really come in handy whilst troubleshooting.

Tricks you can do with your friendly Shift key

The Shift key has a number of special functions:

- ✔ **Disable Automatic Login:** Hold down the left Shift key and hold the mouse button down after the screen lights up.
- ✔ **Prevent your Login Items from running:**
  - • If Tiger displays a *multiuser login screen,* hold down Shift at the login screen while you click the Login button.
  - • If *your iMac doesn't display a login screen,* hold down Shift either when you push your iMac Power button or immediately after the screen blanks during a restart.

Startup keys

Table 19-1 provides the lowdown on startup keys. Hold the indicated key down either *when you push your iMac Power button* or *immediately after the screen blanks during a restart.*

Table 19-1	Startup Keys and Their Tricks
Key	**Effect on Your iMac**
C	Boots from the CD or DVD that's loaded in your optical drive
Media Eject	Ejects the CD or DVD in your optical drive
Option	Displays a system boot menu, allowing you to choose the operating system
Shift	Prevents your Login Items from running
T	Starts your iMac in FireWire Target Disk mode
⌘+V	Show Mac OS X Console messages
⌘+S	Starts your iMac in Single User mode
⌘+Option+P+R	Resets Parameter RAM (PRAM)

Some of the keys/combinations in Table 19-1 might never be necessary for your machine, but you might be instructed to use them by an Apple technician. I'll warrant that you'll use at least the C startup key fairly often.

All hail Disk Utility, the troubleshooter's friend

Tiger's *Disk Utility* is a handy tool for troubleshooting and repairing your hard drive. It's in the Utilities folder within your Applications folder.

Fire up Disk Utility, click the First Aid tab, and you see the rather powerful-looking window shown in Figure 19-2.

Danger, Will Robinson!

Many Disk Utility functions can actually **wipe your hard drives clean of data** instead of repairing them! These advanced functions aren't likely to help you with troubleshooting a problem with your existing volumes anyway.

Remember: Don't use these Disk Utility functions unless an Apple technician *tells* you to use them: *partitioning and erasing drives, setting up RAID arrays,* or *restoring files from disk images.*

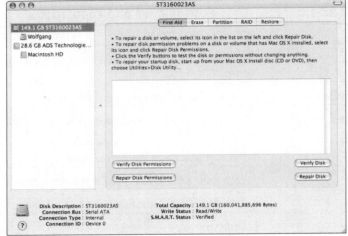

Figure 19-2:
The physician of hard drives — Tiger's Disk Utility.

In the left column of the Disk Utility window, you can see

- ✓ The *physical* hard drives in your system (the actual hardware)
- ✓ The *volumes* (the data stored on the hard drives)

  You can always tell a volume because it's indented underneath the physical drive entry.

- ✓ CD or DVD discs currently loaded on your iMac
- ✓ USB or FireWire Flash drives

For example, in Figure 19-2, I have two hard drives (the 149.1GB and 28.6GB entries), and each of those hard drives has a single volume (the Wolfgang and the Macintosh HD entries, respectively).

The information at the bottom of the Disk Utility window contains the specifications of the selected drive or volume . . . things like capacity, free space, and the number of files and folders for a volume, or connection type and total capacity for a drive.

Repairing disk permissions

Because Tiger is built on a UNIX base, lots of permissions can apply to the files on your drive — that is, who can open (or read or change) every application, folder, and document on your hard drive. Unfortunately, these permissions are often messed up by wayward applications or power glitches. And if the permissions on a file are changed, often applications lock up or refuse to run altogether, or application installers that do a sub-par job of cleaning up after themselves.

I recommend repairing your disk permissions with Disk Utility once a week. (Figure 19-3 shows a permissions repair sweep on my internal hard drive's volume.) Use these steps to repair permissions on your iMac's hard drive:

1. **Save and close any open documents and also make sure that you're logged in with an admin account.**

   Chapter 16 shows you how to log in as an admin user.

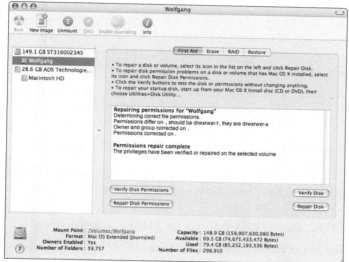

Figure 19-3:
A successful run, using Repair Disk Permissions.

2. **Double-click the Disk Utility icon in the Utilities folder.**

3. **Click the volume that you want to check.**

4. **Click the Repair Disk Permissions button.**

   I don't worry about verifying. If something's wrong, you end up clicking Repair Disk Permissions, anyway. Just click Repair Disk Permissions; if nothing pops up, that's fine.

5. **To finish the process, always reboot after repairing permissions.**

   This shows you whether a problem has been corrected!

Repairing disks

Disk Utility can check the format and health of both hard drives and volumes with Verify Disk — and, if the problem can be corrected, fix any error using Repair Disk.

Using Disk Utility to repair your hard drive carries a couple of caveats:

✔ **You can't verify or repair the *boot disk* or *boot volume*.** This actually makes sense because you're using that disk and volume right now.

To verify or repair your boot hard drive, you need to boot from your Mac OS X installation disc by using the C startup key. (Refer to Table 19-1 for keys that come in handy.) After your iMac has booted using the Mac OS X installation disc, choose the Utilities menu and click Disk Utility.

You should be able to select your boot hard drive or volume, and the Verify Disk and Repair Disk buttons should be enabled.

✔ **You can't repair CDs and DVDs.** CDs and DVDs are read-only media and thus can't be repaired at all (at least by Disk Utility).

If your iMac is having trouble reading a CD or DVD, either wipe the disc with a soft cloth to remove dust, oil, and fingerprints, or invest in a disc-cleaning contrivance of some sort.

If you need to verify and repair a disk or volume, follow these steps:

1. **If you need to repair your *boot drive and volume*, save all your open documents and reboot from either *an external drive* or *your Mac OS X Installation disc*.**

2. **Double-click the Disk Utility icon in the Utilities folder.**

3. **In the list at the left side of the Disk Utility window, click the disk or volume that you want to check.**

4. **Click the Repair Disk button.**

5. **If changes were made (or if you had to boot from a disc or external drive), reboot after repairing the disk or volume.**

Mark's iMac Troubleshooting Tree

As the hip-hop artists say, "All right, kick it." And that's just what my iMac Troubleshooting Tree is here for. If rebooting your iMac hasn't solved the problem, follow these steps in order (until either the solution is found, or you run out of steps — more on that in the next section).

Step 1: Investigate recent changes

This is a simple step that many novice Mac owners forget. Simply retrace your steps and consider what changes you made recently to your system. Here are the most common culprits:

✔ **Did you just finish installing a new application?** Try uninstalling it by removing the application directory and any support files that it might have added to your system. (And keep your applications current with the most recent patches and updates from the developer's Web site.)

From time to time, an application's *preference file* — which stores all the custom settings you make — can become corrupted. Although the application itself is okay, it might act strangely or refuse to launch. To check your preference files, try scanning your iMac's applications with Preferential Treatment, a freeware AppleScript utility by Jonathan Nathan, available from his Web site at http://homepage.mac.com/jonn8/as.

✔ **Did you just apply an update or patch to an application?** Uninstall the application and reinstall it without applying the patch. If your iMac suddenly works again, check the developer's Web site or contact its technical support department to report the problem.

✔ **Did you just update Tiger by using Software Update?** Updating Tiger can introduce problems within your applications that depend on specific routines and system files. Contact the developer of the application and look for updated patches that bring your software in line with the Tiger updates. (And use Software Update in automatic mode to check for Mac OS X updates at least once a week.)

✔ **Did you just make a change within System Preferences?** Return the options that you changed back to their original settings; then consult Chapter 6 for information on what might have gone wrong. (If the setting in question isn't in Chapter 6, consider searching Tiger's online help or the Apple support Web site for more clues.)

✔ **Did you just connect (or reconnect) an external device?** Try unplugging the device and rebooting to see whether the problem disappears. Remember that many peripherals need software drivers to run — and without those drivers installed, they won't work correctly. Check the device's manual or visit the company's Web site to search for software that you might need.

If you haven't made any significant changes to your system before you encountered the problem, proceed to the next step.

Step 2: Run Disk Utility

The preceding section shows how to repair disk permissions on your Tiger boot drive.

If you're experiencing hard drive problems, consider booting from your Mac OS X Installation CD or DVD to run a full-blown Repair Disk checkup on your boot volume.

Should I reinstall Mac OS X?

This question seems to get a lot of attention on Mac-related Internet discussion boards and Usenet newsgroups — and the answer is a definitive *perhaps.* (I know, that's really helpful.)

Here's the explanation. You *shouldn't* lose a single byte of data by reinstalling Mac OS X, so it's definitely okay to try it. However, reinstalling Mac OS X isn't a universal balm that fixes all software errors because the problem that you're encountering might be due to a buggy application, or a hard drive that's going critical, or a video card with faulty memory modules. If the trouble you're having is due to a corrupted Mac OS X System Folder, reinstalling Tiger might or might not fix the problem.

Therefore, the debate rages on. I would certainly follow the iMac Troubleshooting Tree all the way to the end before I would even consider reinstalling Tiger, and I would recommend that you contact an Apple support technician on the Apple Web site before you take this step.

Step 3: Check your cables

Cables work themselves loose, and they fail from time to time. Check all your cables to your external devices — make sure that they're snug — and verify that everything's plugged in and turned on. (Oh, and don't forget to check for crimps in your cables or even Fluffy's teeth marks.)

If a FireWire or USB device acts up, swap cables around to find whether you have a bad one. A faulty cable can leave you pulling your hair out in no time.

Step 4: Check your Trash

Check the contents of your Trash to see whether you recently deleted files or folders by accident. Click the Trash icon on the Dock once to display the contents. If something's been deleted by mistake, drag it back to its original folder, and try running the application again.

I know this one from personal experience. A slight miscalculation while selecting files to delete made an application freeze every time I launched it.

Step 5: Check your Internet, wireless, and network connections

Now that always-on DSL and cable modem connections to the Internet are common, don't forget an obvious problem: Your iMac can't reach the Internet because your ISP is down!

You can check your Internet connection by pinging www.apple.com, as shown in Figure 19-4.

1. **Open your Utilities folder (inside your Applications folder).**

2. **Double-click Network Utility.**

3. **Click the Ping button.**

4. **Enter** www.apple.com **in the Address box.**

5. **Click Ping.**

> You should see successful ping messages similar to those in Figure 19-4. If you don't, your ISP or network is likely experiencing problems.

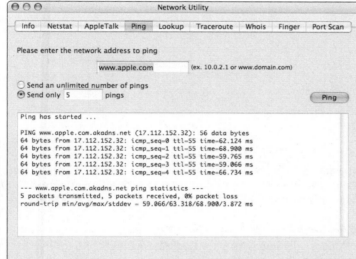

Figure 19-4: Ping apple.com to check your Internet connection.

Step 6: Think virus

If you've made it to this point, it's time to run a full virus scan — and make sure that your antivirus application has the latest updated data files, too. Figure 19-5 illustrates my antivirus application of choice, Virus Barrier X from Intego (www.intego.com), performing a full system scan. (If a virus is detected and your antivirus application can't remove it, try *quarantining* it instead, which basically disables the virus-ridden application and prevents it from infecting other files.)

Step 7: Disable your Login Items

Mac OS X might encounter problems with applications that you've marked as Login Items within System Preferences. In this step, I show you how to identify login problems and how to fix 'em.

Checking for problems

It's time to use another nifty startup key (refer to Table 19-1). This time, hold down Shift during start up (if your iMac doesn't display the Login screen) or hold down Shift at the Login screen while you click the Login button.

Figure 19-5:
Virus
Barrier X,
hard at work
detecting
malicious
infections.

These tricks disable your account's Login Items, which are run automatically every time you log in to your iMac. If one of these Login Items is to blame, your iMac will simply encounter trouble every time you log in.

Finding the Login Item that's causing trouble

If your iMac works fine with your Login Items disabled, follow this procedure for each item in the Login Items list:

1. **Open System Preferences, click Accounts, and then click the Login Items button.**

2. **Delete the item from the list; then reboot normally.**

   You can delete the selected item by clicking the Delete button, which bears a minus sign.

   When your iMac starts up normally with Login items enabled, you've discovered the perpetrator. You'll likely need to delete that application and reinstall it. (Don't forget to add each of the *working* Login items back to the Login items list!)

Step 8: Turn off your screen saver

This is a long shot, but it isn't unheard of to discover that a faulty, bug-ridden screen saver has locked up your iMac. (If you aren't running one of the Apple-supplied screen savers and your computer never wakes up from Sleep mode or hangs while displaying the screen saver, you've found your prime suspect.)

Open System Preferences, click Desktop & Screen Saver, click the Screen Saver button, and then either *switch to an Apple screen saver* or *drag the Start slider to Never.*

If this fixes the problem, you can typically remove the screen saver completely by deleting the offending saver application in the Screen Savers folder inside your Mac OS X Library folder. If you can't find the screen saver application, try typing the saver name in the Spotlight search box.

Step 9: Run System Profiler

Ouch. You've reached Step 9, and you still haven't uncovered the culprit. At this point, you've narrowed the possibilities to a serious problem, like bad hardware or corrupted files in your Mac OS X System Folder. Fortunately, Tiger provides System Profiler, which displays real-time information on the hardware in your system. Click the Apple menu and choose About This Mac; then click More Info. Figure 19-6 illustrates a typical healthy result from one of the Hardware categories, Disc Burning. Click each one of the Hardware categories in turn, double-checking to make sure that everything looks okay.

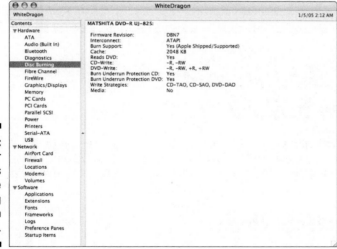

Figure 19-6: Check your iMac's hardware by using System Profiler.

You don't have to understand all the technical hieroglyphics, but if a Hardware category doesn't return what you expect or displays an error message, that's suspicious. (If your iMac doesn't have a specific type of hardware onboard — including Bluetooth, Fibre Channel, PC Cards, PCI Card, or Parallel SCSI hardware — you won't get information from those categories.)

Diagnostics shows whether your iMac passed the Power On self-test.

Take the cover off!

You can diagnose some hardware problems if you remove the back cover from your computer. (I show you how to take the cover off in Chapter 20.)

Carefully reconnect the power cord to the back of the computer and plug it in to the AC socket; then look for the white arrow in the middle of the motherboard. The arrow points to four LED diagnostic lights on the motherboard.

Each diagnostic light indicates a specific condition. To wit

✔ If LED 1 is lit *and* your iMac is turned **off** *and* the power cord is connected, your power supply is working correctly.

✔ If LED 2 is lit *and* your iMac is turned **on** — naturally, the power cord is connected —

it's another indication that your power supply is okay. (Be careful not to touch the internal circuitry of your iMac while it's turned on. It's okay, however, to press the Power button.)

✔ If LED 3 is lit *and* your iMac is turned **on**, a video signal is being generated, and the LCD display is receiving the signal. (Note, however, that this doesn't mean the LCD panel isn't broken — it only indicates the panel is receiving the signal.)

✔ If LED 4 is lit at any time, you've got an overheating problem. This light is always off when your iMac is turned **on** and the temperature is within the correct limits.

Okay, I Kicked It, and It Still Won't Work

Don't worry, friend reader — just because you've reached the end of my iMac tree doesn't mean you're out of luck. In this section, I discuss the online help available on Apple's Web site as well as local help in your own town.

Apple Help Online

If you haven't visited Apple's iMac Support site yet, run — don't walk — to www.apple.com/support/imac, where you can find

✔ **The iMac Troubleshooting Assistant,** which queries you on the symptoms being displayed by your iMac and offers possible solutions

✔ **The latest patches, updates, and how-to tutorials** for the iMac

- ✔ **The iMac and Mac OS X discussion boards,** moderated by Apple

- ✔ **Tools** for ordering spare parts, checking on your remaining warranty coverage, and searching the Apple Knowledge Base

- ✔ **Do-it-yourself instructions** (PDF files) that you can follow to repair or upgrade your iMac

At the time of this writing, Apple is even testing a real-time Web Chat Support system, where you can converse in real-time chat with an Apple technician. So far, I haven't needed it, but it sounds like a winning feature.

Local service, at your service

In case you need to take in your iMac for service, an Apple Store or Apple Authorized Service Provider is probably in your area. To find the closest service, launch Safari and visit

```
http://wheretobuy.apple.com/locator/service.html
```

That's the Find Service page on the Apple Web site. You can search by city and state or ZIP code. The results are complete with the provider's mailing address, Web site address, telephone number, and even a map of the location!

Always call your Apple service provider before you lug your (albeit lightweight) iMac all the way to the shop. Make sure that you know *your iMac's serial number* (which you can display in System Profiler) and *which version of Mac OS X you're using.*

Chapter 20

I Want to Add Stuff

"No iMac is an island." Somebody famous wrote that, I'm sure.

Without getting too philosophical — or invoking the all-powerful Internet yet again — the old saying really does make sense. All computer owners usually add at least one *peripheral* (external device), like a joystick, an iPod, a backup drive, or a scanner. I talk about the ports on your iMac in Chapter 1 . . . those holes aren't there to just add visual interest to the back end of your treasured iMac. Therefore, I cover your USB and FireWire ports (and what you can plug into them) in detail in this chapter.

Ah, but what about the stuff inside your iMac? That's where things get both interesting and scary at the same time. In this chapter, I describe what you can add to the innards of your computer as well as how to get inside there if you work up the courage to go exploring. (Don't tell your family or your friends, but opening up your iMac is as simple as loosening three screws. There's actually nothing to fear whatsoever. Just make it *sound* like *Mission: Impossible,* and folks will crown you their new resident techno-wizard!)

Getting inside Your iMac

This section is short for a reason. Apple designed the world's best all-in-one computer. That even includes making it EZ-Open — forgive me if your treasured supercomputer now reminds you of a longneck beer bottle. (Come to think of it, the level of technical knowledge required to gain access to either one is about the same.)

Here's the step-by-step procedure to reveal the guts of your iMac:

1. **Get ready to operate.**

   a. *Spread a clean towel on a stable work surface, like your kitchen table. (The towel helps protect your screen from scratches.)*

   b. *Find a Phillips screwdriver.*

   c. *Shut down your iMac.*

   d. *Unplug all cables from the computer.*

2. **Tilt the computer over and lay the screen flat on top of the towel.**

   Figure 20-1 shows this.

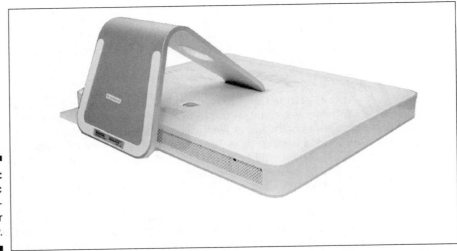

Figure 20-1:
Your iMac
is pre-
pared for
surgery.

3. **Loosen the three screws at the bottom of the computer's case.**

   Apple thought of everything! You can't lose these screws because they're *captive*. They actually stay in the back cover, so don't try to remove them completely.

4. **Grab the metal foot at the bottom of the case and carefully lift the back cover off the computer, as shown in Figure 20-2.**

   Don't touch anything inside the iMac unless you've *grounded* yourself. I cover this safety step in the sidebar "Let's get grounded!"

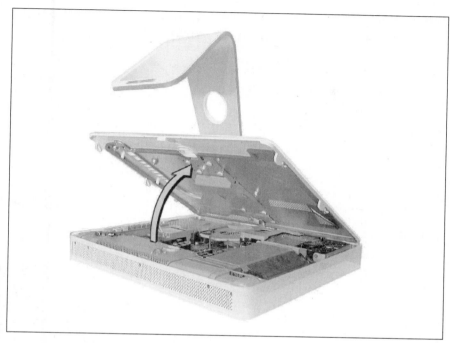

Figure 20-2:
Lift off the
back cover.

5. Stow the cover/foot assembly safely out of reach of kids and cats.

Tah-dah! That wasn't much of a challenge, was it? Here's your chance to gaze with rapt fascination at the bare innards of your favorite computer.

To put the back cover back on, just reverse the steps. (Rather like changing the oil on my Dad's 1970 Ford pickup truck.)

More Memory Will Help

Hey, wait a second. No *however* stuck on the end? You mean for once, there isn't an exception? Aren't all computers different? Just keep in mind this Mark's Maxim:

More memory helps.™

Period. End of statement. No matter what type of computer you own, how old it is, or what operating system you use, adding more memory to your system (to the maximum it supports) significantly improves the performance of your operating system (and practically every application that you run).

Let's get grounded!

Follow one cardinal rule when the unguarded insides of any computer are in easy reach: *Always ground yourself before you touch anything!* Your body can carry enough static electricity to damage the circuitry and chips that make up the brains of your iMac, and touching those parts without grounding yourself is an invitation for disaster.

Grounding yourself is easy to do, right inside your iMac. Just touch the metal cover at the bottom of the case chassis, right next to the power cord socket, for a couple of seconds.

After you ground yourself, you can then safely handle both the internal components of your iMac and any new hardware components that you might be installing (like memory modules or an Airport Extreme card).

If you walk anywhere in the room — hunting for a screwdriver, perhaps, or taking a sip of liquid reinforcement that you've stashed a comfortable distance away — you *must* ground yourself again before you get back to work. *Remember:* You can actually pick up a static charge by simply walking. Go figure.

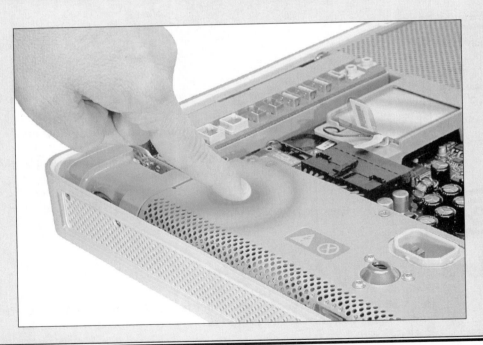

Memory maximizes the power of your computer: The more memory you have, the less data your iMac has to temporarily store on its hard drive. Without getting into virtual memory and other techno-gunk, just consider that extra memory as extra elbowroom for your applications and your documents. Believe me, both Mac OS X and Windows XP efficiently make use of every kilobyte of memory that you can provide.

Figuring out how much memory you have

To see how much memory you have in your computer, click the Apple menu (🍎) and choose About This Mac. Figure 20-3 shows the dialog.

Figure 20-3:
Find out how much memory your iMac has.

Your iMac has sockets for two PC3200 DDR SDRAM memory modules. (Don't fret over what all the abbreviations mean. Rest assured that this memory type is fast.) Currently, these modules are available with up to 1GB of memory, so you can install as much as 2GB of memory in your iMac.

How you plan memory upgrades depends on how much memory you want. If your iMac uses the single default 256MB module supplied by Apple, you have a couple of options:

✔ **Add up to 1GB of RAM** (1280MB total) by inserting a memory module in the empty slot. At the time of this writing, a gigabyte of memory module should set you back about $125 or so.

1280MB of memory is plenty for running applications from the iLife and iWork suites as well as any of the applications bundled with Tiger.

✔ **Install up to 2GB of total memory** by removing the standard 256MB module and inserting high-capacity modules in both slots.

If your primary applications include video editing, game playing, or image editing, you can use all the memory your iMac can hold.

Installing memory modules

I'm happy to report that adding extra memory to your system is one of the easiest internal upgrades that you can perform. Therefore, I recommend that you add your own memory yourself unless you simply don't want to mess with your iMac's internal organs. Your local Macintosh service specialist will be happy to install new RAM modules for you (for a price).

After you remove the back cover from your computer, as shown in the earlier section "Getting inside Your iMac," follow these steps to add extra memory:

1. *Ground thyself!*

   Check out the sidebar, "Let's get grounded!" in this chapter.

2. **Locate the memory modules within your iMac's svelte chassis.**

   Figure 20-4 illustrates their position.

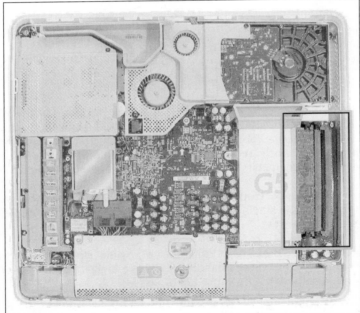

Figure 20-4: The two iMac memory slots are right here.

3. **Remove an existing memory module if you're replacing it.**

   To remove a memory module, gently press down on the two tabs at the ends of the socket (as shown in Figure 20-5) and then pull the module away from the socket.

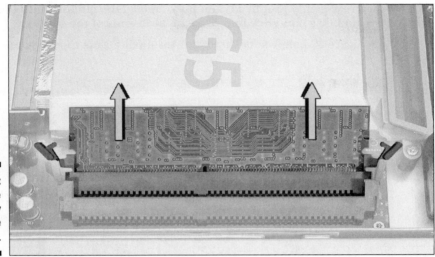

Figure 20-5:
Remove
a memory
module
like a pro.

Save the old module in the static-free packaging that held the new module. Your old RAM (which you can now sell on eBay) will be protected from static electricity.

4. **Position the new module in the socket.**

> *a. Line up the module's copper connectors toward the socket.*

> *b. Line up the notch in the module aligned with the matching spacer in the socket. See what I mean in Figure 20-6.*

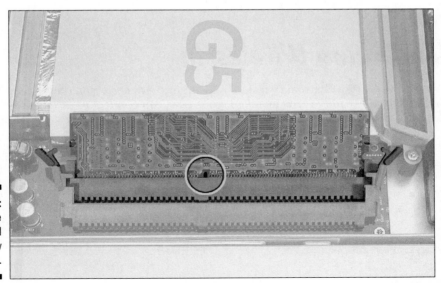

Figure 20-6:
Prepare
to install
the new
module.

5. Press gently (but firmly) on both ends of the module until the module's tabs click into place on both ends of the socket.

Figure 20-7 shows the direction you should press the module.

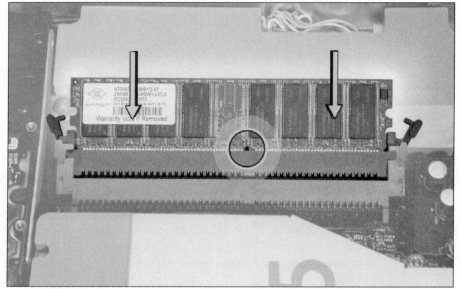

Figure 20-7:
Press the
new RAM
module into
place until
it locks.

6. Replace the back cover.

Read how in the earlier section, "Getting inside Your iMac."

Networking Wirelessly

An AirPort Extreme wireless networking card is a common upgrade. With one of these nifty cards installed, your iMac can connect to an existing wireless network in your home or business — as long as you're in range of the signal, of course — without connecting a single cable.

With the back cover removed from your iMac (read how earlier in this chapter), follow these steps to install an AirPort Extreme wireless card:

1. *Get grounded!*

Check out the sidebar "Let's get grounded!" elsewhere in this chapter.

2. Locate the wireless card channel, as shown in Figure 20-8.

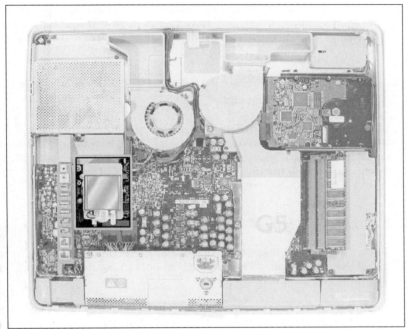

Figure 20-8:
Your AirPort
Extreme
card hangs
out here.

3. **Slide the AirPort card into the channel until you hear a click.**

   The AirPort card fits only one way in the channel. The end of the card should be flush with the guides at each side of the channel, and the jack on the card faces the bottom of the computer.

4. **Connect the round antenna cable to the matching jack at the end of the card.**

5. **Replace the back cover.**

That's it. You're ready to reconnect the cables that you *do* need.

Can I Upgrade My Hard Drive?

This is a trick question. Yes, you can upgrade your hard drive. But before you start cruisin' the Internet for a 320GB monster, I have two suggestions:

- ✔ **Don't upgrade your internal hard drive yourself.**

- ✔ **Be sure you really need a hard drive upgrade.**

  Apple's pretty generous when configuring hard drive storage for its base systems. (Current models run with either an 80GB or a 160GB drive.)

Most folks simply don't need more than 80GB of hard drive space. You're likely to find that you still have plenty of elbowroom for a typical family's needs on your hard drive unless you're heavily into

- Digital video (DV)
- Cutting-edge video games
- Tons of digital audio

If you're short on hard drive space, clean up your existing hard drive by deleting all the crud you don't need, such as game and application demos, duplicate or "work" copies of images and documents, archived files you've downloaded from the Internet, and the contents of your Trash.

Consider your external options

If you do need additional hard drive space, I recommend using an external drive! Use a high-speed FireWire or USB port to connect a second hard drive the quick and easy way.

Most of today's FireWire and USB peripherals don't even require the driver software that Mac old-timers remember with such hatred. You simply plug in a FireWire or USB device, and it works. You can move your external drive between different Macs with a minimum of fuss and bother.

An external hard drive can do anything that your internal hard drive can do. You can boot from it, for example, or install a different version of Mac OS X (great for beta testers like me).

There's one problem with external drives: Data transfers more slowly this way than via an internal drive. That's why most Mac owners use their external drives for storing little-used documents and applications. Their favorite applications and often-used documents are housed on the internal drive.

Putting a port to work

An iMac carries two kinds of high-speed ports. These are very similar in performance and operation. Either one is a good match for connecting any external device.

USB 2.0

The USB standard is popular because it's just as common in the PC world as in the Mac world. (Most PCs don't have a FireWire port.) Your iMac carries its USB 2.0 ports on the back of the case. Hardware manufacturers can make one USB device that works on both types of computers.

I heartily recommend that you avoid using any USB 1.1 devices (except, perhaps, a USB 1.1 keyboard or mouse). USB 1.1 is very slow compared with the USB 2.0 standard (although you can connect a USB 1.1 device to a USB 2.0 port with no problem at all). You should buy only USB 2.0 external hard drives, CD/DVD recorders, or Flash drives. The USB ports on the back of the standard Apple wired keyboard are USB 1.1 ports, which work fine with slower stuff like scanners, printers, and digital cameras. 'Nuff said.

FireWire 400

FireWire (also called *IEEE 1394*) is the best port for most digital video camcorders. Use your FireWire port for connecting external drives to your iMac — you'll find them on the back of your iMac's case.

Your iMac *does not* have FireWire 800 ports. (FireWire 800 is twice as fast as FireWire 400.) The physical connector is shaped differently, and buying a FireWire 800 device for your iMac is an expensive mistake.

Connecting an external drive

With FireWire or USB, you can install an external hard drive without opening your iMac's case:

1. **Connect the FireWire or USB cable betwixt the drive and your computer.**

2. **Plug the external drive into a convenient surge protector or UPS (uninterruptible power supply).**

3. **Switch on the external drive.**

4. **If the drive is unformatted, partition and format the external drive.**

    The drive comes with instructions or software for you to do this.

    The drive immediately appears on the Desktop.

Figure 20-9 illustrates my Mac OS X Desktop with my FireWire drive on board (complete with distinctive FireWire icon).

Gotta have internal

If you decide that you have to upgrade your existing internal hard drive — or if your internal drive fails and needs to be replaced — I strongly recommend that you take your iMac to an authorized Apple service center and allow the techs there to sell you a drive and make the swap. Here are three darned good reasons why:

✔ **Selection:** If you're worried about picking the proper drive, an Apple technician can order the right drive type and size for you . . . no worries.

✔ **Difficulty:** Swapping a hard drive in your iMac isn't anywhere as easy as adding RAM modules. You have to remove the optical drive first, for example, which can be very intimidating.

✔ **Backup:** That very same Apple service technician can back up all the data on your existing drive and move it to the new drive, so you won't lose a single document. That will save you time and possible angst.

If you're an experienced and confident techno-soul, you can find a PDF file detailing how you can remove your internal hard drive within the Support section of the Apple Web site (`www.apple.com/support/imac`).

Make certain that you've got a complete and up-to-date backup of your data before you remove your existing hard drive! Otherwise, you're walking into a field of land mines without a map.

Attractive Add-Ons

These USB and FireWire toys might add a cord to your collection at the back of your iMac, but they're well worth the investment, and they can really revolutionize how you look at technologies like television, digital audio, and computer gaming.

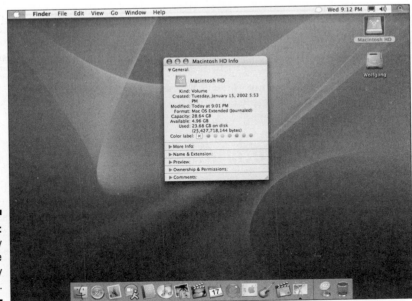

Figure 20-9:
That's my FireWire drive, ready for action.

Game controllers

If you're ready to take a shot at the enemy — whether they be Nazi soldiers, chittering aliens, or the latest jet fighters — you'll likely find your keyboard and mouse somewhat lacking. (And if that enemy happens to be a friend of yours playing across the Internet, you'll be ruthlessly mocked while you're fumbling for the right key combination.) Instead, either *pick up a USB joystick or gamepad* or *invest in a really whiz-bang game controller* like the Belkin Nostromo n50 SpeedPad ($35 from www.belkin.com), which incorporates a mini-keyboard and gamepad. (You can configure the keys on the Nostromo for each game you play!)

Video controllers

For armchair directors, specialized USB digital video controllers make editing easier. The ShuttleXpress from Contour Design (www.contourdesign.com) provides a five-button jog control that can be configured to match any DV editor. For $50, you'll have the same type of editing controller as dedicated video-editing stations costing several thousand dollars.

TV hardware

To watch (and record) the signal from your satellite or cable on your iMac, use an EyeTV digital video recorder from Elgato Systems (www.elgato.com) and avoid shelling out for a TiVo. The units include a 124-channel TV tuner and built-in MPEG encoder, so you can pause live TV and schedule recording times. EyeTV has a couple of products for your iMac: *EyeTV USB* ($169) and *EyeTV 200* ($329; this model uses a FireWire connection and a better MPEG encoder so you can capture DVD-quality video).

Audio hardware

Ready to put GarageBand to the test with your favorite version of *Chopsticks?* You'll need a USB keyboard; consider the eKeys 37 from M-Audio (www.m-audio.com), which retails for a mere $60. It provides 37 keys and uses a USB connection.

Another neat audio favorite of mine is the USB-powered radioSHARK from Griffin Technology (www.griffintechnology.com), which allows you to add AM/FM radio to your Mac, complete with recording capability, a pause feature, and scheduled recording, all for $70.

DVD recording

If you crave today's hottest DVD recording technology, look no farther than LaCie's 16X d2 DVD-RW/+RW dual-layer/dual-format DVD recorder! This FireWire jewel can burn 8.5GB of data onto a single disc, and ships complete with Roxio's Toast recording application. Read all the details at the LaCie site at www.lacie.com, where you can pick one up for about $200.

Chapter 21

Tackling the Housekeeping

*N*othing runs better than a well-oiled machine — and Tiger is no exception. With a little maintenance, you can ensure that your iMac is performing as efficiently as possible.

In this chapter, I demonstrate how you can make good use of every byte of storage space provided by your hard drive, and how to back up and restore that hard drive to an external drive or a DVD. Your hard drive also benefits from a periodic scan for permission errors.

Tiger's new Automator application is a great housekeeping tool: It allows your iMac to perform tasks automatically that used to require your attention. I show you how you can create Automator applications and set them up to run by themselves. (It sounds a little spooky, but you'll have a ball!)

And it's important to never forget about updating Mac OS X itself. But then again, if you configure Software Update to run automatically, you can live life free and easy, watching your favorite soaps and eating ice cream (or yogurt — your pick).

Cleaning Unseemly Data Deposits

Criminy! Where does all this stuff *come* from? Suddenly that spacious 80GB hard drive has 3GB left, and you start feeling pinched.

Before you consider buying a new external hard drive or upgrading your internal hard drive, take the smart step: "Sweep" your hard drive clean of unnecessary and space-hogging software.

Getting dirty (Or, cleaning things the manual way)

If you're willing to dig into your data a little, there's no reason to buy additional software to help you clean up your hard drive. All you really need is the willpower to announce, "I simply don't need this application any longer." (And sometimes, that's tougher than it might seem.)

Unnecessary files and unneeded folders

Consider all the stuff that you probably don't really need:

- Game demos and shareware that you no longer play (or even remember)
- Movie trailers and other QuickTime video files that have long since passed into obscurity
- Temporary files that you created and promptly forgot
- Log files that chronicle application installations and errors
- StuffIt archives that you downloaded and no longer covet
- iTunes music that no longer appeals to your ear

How hard is it to clean this stuff off your drive? Easier than you might think!

- Files are easily deleted.
- You can get rid of at least the lion's share of any application (often the whole application) by deleting its application folder that was created during the installation process.

Removing an application or file from your hard drive is usually two simple steps:

1. **Display the file or application folder in a Finder window.**

2. **Delete the file or folder with one of these steps:**

   - Drag the icon to the Trash.
   - Press ⌘+Delete.
   - Select the icon and click the Delete button on the Finder toolbar (if you've added one).

Truly, no big whoop.

Mac owners like you and I can once again feel superior to the XP Zombies because most Mac OS X applications don't need a separate, silly "uninstall" program. In fact, Macintosh software developers have always followed a simple general rule: All (or virtually all) of an application's support data should reside in a single folder.

Don't forget to actually *empty* the Trash, or you'll wonder why you aren't regaining any hard drive space. (Tiger works hard to store the contents of the Trash until you manually delete it, just in case you want to undelete something.) To get rid of that stuff permanently and reclaim the space

1. **Click the Trash icon on the Dock and hold the mouse button down until the pop-up menu appears.**

2. **Choose Empty Trash.**

Associated files in other folders

Some applications install files in different locations across your hard drive. (Applications in this category include Microsoft Office and Photoshop.) How can you clear out these "orphan" files after you delete the application folder?

The process is a little more involved than deleting a single folder, but it's still no big whoop. Here's the procedure:

1. **Click the Search text box in a Finder window.**

2. **Type the name of the application in the Search text box.**

   Figure 21-1 shows this search. I want to remove Corel Painter, so I searched for

   • Every file that has the word *Painter* in its name

   • Every HTML and PDF document that contains the word *Painter*

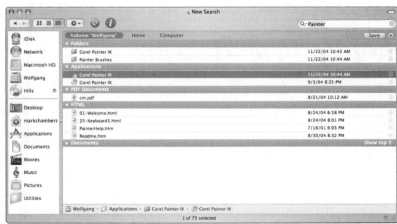

Figure 21-1: Mining a hard drive for additional files to delete.

3. **Decide which of these files belong to the to-be-deleted application.**

   Be sure that the files you choose to delete are part of the deleted application. For example, a text file with the name *Michelangelo, That Famous Painter* might not be part of Corel Painter.

   Many associated files either

   - Have the same icon as the parent application
   - Are in the Preferences, Caches, or Application Support folders

4. **Click the associated file(s) that you want to delete in the Search Results window and drag them to the Trash.**

   Don't empty the Trash immediately after you delete these files. Wait a few hours or a day. If you find that you've deleted a file you need, you can easily restore it from the Trash.

Using a commercial cleanup tool

If you'd rather use a commercial application to help you clean up your hard drive, a number of them are available — but most are shareware and perform only one task. For example, Doublet Scan from Hyperbolic Software (www. hyperbolicsoftware.com) finds only duplicate files on your hard drive, matching by criteria such as filename, size, and extension. It's a good tool at $30.

For a truly comprehensive cleanup utility, I recommend Spring Cleaning from Allume Systems (www.allume.com) — the same folks that produce the archiving utility StuffIt. Figure 21-2 illustrates the main menu of Spring Cleaning, which sells for $50. Not much crud squeaks by all those search routines, including duplicates, orphan preference files, and log files. Spring Cleaning even includes a separate feature called MacUninstaller that can help automate the steps that I cover in the preceding section.

Backing Up Your Treasure

Do it.

I'm not going to lecture you about backing up your hard drive . . . well, perhaps just for a moment. Imagine what it feels like to lose *everything* — names, numbers, letters, reports, presentations, saved games, photographs, and music. Then ask yourself, "Self, isn't all that irreplaceable stuff worth just a couple of hours every month?"

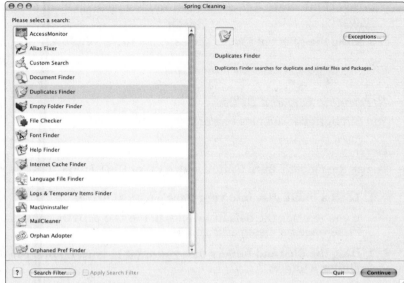

Figure 21-2:
Spring
Cleaning
helps keep
your data
ranch
squeaky
clean.

Time for a Mark's Maxim:

> ***Back up.* On a regular basis. Then store those DVDs or that external back-up device somewhere safe, away from calamities.™**

Take my word for it — you will thank me some day!

You can back up your files either by saving them or by creating a backup image.

Saving files

The simplest method of backing up files is simply to copy the files and folders to an external hard drive or a CD or DVD. Nothing fancy, but it works.

External hard drive

If you have an external hard drive on your iMac, you can drag files to it from the internal hard drive:

1. **Open separate Finder windows for**
   - The external hard drive
   - The internal hard drive

> 2. **Select the desired files that you want to back up from your internal drive.**
>
> 3. **Drag the selected files to the external drive window.**

Chapter 20 covers external hard drives.

Recordable CDs and DVDs

You can burn backup files to a recordable CD or DVD.

Finder

To use the Finder's Burn feature with a CD or DVD, follow these steps:

1. **Load a blank disc into your iMac's optical drive.**

   If you're using the default settings in the CDs & DVDs pane in System Preferences, a dialog asks you for a disc name.

2. **Drag the files and folders that you want to back up into the disc's Finder window.**

   They can be organized any way you like.

3. **Click File and choose Burn Disc from the menu.**

4. **Choose the fastest recording speed possible.**

5. **Click Burn.**

Other recording applications

If you've invested in Toast Titanium from Roxio (www.roxio.com) or another CD/DVD recording application, you can create a new disc layout to burn your backup disc.

You can save that disc layout and use it again in the future. This simplifies the process of backing up the same files in the future (if you don't move folders or files from their current spot).

Saving images

Tiger's Disk Utility can create a basic backup on a disc image. You won't have to buy a commercial backup application.

Disk Utility doesn't have cool scheduling features or automatic restores, so you have to select and drag stuff manually. If you want features like automatic scheduling or support for multiple backup sets, you need a commercial backup utility like Retrospect Backup.

Creating backups

A *backup image* is actually a single file that contains multiple files and folders — rather like a StuffIt archive but easily mounted or restored on any Mac running Tiger.

The image can be created on

- ✔ **A CD, a DVD, or an external hard drive**
- ✔ **Your iMac's built-in hard drive**

  If you back up on the built-in hard drive, you'll lose *both* your live files and your backup if something happens to that hard drive. Rather unwise, if you think about it.

Follow these steps to create the image on your internal hard drive:

1. **Open a Finder window, click Applications, and then click Utilities.**

2. **Double-click the Disk Utility icon.**

   The Disk Utility window appears.

3. **Choose File➪New.**

   The Image Type options pop-up menu appears.

4. **Select the desired image type from the pop-up menu:**

   - *If you're backing up several folders or an entire volume,* choose Blank Image from the pop-up menu.

     The New Blank Image dialog that you see in Figure 21-3 appears.

   - *If you're backing up only the contents of a single folder,* choose Image from Folder.

     With this option, you won't have to drag things. Disk Utility simply copies everything in the folder that you select — whether all your crown jewels are in a single folder or you copy everything that you want to back up into a single folder.

     This is a neat way of backing up MP3 files in your iTunes folder.

5. **Enter the necessary information on the New Blank Image dialog:**

   a. *Type a name for the image in the Save As box.*

   b. *Choose a location from the Where pop-up menu.*

   c. *Choose a size for the image file.*

      I recommend that you select a size at least 10MB larger than the total size of the files that you want to backup. (That way, you won't run out of space when you realize that you didn't include your digital photographs of downtown Fresno.) To do this, select the file(s) or volume that you're going to back up and press ⌘+I to display the Get Info dialog, from which you can see the total size for the selected items listed in the dialog.

You can choose sizes that match the capacity of either a CD (660MB) or a DVD (4.7GB).

d. Choose whether you want the image to be encrypted for security.

I like to leave a backup image unencrypted so I don't have to remember a password.

If you encrypt an image and you forget the password, you cannot recover that data!

6. Set Format to Read/Write Disk Image.

7. Click the Create button.

The Disk Utility displays a progress bar to indicate how long the process will take.

8. Open two windows to drag and drop files:

a. Open a Finder window and navigate to the desired location.

b. Double-click the Image icon on your Desktop.

The disc image displays its blank vista in a separate window.

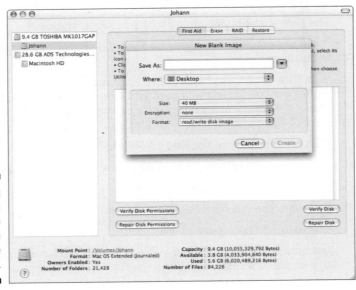

Figure 21-3: Preparing a blank image file as a simple backup.

9. **Select the files and folders that you want to copy in the Finder window.**

10. **Drag the selected files and folders from the Finder window to the image window.**

An image file operates just like any other hard drive or optical drive on your iMac. You can eject it either by dragging the icon to the Trash or by selecting it and then pressing ⌘+E. However, if you log off, turn off, or restart your iMac, the image icon disappears — you have to navigate to the location where you stored it and double-click the image file to mount it on your Desktop again.

Restoring from backup

If you have to use your backup, you can use Disk Utility's Restore feature. Follow these steps:

1. **Mount the disc image by double-clicking the image icon in a Finder window.**

   The disc image icon appears on your Desktop.

2. **Launch the Disk Utility by double-clicking its icon in the Utilities folder.**

3. **Click the backup image icon at the left side of the window; then click the Restore button (see Figure 21-4).**

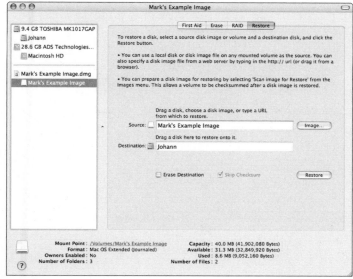

Figure 21-4:
Restoring files from an image — good thinking on your part!

4. **Drag the image icon to the Source box.**

5. **Drag the destination disk to the Destination box.**

   Make doggone sure that the Erase Destination check box is disabled (clear)!

   The only time to use Erase Destination is when you're restoring your data onto an empty, formatted drive. And that's not today.

6. **Click Restore.**

Commercial backup programs

If you prefer your backups to be automated on a regular schedule and you'd be happier with all the bells and whistles of a commercial application, scads of backup applications are on the shelves at your local Software Hut. These applications make it much easier to back up your entire drive in one fell swoop, without dragging anything or any manual labor involved.

My favorite backup application has always been Dantz Retrospect (www.dantz.com), as shown in Figure 21-5, which sells for the princely sum of $129. The application can back up to tape drives, external hard drives, CDs and DVDs, and even a host FTP server over the Internet.

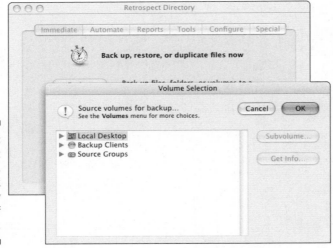

Figure 21-5: Dantz Retrospect, hard at work ensuring my peace of mind.

Maintaining Hard Drive Health

Shifty-eyed, sneaky, irritating little problems can bother your hard drive: *permissions errors*. Incorrect disk and file permissions can

- Make your iMac lock up
- Make applications act screwy (or refuse to run at all)
- Cause weird behavior within a Finder window or System Preferences

To keep Tiger running at its best, I recommend that you fix permissions errors at least once a week.

To fix any permissions errors on your system, follow these steps:

1. **Open a Finder window, click Applications, and then click Utilities.**

2. **Double-click the Disk Utility icon.**

3. **Click the volume at the left that you want to check.**

4. **Click the Repair Disk Permissions button.**

   Disk Utility does the rest and then displays a message about whatever it has to fix. (When will someone invent a *car* with a Repair Me button?)

What causes permissions errors?

Permission errors are usually introduced on your system when a faulty installer makes a mistake copying files to your system. Sometimes, the application itself has a bug that produces errors when it tries to open or close files or use Mac OS X system functions. Fortunately, you don't really have to investigate what causes a permission error. (That's good because you and I aren't likely to understand such techno-gibberish, anyway.) You just need to know that Disk Utility fixes the errors.

Here's a little-known fact about Mac OS X: Your start-up disk is automatically checked for most errors every time you start (or restart) your iMac. Therefore, you don't have to worry about hard drive errors "creeping up" over time, like they do under Windows. Each time you start your iMac, it's like you're running Disk Utility's Repair Disk feature automatically.

Didn't I *tell* you this operating system was the best on planet Earth?

Automating Those Mundane Chores

One new feature in Tiger — Automator — has generated a lot of excitement. Automator can create applications with a compiled form of AppleScript. That might sound daunting — akin to building your own nuclear submarine single-handedly over a long weekend — but Automator is actually easy to use. Heck, you might find it downright *fun!*

Building Automator applications

Automator applications are built by using a drag-and-drop approach. If you're familiar with how iMovie works, you'll feel right at home here; the tasks that you arrange in the Automator window run sequentially, just like the video clips that you drag into an iMovie window.

You can create a simple Automator application with these steps:

1. **Open the Finder menu.**

2. **Press ⌘+N to open a new Finder window.**

3. **Click the Applications folder in the Finder window Sidebar (housed on the left side of the window).**

4. **Double-click the Automator icon.**

   The Automator window appears, as shown in Figure 21-6.

5. **In the Library column, click the Tiger application that you want automated.**

   A list of actions appears that you can perform with that application.

6. **Drag the desired action into the Workflow area (right side).**

   If the action that you selected can be modified with any criteria, you can change the settings to your heart's content.

7. **Click Run to test your script.**

   Figure 21-7 illustrates a script that I designed. It automatically downloads new photos from my digital camera, creates a new iPhoto album with those images, and then displays them and allows me to mark them as Approved or Rejected, with an option to delete them. Pretty slick stuff for ten minutes worth of work and testing, wouldn't you say? (I call it *Mark's Photo Processor* . . . which I'm sure someday will make me a millionaire!)

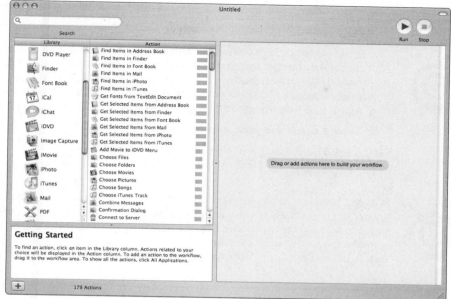

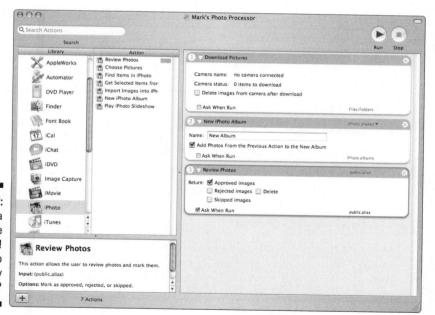

8. **If the script runs properly, press ⌘+Shift+S to save your application.**

   Automator displays a Save As dialog.

   If the script croaks or doesn't work quite the way you intended, you can remove and rearrange actions to your heart's content. (To remove an action, click the X button in the upper right of the action block.) You might also consider tweaking the action-specific settings or using the Ask When Run option to make sure that an action gets the right input.

9. **Type a name for your new program.**

10. **Click File Format and then choose Application.**

11. **Click Save.**

You can build an Automator application that uses values that you type (a software developer calls it your *input*) each time you run it. To set your application for manual input, enable the Ask When Run check box. This allows your application to prompt you with a dialog requesting the necessary values (such as an iTunes playlist or a specific folder on your hard drive).

Running applications at start up

If your Automator application should run every time you log in, follow these steps to set it up as a Login Item:

1. **Open System Preferences.**

2. **Display the Accounts pane.**

3. **Click the Login Items button.**

4. **Click the plus button at the bottom of the list.**

5. **Navigate to the location of your new Automator application.**

6. **Click Add.**

   Now your Automator application is *really* automatic. Watch your significant other gape in amazement as your iMac begins to work without you touching the keyboard!

Many third-party applications have their own Automator actions after installation. Check the developer's Web site often to see whether additional Automator applications have been added that you can download.

Updating Mac OS X Automatically

I prefer my iMac to take care of cleaning up after itself, so updating Tiger should be automatic as well. In Mac OS X Tiger, operating system updates are performed by the Software Update application.

Software Update uses the Internet, so you need an Internet connection to shake hands with the Apple server and download any updates.

Software Update can be found in two convenient spots:

✔ **The Apple menu:** Click the Apple menu (🍎) and then click Software Update, which displays the Update dialog and alerts you to anything new that's available.

✔ **System Preferences:** Click the Software Update icon to display the Software Update pane that you see in Figure 21-8.

Figure 21-8:
Setting up
Software
Update
to launch
itself . . . all
by itself.

If you take the System Preferences route, you can set Software Update to check for updates automatically:

　a. Mark the Check for Updates check box to enable it.

　b. Choose the time period from the Check for Updates pop-up menu.

Software Update covers every Apple application, so I usually check once a day just to make sure that I don't miss anything.

If something needs to be updated, the program alerts you, either automatically downloading the update(s) or displaying a dialog letting you know what you can patch (depending on the settings you choose in the System Preferences Software Update pane).

You can even check for updates immediately from System Preferences. That, dear reader, is just plain thoughtful design.

Part VII

The Part of Tens

In this part . . .

Ah, what book in the *For Dummies* series is truly complete without the infamous Part of Tens? Here you find lots of this author's raw opinion: my recommendations for the best Mac applications, the best tips for boosting your computer's performance, and even Ten Things to Avoid Like the Plague.

Chapter 22

Ten Applications
You Can't Do Without

Applications make the world go around! It's the truth — and although Tiger gets much of the glory for its elegant design and power, you can't really do much productivity-wise from your Desktop without a snappy application. I'm sure that the Laws of Gravity, Magnetism, and Murphy are all controlled somewhere in the cosmos by one heck of a piece of software. (Who owns the Celestial Supercomputer, I don't know . . . but I'll bet it uses a processor.)

I dedicate this Part of Tens chapter to listing applications that every Mac owner should know about. Even if you don't use one or two of these great tools now, you'll likely realize that you need and want them in the future.

Most of these applications are actually installed right along with Mac OS X — they're *free* — but some of the software in this chapter is commercial, so you have to pay for those items. I make sure that you know which are free and which are not.

Applications

This section presents a regular smorgasbord of six applications, running the gamut from DVD entertainment to productivity software. (I've even heard tell that you can run Windows XP on your iMac . . . and leave it to Bill and his cronies to sell you the application!)

Some of these applications are built in to Mac OS X — read that as *free* — whilst others you must buy. I note here which is which and give you a ball-park price for the commercial stuff.

DVDs and CDs

Half the time we're watchin' 'em, and the other half of the time we're burnin' 'em — DVDs, that is. Apple has always had superior support for DVD hardware; after all, the SuperDrive has been a feature (or featured upgrade) for Macintosh computers for years now. Come explore the best two DVD applications around for your Tiger machine.

Watching DVD movies with aplomb

Face it — that gorgeous 17" or 20" flat-panel monitor on your iMac is perfect for watching DVD movies. (Psst . . . it's okay . . . you can fib to your significant other and your friends that you're using your new supercomputer for work. I own an iMac, too, so I understand. *It's an iMac thing.*)

Thanks to our good friends in Cupertino, you'll find that Tiger's DVD Player does a great job at screening all your favorite DVD films:

- ✔ You can either display your movie in a window or use the entire screen (especially nice for widescreen titles).

- ✔ If your movie includes different audio tracks, subtitles, and camera angles, you can control them all from the spiffy remote control that appears onscreen whenever you move your mouse.

- ✔ You can step through the video frame by frame or in slow motion to see the martial arts action that you missed in the theater.

By default, DVD Player runs automatically when you load a DVD-Video disc (DVD-V), including those that you create yourself with iDVD or Roxio Toast.

I especially like the feature that remembers whether you've viewed a disc already and also gives you the opportunity to restart the film where you left off.

Yes, they really named it Toast

Until the advent of Mac OS X and the iLife suite, recording audio and data CDs or DVD-Vs on your Mac required a third-party application. The Cadillac of recording software for the Mac was, is, and will likely always be the unlikely named Toast, from Roxio (www.roxio.com). The latest version is Toast 6 Titanium, available online for about $65.

The built-in recording features in iTunes and iDVD are certainly fine, and the discs that these two applications produce are compatible with any audio CD player or DVD player that you're likely to find. However, you'll need Toast to

✔ **Produce specialized types of discs, such as**

- Hybrid discs that store both Mac and PC data

- ISO 9660 discs for UNIX and Linux machines

- Mixed-mode and enhanced CDs that carry both audio and data

- Video CDs and Super Video CDs

✔ **Copy an existing CD or unprotected DVD**

✔ **Mount a DVD image as if it were a physical disc that you've loaded into your iMac's optical drive — definitely a plus if you**

- Play games

- Restore from backup images

✔ **Recognize older external optical drives that might not be supported within Tiger or the iLife suite**

For a comprehensive guide to using Toast to create all these types of specialized discs, look no farther than my book *CD & DVD Recording For Dummies*, 2nd Edition (Wiley). It covers Toast Titanium like a layer of syrup.

Management and communication

Both iCal and Apple Mail are mighty applications, bent on organizing something: your time, calendar, and/or your Internet e-mail traffic. (They do a great job, too.) Apple provides both in Mac OS X, so you can keep your credit card in your pocket or purse.

Coverage on iLife applications isn't in this chapter because I cover 'em in depth elsewhere in the book. See all the chapters in Part IV.

Staying on top of things with iCal

iCal is one of those oddities in the computer world. Unlike iTunes or iMovie, it's not particularly sexy (in a multimedia way), and it doesn't get oodles of coverage in the glossy Macintosh magazines. Yet everybody eventually ends up using it. Sooner or later, every Mac owner appreciates iCal as an unsung hero. (And a free unsung hero to boot.)

Unfortunately, iCal can't enter events for you — and take my word for it, the Data Elves aren't going to show up and magically type for you — so you have to create events manually. After they're in the iCal database, however, you can

- ✔ Set alarms for specific events.
- ✔ Add notes for each event.
- ✔ Print a calendar.
- ✔ Set repeating events on a regular schedule.

By default, iCal includes two calendars — Home and Work — but you can set up as many separate calendars as you like, for scheduling everything from soccer seasons to DVD releases.

Oh, and don't forget about the To Do items, which keep you focused on the tasks that really matter. You can easily sort To Do items by priority or due date; you can also hide items with due dates outside the current calendar page.

If you're a .Mac member, you can publish any calendar online that other folks can then subscribe to (great for clubs and organizations). Or, you can publish your calendar on any Web server that supports WebDAV functionality. Check with your site's Webmaster (or call your Internet service provider) to see whether you can offer an iCal calendar on your Web site. I discuss Apple's .Mac service at length in Chapter 9.

One doggone good e-mail application

Ask yourself this question: "Am I taking my e-mail application for granted?" Sure, e-mail might not take center stage in the computer magazines these days, but consider what your life would be like with a substandard, whip-and-buggy e-mail application — almost as bad as no e-mail at all.

The best e-mail applications (like Apple Mail) have powerful, trainable spam filters that improve automatically as you manually check your junk mail. A first-class performer (like Apple Mail) offers fully automated scripting for common tasks, snazzy fonts and colors, and the ability to create HTML-format messages with embedded images and objects. Are you seeing a pattern here?

One of my favorite recent additions to Apple Mail is the ability to organize your messages by *threads*. (In plain English, a thread groups replies together so that they can be read as an actual discussion.) Anyone who frequents Usenet newsgroups or Web discussion sites recognizes a threaded view as easier to read than a traditional sequential display, especially when your mail is heavy on replies and includes ongoing conversations with several folks involved.

It's free, it's fun, and it's fashionable — go, Apple Mail, go!

Productivity

Sooner or later, you're going to need grown-up, respectable documents out of your iMac, or you might need to run an absolutely-gotta-have-it-application-that's-not-available-for-Macs. (I actually run into very few of those.) In this section, I cover two of my favorite productivity applications — Virtual PC and Apple Works — and the serious stuff they can do.

Sweet! I'm running Windows XP on my iMac!

Okay, even I'll admit that there are fewer applications available to Macs than PCs running Windows — and practically every Mac owner on the planet has one or two PC programs that make life easier. Luckily, Microsoft offers a solution: Virtual PC 7 for Mac (www.microsoft.com/mac). The program sells for about $225, which includes a licensed copy of Windows XP Professional. This nifty program can easily run most Windows XP programs, complete with support for external USB devices, Ethernet networks, the Internet, and your Mac's printer.

Windows programs don't even know the difference because Virtual PC for Mac simulates an entire PC (complete with a virtual video card, sound card, Pentium processor, and PS/2 keyboard and mouse)!

Virtual PC for Mac has its limitations:

✔ **You won't be running the latest 3-D games.**

✔ **You can't watch DVD movies in Windows.**

✔ **Your Windows applications will be nowhere near as fast as if you were actually running them on a real PC.**

 However, with the processor in your iMac and at least a gigabyte of memory, Virtual PC runs tolerably well. And it's better than kissing that must-have Windows program goodbye, right?

Make sure that your iMac has at least 512MB of RAM before you consider buying Virtual PC for Mac. Anything less, and your Windows applications will simply run snail-slow.

You can install

✔ **More than one version of Windows**

 I have both Windows XP and Windows 2000 running on my system.

✔ **Almost any other operating system that's ever been produced for the PC**

 I have a Red Hat Linux drive.

Virtual PC for Mac makes it easy to shut down a virtual computer — it's akin to hibernating a laptop computer — keeping your open documents intact. When you reload your virtual Windows machine, you're right back at the exact same point that you shut down.

For the scoop on Virtual PC for Mac, visit Microsoft's Macintosh Web site at www.microsoft.com/mac.

You can quote me: I like AppleWorks

I wish I had a dime for every time I've read or heard about how the Macintosh version of Office is so indispensable to every Mac owner and how it should be an automatic purchase at the moment you buy your computer. I'll admit, the applications that make up Office are superb — I'm writing with Word at this moment — but every new Mac owner should try AppleWorks *before* jumping onto the Microsoft productivity bandwagon.

Why? Well, to be honest, most computer owners simply don't use or need all the features and hoo-hah that's built into the Mac Office applications! For example, if all you produce on paper are simple letters, typical schoolwork, or brochures for your home business, Word might be an expensive case of overkill.

As an author, I confess that I use all the power that Word has to offer — and my publisher requires me to use it, so I shelled out the cash. However, I exchange Word and AppleWorks documents all the time with my friends who use AppleWorks.

The same goes for Excel and PowerPoint. AppleWorks can create spreadsheets, databases, drawings, paintings, and presentations. Talk about a Swiss Army knife!

The only Mac Office 2004 application that AppleWorks doesn't match is Entourage, and the combination of Apple Mail, iCal, and Address Book does the same job.

AppleWorks offers templates and assistants that are similar to those in Office, so creating all sorts of specialized business and personal documents is easy. You can also use your Internet connection to view new templates online, join the AppleWorks Users Group (AWUG for short), pick up free clip art, or read the latest AppleWorks eNews newsletter.

So go ahead, visit your Applications folder and give AppleWorks a try — it's fast, it's free, and I think you'll be pleasantly surprised.

System Stuff

Ah, utilities. . . . I love 'em almost as much as I crave games. I think that most iMac power users would agree with me when I say that a well-maintained Mac is a wonderful machine. To that end, the utilities you find in this last section help keep your hardware, software, and files in tip-top shape.

Maintenance

Although I devote Chapter 21 to the joys of maintenance, I want to mention the following two applications again, just to make sure you remember them. (The alternative is a tattoo, which is probably overkill.)

Disk repair and so very much more

If you're not already using Disk Utility, you should. On a regular basis. *Really.*

"But Mark!" you exclaim, "Isn't it true that Mac OS X automatically checks the startup disk for file system errors each time my Mac starts up, and repairs any problems that it finds?" Yes, indeed it does — you can feel good about the health of your startup drive. But what about any external drives that you might be using? When's the last time you checked them?

Oh, and don't forget the most important function (in my opinion) that Disk Utility offers: the ability to fix file and folder permission problems. This is why I recommend that you launch Disk Utility and check your Mac OS X startup drive on a weekly basis. Permission problems can cause your applications to act like they're on mind-altering drugs or even lock you out of using those applications altogether! Chapter 19 shows you how to squash permission errors.

Of course, there's more to Disk Utility, but you're not likely to use heavy-duty functions like partitioning or RAID management very often. These are advanced features that one normally uses only when initializing a new hard drive.

If you haven't backed up your hard drive — and you know that you should — consider creating a *drive image,* ready to restore in case of trouble. Many Mac owners consider this all the hard drive backup functionality that's really necessary (instead of buying a commercial backup system like Retrospect). For the scoop on using image files for backup, check out Chapter 21.

"Back, viruses, stay back!" I say!

Blah, blah, blah. . . . Unless you've been living in a cave in the Himalayas for the last decade, you already know what I'm going to say about how important it is to protect your iMac from viral infection. I'll save the keystrokes for the next application.

Get yourself an antivirus application — one that automatically checks the discs that you load as well as the stuff that you download. (I use Norton AntiVirus for Macintosh, www.symantec.com, which is about $65 online.) Set it to automatically download the latest virus definition files from the Internet and scan your entire system once a month. Subscribers to Apple's .Mac service, which I cover in Chapter 9, get Virex (another popular antivirus application) as part of their membership.

Now you can relax.

Files

Care to compress a folder full of files to save space on your hard drive or maybe send them via e-mail? Perhaps you'd like to use the keyboard and the power of UNIX to perform file manipulation miracles that are practically impossible by using the mouse. Either way, the applications in this final section have you covered.

We laugh at Zip files

In the Windows universe, the WinZip archive file is king, followed by WinRAR and a host of other different archiving formats.

For Mac owners, however, Zip files have never been hot stuff (horrible pun intended). StuffIt, from Allume Systems (www.stuffit.com), has always been the archive format standard under Mac OS X.

The latest version 9 of StuffIt Deluxe will set you back $80, but it's worth every penny for the convenience and flexibility that archives bring to your Desktop:

- ✔ **Industrial-strength data encryption to secure your archives**
- ✔ **One-click automatic backup**

  As a .Mac subscriber, I like that the application allows you to back up to your iDisk.

- ✔ **Archive browsing without actually expanding (a real timesaver)**
- ✔ **Direct burn of archived data to CD or DVD**

Archives explained in a small space

An *archive* is a single file that can hold data in a compressed format. Archives offer these advantages:

✔ **Take less disk space**

✔ **Download faster**

✔ **Can hold multiple files and folders**

This is great for easily creating backups or sending a number of images through e-mail as a single attachment.

When you're ready to use the data, you simply *unarchive* the file, which expands the items and restores them to their original form.

Oh, by the way, StuffIt Deluxe also opens and creates Zip files. You know, just in case you have to share files with The Great Unwashed Windows Horde.

Doing the command line dance

This must-have application is a little different from the others: You have to type your commands manually, and there are no icons or fancy graphics. You're in the character-based *Twilight Zone,* and only the bravest of Mac novices will venture there.

However, when you launch the Terminal application, you open a window into the UNIX core that lies underneath Mac OS X. Suddenly you can do wondrous things that you can't do from the Finder menu:

✔ You can manipulate hidden and hard-to-reach files, like preference files.

✔ You can work with UNIX applications like File Transfer Protocol (FTP) and the Apache Web server.

✔ If you're familiar with wildcards and the command line hieroglyphics that make up UNIX, you can manage your files with a speed that no graphical user interface can match. (That's a DOS feature I still miss.)

Before you make your move into UNIX, I highly recommend that you grab a companion and guide for the journey. A good pick is *UNIX For Dummies,* 5th Edition, by John R. Levine and Margaret Levine Young (Wiley). Without a learning tool that you can use to teach yourself, Terminal is a very lonely window indeed.

Chapter 23

Ten Ways to Speed Up Your iMac

- -

In This Chapter

▶ Adding memory

▶ Using spoken commands

▶ Defragmenting your drive

▶ Banishing the desktop background

▶ Using column mode

▶ Customizing the Dock

▶ Using keyboard shortcuts

▶ Customizing your Finder windows

▶ Launching recent applications and documents

▶ Using the Go menu

- -

*E*ven an iMac can always go just a bit faster . . . or *can* it? There's actually a pretty short list of tweaks that you can apply to your iMac's hardware to speed it up, and these suggestions are covered in this chapter.

You can also speed up Tiger (the latest Mac OS X version) considerably by customizing things like your Desktop and your Finder windows, which makes it easier to spot and use your files, folders, and applications. That's in this Part of Tens chapter, too.

Finally, you can enhance your efficiency and make yourself a power user by tweaking *yourself.* (Sounds a bit tawdry or even painful, but bear with me, and you'll understand.) If you haven't delved into things like keyboard shortcuts, the Recent menu, and the Go menu, you'll find that you're taking a number of extra steps that you can eliminate. Soon you'll be the fastest component in your whole system! I recommend how you can speed yourself up in this chapter as well.

Nothing Works Like a Shot of Memory

Okay, maybe *shot* is the wrong word, but adding additional memory to your iMac (by either replacing or adding a memory module) is the single surefire way to speed up the performance of your entire system. That includes every application, as well as Tiger itself.

Why does additional memory provide such a boost? With more memory, your iMac can hold more of your documents and data in memory, and thus has to store less data temporarily on your hard drive. It takes your iMac much less time to store, retrieve, and work with data when that data is in RAM rather than on your hard drive. That's why your system runs faster when you can fit an entire image in Photoshop in your iMac's system memory

By the way, this tweak works on any computer running Mac OS X, Windows XP, or Linux/UNIX — they all automatically take advantage of as much memory as you can toss their way. My iMac has more than 1GB of memory, and you can sure tell the difference from the 256MB that it originally shipped with. It's like comparing a Humvee with a Ferrari! (For details on installing more memory, visit the friendly confines of Chapter 20.)

Hold a Conversation with Your iMac

Your iMac can speak any text to you through the Services menu, but that's generally not a big timesaver. (Neat for the kids, I admit, just like spoken alerts — more on this later in this section.) However, many Mac owners will attest that you *can* significantly increase your own efficiency by using the Speakable Items feature, which allows you to speak common commands within applications and Finder windows. Your voice is indeed faster than either your mouse or your fingers! Common commands in the Speakable Items folder include "Log me out," "Get my mail," "Hide this application," and "Open my browser." You won't find them on your local radio station's Top 40 countdown, but they're popular among the Mac set.

To enable Speakable Items, choose System Preferences➪Speech and then select the On radio button next to Apple Speakable Items to enable speech recognition. You'll see the feedback window appear, which includes a convenient sound level meter that you can use to adjust the volume of your voice. Remember, by default, that the speech recognition system is active only when you press and hold the Esc key.

It takes a little practice to enunciate the King's English properly — your iMac is a bit finicky when it comes to recognizing a Texas drawl — but the effort pays off when you realize just how much faster things are moving when you're sitting at your computer.

When you're looking at the Speech pane, click the Spoken User Interface tab and then select the Speak the Alert Text check box to enable it. This activates spoken alerts. I think they're cool. (Any message that's displayed in a dialog will now be spoken automatically.) Enable the Selected Text When the Key is Pressed check box to specify a key that will speak highlighted text in your applications, which is perfect for messing with your co-worker's minds in the office.

Vamoose, Unwanted Fragments!

Apple would probably prefer that I not mention disk fragmentation because Tiger doesn't come with a built-in defragmenting application. (Go figure.)

To keep your hard drive running as speedily as possible, I recommend defragmenting at least once a month. You can use third-party applications like Micromat's Drive 10 and TechTool Pro (www.micromat.com) to defragment your drive.

Keep Your Wallpaper Simple

It's funny that I still include this tip in a chapter dedicated to improving performance — after all, I recommended using a solid color background in my first books on Mac OS 8 and Windows 98! Just goes to show you that some things never change.

Even with the high-powered video cards in today's iMacs, it still takes time for Tiger to redraw your Mac OS X background when you close or hide an application window. And if you're running a number of heavy-duty applications (like Final Cut Pro HD and Photoshop), you can actually see the block of video memory "blank out" for a few seconds while things grind along. The slowdown is worse when you're using a huge true-color image as a background at 1680 x 1050 on your iMac with the 20" screen. Think about all those pixels, and you'll likely get a headache, too.

Therefore, if you're interested in running your system as fast as it will go, choose a solid-color background from the Desktop & Screen Saver pane in System Preferences. (In fact, there's even a separate category that you can pick called Solid Colors.)

Defraggle rocks

What's fragmentation? Here's the short version: The longer you use your hard drive (and the more often you create and delete files), the more fragmented that files become on your hard drive, and the longer they take to read. A disk defragmenting application reads all the files on your drive and rewrites them as continuous, contiguous files, which your machine can read significantly faster.

Column Mode is for Power Users

One of my favorite features of Mac OS X is the ability to display files and folders in column view mode. Just click the Column button in the standard Finder window toolbar, and the contents of the window automatically align in well-ordered columns.

So why is column mode so doggone fast? Just imagine drilling through several layers of folders to get to a specific location on your hard drive — for example, Users/chambers/Music/iTunes/iTunes Music, which I visit on a regular basis. If you use icon view, you have to double-click so often that you'll have to give your mouse button a rest. List view really isn't that much better because the folder contents keep expanding, and you have those doggone expanding/collapsing triangles to deal with.

In column mode, however, a single click drills a level deeper, and often you won't even have to use the Finder window's scroll bars to see what you're looking for. Files and folders appear in a logical order (unlike icon mode) without changing the layout of the window (unlike list mode). I think you'll find column mode both faster and less confusing, which will move you a little closer to your ultimate goal of power-user status.

Make the Dock Do Your Bidding

Every Mac owner considers the Mac OS X Dock a good friend: It's a control center, a status display, and an organizer all rolled into one. But when's the last time you customized it — or have you ever made a change to it at all?

You can drag files and folders to the Dock, as well as Web URLs, applications, and network servers. You can also remove applications and Web URLs just as easily by dragging the icon from the Dock and releasing it on your Desktop (producing that cool puff of animated smoke that someone in Cupertino is likely still very proud of to this very day).

I find that I make a significant change to my Dock icons at least once every week. I find nothing more convenient than placing a folder for each of my current projects in the Dock or adding applications to the Dock that I might be researching for a book or demonstrating in a chapter.

You can position the Dock at either side of the Desktop or even hide the Dock from sight entirely to give yourself an extra strip of space on your Desktop for application windows. Click the Apple menu (🍎) and choose Dock. From the submenu that appears, you can choose either Position on Left or Position on Right, or you can choose Turn Hiding On to instruct the Dock to perform its vanishing act. You can also toggle the Dock's magnifying feature on and off from this menu.

It All Started with Keyboard Shortcuts

Ask a computing dinosaur like me (who started computing before the arrival of the IBM-PC) how you can spot a *true* power user, and you're likely to get the same answer: Watch how the person uses keyboard shortcuts. A real power user makes use of every keyboard shortcut available, committing those key sequences to memory.

Heck, keyboard shortcuts have been around since the days of WordStar and VisiCalc, back when a mouse was still a living rodent. Although selecting a command from a menu might be intuitive, it's also very time-consuming compared with a simple press of a few keys. The same action gets performed, but if you add up all those seconds of mouse-handling that you save by using keyboard shortcuts, you'll see that you can save hours of productive time every year.

You're likely already using some keyboard shortcuts, like the common editing shortcuts ⌘+C (Copy) and ⌘+V (Paste). When I'm learning a new application, I often search through the application's online help to find a keyboard shortcut table and then print out that table as a quick reference.

Hey, You Tweaked Your Finder!

Here's another speed enhancer along the same lines as my earlier tip about customizing your Dock: You can also reconfigure your Finder windows to present you with just the tools and locations that you actually use (rather than what Apple *figures* you'll use).

For example, you can Control-click (or right-click) the toolbar in any Finder window and choose Customize Toolbar. By default, Tiger's Finder toolbar includes only the default icon set that you see at the bottom of the sheet, but you can drag and drop all sorts of useful command icons onto the toolbar: Burn (for CDs and DVDs), Delete (which sends the highlighted files or folders to the Trash), and Get Info (the same result as pressing ⌘+I). You can save space by displaying small-size icons, too.

The Finder window sidebar is a healthy, no-nonsense repository for those locations that you constantly visit throughout a computing session. For example, I have both a Games folder and a Book Chapters folder that I use countless times every day — it's important to balance work with pleasure, you know — and I've dragged both of those folders to the Sidebar. Now I can immediately jump to either folder from any Finder window or Open/Save File dialog with a single click of the mouse . . . speedy indeed!

Keep in Touch with Your Recent Past

Click that Apple menu, and use that Recent Items menu! I know that sounds a little *too* simple, but I meet many new Apple computer owners every year who either don't know that the Recent Items menu exists or forget to use it. You can access both applications and documents that you've used within the last few days.

Most computer users turn to the same applications over and over, and to the same documents several times in each computing session. You can put these items in your Dock or your Finder Sidebar, but they're also available from the Recent Items menu (and you don't have to physically drag things willy-nilly around your Desktop). Consider the Dock and Finder Sidebar as permanent or semipermanent solutions, and the Recent Items menu as more of a temporary solution to finding the stuff that you're working on right now.

Go Where the Going Is Good

To round out this Part of Tens chapter, I recommend another little-known (and under-appreciated) Finder menu feature (at least among Macintosh novices): the Go menu, which is located on the Finder menu.

The Go menu is really a catchall, combining the most important locations on your system (like your Home folder and your iDisk) with folders that you've used recently. Plus, the Go menu is the place where you can connect to servers or shared folders across your local network or across the Internet.

Pull down the Go menu today — and don't forget to try out those spiffy keyboard shortcuts you see listed next to the command names. (For example, press ⌘+Shift+H to immediately go to your Home folder.) And if a Finder window isn't open at the moment, a new window opens automatically — such convenience is hard to resist!

Chapter 24

Ten Things to Avoid Like the Plague

*I*f you've read other books that I've written in the *For Dummies* series, you might recognize the title of this chapter — it's a favorite Part of Tens subject of mine that appears often in my work. I don't like to see any computer owner fall prey to pitfalls. Some are minor — like keeping your iMac clean — while others are downright catastrophic, like providing valuable information to persons unknown over the Internet.

All these potential mistakes, however, share one thing in common: They're *easily prevented* with a little common sense, as long as you're aware of them. That's my job — in this chapter, I fill in what you need to know. Consider these pages as experience gained easily!

Man, That Is the Definition of Sluggish

Let's see, what could I be talking about? Oh, yes . . . only a USB 1.1 external hard drive or CD-ROM drive could be as slow as a turtle on narcotics.

Unfortunately, you'll still find countless examples of USB 1.1 storage hardware hanging around. eBay is stuffed to the gills with USB 1.1 hard drives, and your family and friends will certainly want to bestow that old 4x CD-RW drive to you as a gift. (This is one that you should politely refuse immediately, just like your Aunt Harriet's woebegone fruitcake.) These drives were considered cool in the early days of the colorful iMac G3, when USB was a brand-new technology. Today, however, a USB 1.1 hard drive is simply a slow-as-maple-syrup-in-January embarrassment.

Plenty of great USB 1.1 devices are around these days, like joysticks, keyboards, mice, and other controllers, along with printers and scanners that work just fine with slower transfer rates. But if a peripheral's job is to store or move data *quickly* — including hard drives, network connections, CD-ROM, drives, and USB Flash drives — then give a USB 1.1 connection a wide berth, opting instead for a USB 2.0 or FireWire device.

Phishing Is No Phun

No, that's not a misspelling. In the latest Internet lingo, *phishing* refers to an attempt by unsavory characters to illegally obtain your personal information. If that sounds like an invitation to identity theft, it is — and thousands of sites have defrauded individuals like you and me (along with banks and credit card companies) out of billions of dollars.

A phishing scam works like this: You get an e-mail purporting to be from a major company or business, like eBay, a government agency, or a major credit card company. The message warns you that you have to update your login or financial information to keep it current, or that you have to validate your information every so often — and even provides you with a link to an official-looking Web page. After you enter information on that bogus page, it's piped directly to the bad guys, and they're off to the races.

Here's a Mark's Maxim that every Internet user should take to heart:

> **No *legitimate* company or agency will solicit your personal information through an e-mail message!™**

Never respond to these messages. If you smell something phishy, open your Web browser and visit the company's site (the *real* one) directly; then contact the company's customer support department. They'll certainly want to know about the phishing expedition, and you can help by providing them with the e-mail and Web addresses used in the scam.

In fact, sending any valuable financial information through unencrypted e-mail — even to those whom you know and trust — is a bad idea. E-mail messages can be intercepted or can be read from any e-mail server that stores your message.

Put Floppy Disks to Rest

Did you know that the Apple iMac was the first model produced by a major computer manufacturer that didn't include a floppy drive? Apple always looks ahead five years when it develops a new computer model, and the good folks in Cupertino accurately predicted the demise of the stodgy 1.44MB floppy disk. Why kill off such a computing icon? For a number of very good reasons:

✔ **Like the weather:** Floppy disks are downright unreliable because they are easily demagnetized.

✔ **Compatibility:** A floppy disk that reads and writes fine on one machine might not be readable in another.

✔ **Capacity:** Floppies don't store much, either.

✔ **Germ-ridden:** Floppies make great "tour buses" for viruses.

✔ **Lack of speed:** Oh, and don't forget that floppies are the slowest form of storage around.

Unfortunately, most PC owners have a shoebox full of floppies with data that might (or might not) still be important, so the floppy continues to persist, like the human appendix. I'm just doing my part to help the evolution of the personal computer by letting you know just how lousy the floppy really is.

If you still need a portable storage bin of some sort to carry from computer to computer, I heartily recommend that you pick up a USB Flash drive. These drives hold anywhere from 64MB to 2GB, and they work in any USB port. (And they're downright warp-drive fast when compared with a floppy disk, especially the USB 2.0 variety.)

Do You Really Want a Submerged Keyboard?

Your answer should be an unequivocal "No!" — and that's why everyone should make it a rule to keep all beverages well out of range of keyboards, speakers, mice, iSight cameras, and any other piece of external hardware. Especially when kids or cats are in close proximity to your iMac.

Cleaning up a hazardous soda spill is hard enough in the clear, but if that liquid comes in contact with your iMac, you're likely to be visited with intermittent keyboard problems (or, in the worst-case scenario, a short in an external peripheral or your iMac's motherboard).

Suffice it to say that 12 inches of open space can make the difference between a simple cleanup and an expensive replacement!

Don't Use Antiquated Utility Software

Mac OS 9 was (and still is) a great operating system for older iMacs, but if you're using Mac OS X, you must turn in your older utility programs — for example, an older copy of Symantec's Norton Utilities that supports only Mac OS 9. These older disk utility applications can actually do more damage than good to a hard drive under Mac OS X.

A number of things changed when Apple made the leap to Mac OS X, including subtle changes to disk formats, memory management within applications, and the maximum supported size of a hard drive. Add to these changes the fact that all Mac OS 9 applications have to run in Classic mode — which can cause a disk utility to assume that it has full access to a hard drive when it actually doesn't — and you could find yourself with corrupted data. Sometimes a complete operating system reinstall is necessary.

Now that you're using Mac OS X, make sure that you diagnose and repair disk and file errors using only a utility application that's specifically designed to run in Tiger, like TechTool Pro from Micromat (www.micromat.com). Your iMac's hard drive will definitely thank you.

Don't Endorse Software Piracy

This one's a real no-brainer — remember, Apple's overall market share among worldwide computer users currently weighs in at less than 10 percent. Software developers know this, and they have to expect (and *receive*) a return on their investment, or they're going to find something more lucrative to do with their time. As a shareware author, I can attest to this firsthand.

Pirated software seems attractive — the price is right, no doubt about it — but if you use an application without buying it, you're cheating the developer, who will find Macintosh programming no longer worth the time and trouble. An iMac is a great machine, and Tiger is a great operating system, but even the best hardware and the sexiest desktop won't make up for an absence of good applications. Pay for what you use, and everyone benefits.

Call It the Forbidden Account

You might never have encountered the *root*, or *System Administrator*, account within Mac OS X — and that's always A Good Thing. Note that I'm not talking about a standard administrator (or admin) account here. Every iMac needs at least one admin account (in fact, it might be the only visible account on your computer), and any standard user account can be toggled between standard and admin status with no trouble at all.

The root account, though, is a different beast altogether, and that's why it's disabled by default. All UNIX systems have a root account; because Tiger is based on a UNIX foundation, it has one, too. Anyone logging in with the root account can do *anything* on your system, including deleting or modifying files in the System folder (which no other account can access). Believe me, deliberately formatting your hard drive is about the only thing worse than screwing up the files in your System folder.

Luckily, no one can accidentally access the root/System Administrator account. In fact, you can't assign the root account with System Preferences; you must use the NetInfo Manager application in Utilities (within your Applications folder). Unless an Apple support technician tells you to enable and use it, you should promptly forget that the root account even exists.

Don't Settle for a Surge Suppressor

Technically, there's nothing wrong with using a surge suppressor to feed power to your iMac and all your external peripherals, but it doesn't do the *entire* job. Your system is still wide open to problems caused by momentary brownouts, not to mention a full-fledged blackout. Losing power in the middle of a computing session will likely lead to lost documents and might even result in disk or file errors later. With a UPS *(uninterruptible power supply)* you can rest easy knowing that your iMac will have a few minutes more of "ilife," running on battery power until you can close your documents normally and shut down your computer without trauma.

Most Mac owners know about the backup battery power that a UPS provides, but they don't know about the extra work performed by most UPS units: filtering your AC current. Without a filtering UPS, your iMac's power is susceptible to electronic noise (think about a vacuum being used next to a TV set) and momentary current spikes that can eventually cause problems over time. A simple surge suppressor doesn't provide this feature.

These days, you'll find good UPS models for under $150, so there's no reason not to give your iMac the AC power protection that it deserves!

Refurbished Hardware Is No Deal At All

Boy, howdy, do I hate refurbished stuff. To quote someone famous, "If the deal sounds too good to be true, it probably is."

Examine what you get when you buy a refurbished external hard drive. It's likely that the drive was returned as defective, of course, and was then sent back to the factory. There the manufacturer probably performed the most cursory of repairs (just enough to fix the known problem), perhaps tested the unit for a few seconds, and then packed it back up again. Legally, retailers can't resell the drive as a new item, so they have to cut the price so low that you're willing to take the chance.

Before you spend a dime on a bargain that's remanufactured — I can't get over that term — make sure that you find out how long a warranty you'll receive, if any. Consider that the hardware is likely to have crisscrossed the country at least once, and that it's likely to have picked up a few bumps and bruises during its travels. Also, you have no idea how well the repairs were tested or how thoroughly everything was inspected.

I don't buy refurbished computers or hardware, and most of the tales that I've heard of such behavior have ended badly. Take my advice and spend the extra cash on trouble-free, brand-new hardware that has a full warranty.

iMacs Appreciate Cleanliness

Clean your machine. Every computer (and every piece of computer hardware) appreciates a weekly dusting. Remember, many older iMac models didn't have internal fans, so a shroud of insulating dust (or cooling vents blocked by accumulated crud) could raise the internal temperature to a dangerous level. Even with a fan, dust is an insidious enemy within the confines of your computer's case; I know Mac owners who celebrate each passing year by opening up their machines to blow them clean of dust bunnies with a can of compressed air. (I'm one of them, as a matter of fact.) You'll find instructions on how to open your case in Chapter 20.

Adding memory to your iMac, or perhaps a new AirPort Extreme wireless card? Take advantage of the chance and use that trusty can of compressed air to clean up things.

On the outside of your iMac, your screen should be cleaned at least once every two or three days — that is, unless you like peering through a layer of dust, fingerprints, and smudges. Never spray anything — cleaners, water, anything! — directly on your screen or your iMac's case. I highly recommend the premoistened LCD cleaning wipes typically used for notebook computers, which safely clean your iMac's monitor.

Your iMac's case really doesn't need a special cleaning agent — in fact, you shouldn't use any solvents at all — but a thorough wiping job with a soft cloth should keep your case in spotless shape.

Index

Notes

BUSINESS, CAREERS & PERSONAL FINANCE

0-7645-5307-0

0-7645-5331-3 *†

Also available:

- Accounting For Dummies †
  0-7645-5314-3
- Business Plans Kit For Dummies †
  0-7645-5365-8
- Cover Letters For Dummies
  0-7645-5224-4
- Frugal Living For Dummies
  0-7645-5403-4
- Leadership For Dummies
  0-7645-5176-0
- Managing For Dummies
  0-7645-1771-6

- Marketing For Dummies
  0-7645-5600-2
- Personal Finance For Dummies *
  0-7645-2590-5
- Project Management For Dummies
  0-7645-5283-X
- Resumes For Dummies †
  0-7645-5471-9
- Selling For Dummies
  0-7645-5363-1
- Small Business Kit For Dummies *†
  0-7645-5093-4

HOME & BUSINESS COMPUTER BASICS

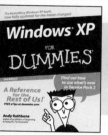

0-7645-4074-2

0-7645-3758-X

Also available:

- ACT! 6 For Dummies
  0-7645-2645-6
- iLife '04 All-in-One Desk Reference
  For Dummies
  0-7645-7347-0
- iPAQ For Dummies
  0-7645-6769-1
- Mac OS X Panther Timesaving
  Techniques For Dummies
  0-7645-5812-9
- Macs For Dummies
  0-7645-5656-8

- Microsoft Money 2004 For Dummies
  0-7645-4195-1
- Office 2003 All-in-One Desk Reference
  For Dummies
  0-7645-3883-7
- Outlook 2003 For Dummies
  0-7645-3759-8
- PCs For Dummies
  0-7645-4074-2
- TiVo For Dummies
  0-7645-6923-6
- Upgrading and Fixing PCs For Dummies
  0-7645-1665-5
- Windows XP Timesaving Techniques
  For Dummies
  0-7645-3748-2

FOOD, HOME, GARDEN, HOBBIES, MUSIC & PETS

0-7645-5295-3

0-7645-5232-5

Also available:

- Bass Guitar For Dummies
  0-7645-2487-9
- Diabetes Cookbook For Dummies
  0-7645-5230-9
- Gardening For Dummies *
  0-7645-5130-2
- Guitar For Dummies
  0-7645-5106-X
- Holiday Decorating For Dummies
  0-7645-2570-0
- Home Improvement All-in-One
  For Dummies
  0-7645-5680-0

- Knitting For Dummies
  0-7645-5395-X
- Piano For Dummies
  0-7645-5105-1
- Puppies For Dummies
  0-7645-5255-4
- Scrapbooking For Dummies
  0-7645-7208-3
- Senior Dogs For Dummies
  0-7645-5818-8
- Singing For Dummies
  0-7645-2475-5
- 30-Minute Meals For Dummies
  0-7645-2589-1

INTERNET & DIGITAL MEDIA

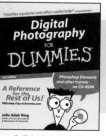

0-7645-1664-7

0-7645-6924-4

Also available:

- 2005 Online Shopping Directory
  For Dummies
  0-7645-7495-7
- CD & DVD Recording For Dummies
  0-7645-5956-7
- eBay For Dummies
  0-7645-5654-1
- Fighting Spam For Dummies
  0-7645-5965-6
- Genealogy Online For Dummies
  0-7645-5964-8
- Google For Dummies
  0-7645-4420-9

- Home Recording For Musicians
  For Dummies
  0-7645-1634-5
- The Internet For Dummies
  0-7645-4173-0
- iPod & iTunes For Dummies
  0-7645-7772-7
- Preventing Identity Theft For Dummies
  0-7645-7336-5
- Pro Tools All-in-One Desk Reference
  For Dummies
  0-7645-5714-9
- Roxio Easy Media Creator For Dummies
  0-7645-7131-1

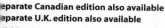

WILEY

SPORTS, FITNESS, PARENTING, RELIGION & SPIRITUALITY

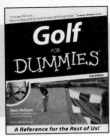

0-7645-5146-9

0-7645-5418-2

Also available:
- Adoption For Dummies
  0-7645-5488-3
- Basketball For Dummies
  0-7645-5248-1
- The Bible For Dummies
  0-7645-5296-1
- Buddhism For Dummies
  0-7645-5359-3
- Catholicism For Dummies
  0-7645-5391-7
- Hockey For Dummies
  0-7645-5228-7

- Judaism For Dummies
  0-7645-5299-6
- Martial Arts For Dummies
  0-7645-5358-5
- Pilates For Dummies
  0-7645-5397-6
- Religion For Dummies
  0-7645-5264-3
- Teaching Kids to Read For Dummies
  0-7645-4043-2
- Weight Training For Dummies
  0-7645-5168-X
- Yoga For Dummies
  0-7645-5117-5

TRAVEL

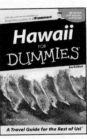

0-7645-5438-7

0-7645-5453-0

Also available:
- Alaska For Dummies
  0-7645-1761-9
- Arizona For Dummies
  0-7645-6938-4
- Cancún and the Yucatán For Dummies
  0-7645-2437-2
- Cruise Vacations For Dummies
  0-7645-6941-4
- Europe For Dummies
  0-7645-5456-5
- Ireland For Dummies
  0-7645-5455-7

- Las Vegas For Dummies
  0-7645-5448-4
- London For Dummies
  0-7645-4277-X
- New York City For Dummies
  0-7645-6945-7
- Paris For Dummies
  0-7645-5494-8
- RV Vacations For Dummies
  0-7645-5443-3
- Walt Disney World & Orlando For Dummies
  0-7645-6943-0

GRAPHICS, DESIGN & WEB DEVELOPMENT

0-7645-4345-8

0-7645-5589-8

Also available:
- Adobe Acrobat 6 PDF For Dummies
  0-7645-3760-1
- Building a Web Site For Dummies
  0-7645-7144-3
- Dreamweaver MX 2004 For Dummies
  0-7645-4342-3
- FrontPage 2003 For Dummies
  0-7645-3882-9
- HTML 4 For Dummies
  0-7645-1995-6
- Illustrator CS For Dummies
  0-7645-4084-X

- Macromedia Flash MX 2004 For Dummies
  0-7645-4358-X
- Photoshop 7 All-in-One Desk
  Reference For Dummies
  0-7645-1667-1
- Photoshop CS Timesaving Techniques
  For Dummies
  0-7645-6782-9
- PHP 5 For Dummies
  0-7645-4166-8
- PowerPoint 2003 For Dummies
  0-7645-3908-6
- QuarkXPress 6 For Dummies
  0-7645-2593-X

NETWORKING, SECURITY, PROGRAMMING & DATABASES

0-7645-6852-3

0-7645-5784-X

Also available:
- A+ Certification For Dummies
  0-7645-4187-0
- Access 2003 All-in-One Desk
  Reference For Dummies
  0-7645-3988-4
- Beginning Programming For Dummies
  0-7645-4997-9
- C For Dummies
  0-7645-7068-4
- Firewalls For Dummies
  0-7645-4048-3
- Home Networking For Dummies
  0-7645-42796

- Network Security For Dummies
  0-7645-1679-5
- Networking For Dummies
  0-7645-1677-9
- TCP/IP For Dummies
  0-7645-1760-0
- VBA For Dummies
  0-7645-3989-2
- Wireless All In-One Desk Reference
  For Dummies
  0-7645-7496-5
- Wireless Home Networking For Dummies
  0-7645-3910-8

HEALTH & SELF-HELP

0-7645-6820-5 *†

0-7645-2566-2

Also available:

Alzheimer's For Dummies
0-7645-3899-3

Asthma For Dummies
0-7645-4233-8

Controlling Cholesterol For Dummies
0-7645-5440-9

Depression For Dummies
0-7645-3900-0

Dieting For Dummies
0-7645-4149-8

Fertility For Dummies
0-7645-2549-2

Fibromyalgia For Dummies
0-7645-5441-7

Improving Your Memory For Dummies
0-7645-5435-2

Pregnancy For Dummies †
0-7645-4483-7

Quitting Smoking For Dummies
0-7645-2629-4

Relationships For Dummies
0-7645-5384-4

Thyroid For Dummies
0-7645-5385-2

EDUCATION, HISTORY, REFERENCE & TEST PREPARATION

0-7645-5194-9

0-7645-4186-2

Also available:

Algebra For Dummies
0-7645-5325-9

British History For Dummies
0-7645-7021-8

Calculus For Dummies
0-7645-2498-4

English Grammar For Dummies
0-7645-5322-4

Forensics For Dummies
0-7645-5580-4

The GMAT For Dummies
0-7645-5251-1

Inglés Para Dummies
0-7645-5427-1

Italian For Dummies
0-7645-5196-5

Latin For Dummies
0-7645-5431-X

Lewis & Clark For Dummies
0-7645-2545-X

Research Papers For Dummies
0-7645-5426-3

The SAT I For Dummies
0-7645-7193-1

Science Fair Projects For Dummies
0-7645-5460-3

U.S. History For Dummies
0-7645-5249-X

Get smart @ dummies.com®

- **Find a full list of Dummies titles**
- **Look into loads of FREE on-site articles**
- **Sign up for FREE eTips e-mailed to you weekly**
- **See what other products carry the Dummies name**
- **Shop directly from the Dummies bookstore**
- **Enter to win new prizes every month!**

Separate Canadian edition also available
Separate U.K. edition also available

Available wherever books are sold. For more information or to order direct: U.S. customers visit www.dummies.com or call 1-877-762-2974.
U.K. customers visit www.wileyeurope.com or call 0800 243407. Canadian customers visit www.wiley.ca or call 1-800-567-4797.